Louisiana's Legal Heritage

STUDIES IN LOUISIANA CULTURE

Robert R. Macdonald

Series Editor

BOOKS IN THE SERIES

LOUISIANA'S BLACK HERITAGE

Edited by
Robert R. Macdonald, John R. Kemp, Edward F. Haas

LOUISIANA'S LEGAL HERITAGE

Edited by
Edward F. Haas

Louisiana's Legal Heritage

Edited By

Edward F. Haas

Foreword By

Robert R. Macdonald

Published for the Louisiana State Museum
By
The Perdido Bay Press
Pensacola, Florida

1983

This publication is sponsored by the Louisiana Museum Foundation through a grant from the Louisiana Committee for the Humanities.

Library of Congress Cataloging in Publication Data

Louisiana's legal heritage.

Includes bibliographical references and index.

Contents: Louisiana's legal heritage / Edward F. Haas -- *Le mari est seigneur:* marital laws governing women in French Louisiana / Vaughan Baker, Amos Simpson, and Mathé Allain -- Do it! Don't do it! : Spanish law on sex and marriage / Jack D. L. Holmes -- [etc.]

1. Law--Louisiana--History and criticism--Addresses, essays, lectures. I. Haas, Edward F. II. Louisiana State Museum.

KFL78.L68 1983 349.763'09 83-13566

ISBN 0-933776-12-8 347.63009

CONTENTS

LIST OF ILLUSTRATIONS

Page

CONTRIBUTORS

VAUGHAN BAKER SIMPSON is the director of the Women in Louisiana Collection at the Center for Louisiana Studies, University of Southwestern Louisiana. Among her works are studies in women's history and the French influence in Louisiana.

AMOS E. SIMPSON is Godchaux Honor Professor of History at the University of Southwestern Louisiana. He is a specialist in modern European history and the Civil War and Reconstruction in Louisiana.

MATHÉ ALLAIN teaches French at the University of Southwestern Louisiana. She has written extensively on Louisiana history.

JACK D. L. HOLMES is the director of the Louisiana Collection Series. His many works on colonial Louisiana include *Gayoso: The Life of a Spanish Governor in the Mississippi Valley, 1789-1799* and *A Guide to Spanish Louisiana, 1762-1802.*

HANS W. BAADE is Hugh Lamar Stone Professor of Civil Law at the University of Texas, Austin. A student of international law and Spanish colonial legal institutions, he has written several articles on the law in early Louisiana.

A. N. YIANNOPOULOS is W. R. Irby Professor of Law at Tulane University. He is a leading authority on comparative law in the modern world and the Louisiana civil law system.

RICHARD H. KILBOURNE, JR. practices law in Louisiana. A former associate at the Center of Civil Law Studies, Paul M. Hebert Law Center, Louisiana State University, Baton Rouge, he is the author of *Louisiana Commercial Law: The Antebellum Period.*

GEORGE DARGO holds a doctorate in United States history from Columbia University and now teaches at the New England School of Law. He is the author of *Roots of the Republic: A New Perspective on Early American Constitutionalism; Jefferson's Louisiana: Politics and the Clash of Legal Traditions;* and *Law in the New Republic: Private Law and the Public Estate.*

RONALD M. LABBÉ is associate professor of political science at the University of Southwestern Louisiana. He is a specialist in American constitutional law and the Louisiana judicial system.

OTTO H. OLSEN is professor of history at Northern Illinois University. A student of the Reconstruction era and race relations in the United States, he is the author of *Carpetbagger's Crusade: The Life of Albion W. Tourgee* and the editor of *The Thin Disguise: Plessy v. Ferguson; Turning Point in Negro History* and *The Reconstruction and Redemption of the South: An Assessment.*

WARREN M. BILLINGS is professor of history at the University of New Orleans and the historian of the Louisiana Supreme Court. Among his works are *The Old Dominion in the Seventeenth Century: A Documentary History of Virginia, 1606-1689* and numerous articles on the law in early American history.

This volume is dedicated to the Memory of

Mary Julie Barrois

ACKNOWLEDGMENTS

Because the preparation of an anthology of historical essays is essentially history by committee, its publication necessarily requires the assistance of numerous individuals and institutions. *Louisiana's Legal Heritage* is no exception to this rule. Its publication marks the culmination of an extensive project on Louisiana legal history that also included a symposium and an interpretive exhibition. A generous grant from the Louisiana Committee for the Humanities funded this multifaceted endeavor. The Board of Directors of the Louisiana State Museum and the Louisiana Museum Foundation encouraged the project and provided important administrative support. Camille Loomis, Development Officer for the Louisiana Museum Foundation, deserves special thanks for her assistance. Among the staff members of the Louisiana State Museum who made significant contributions to the project are Freida Morford, Marie Grather, Walter Grather, John Burton Harter, Timothy Chester, Rose Lambert, Julie Barrois, Steven Reinhardt, Susan Lemann, Hazel Browinski, Maxine Blum, Gary Plum, Lee Bates, Penfield Cowan, Norbert Raacke and Charles dela Gueronniere. Joseph D. Castle, Curator of Cartography and Manuscripts at the Louisiana Historical Center, and Stephen Webre of Louisiana Tech University, former Curator of Manuscripts at the Louisiana Historical Center, prepared the colonial section of the interpretive exhibition and performed many other vital tasks that no one else wanted to do.

Several individuals and organizations contributed to the success of the interpretive exhibition. Clive Hardy and Marie Windell of the University of New Orleans Department of Archives and Manuscripts; Mr. and Mrs. A. L. Schlessinger, of New Orleans; M. Stone Miller of the Louisiana State University Department of Archives and Manuscripts; Wilbur Meneray of the Tulane University Department of Special Collections; Collin B. Hamer, Jr. and Wayne Everard of the New Orleans Public Library Louisiana Department; and Susan Cole of the Historic New Orleans Collection arranged the loan of items from their respective collections and offered valuable suggestions. Special thanks must additionally go to Chief Justice John A. Dixon and Clerk Frans J. Labranche, Jr., of the Louisiana Supreme Court for their enthusiastic support.

Several historians and legal scholars made outstanding contributions to the symposium. Raphael J. Rabalais, Jr. of the Loyola University School of Law and Alain A. Levasseur of the Paul M. Hebert Law Center, Louisiana State University, warrant particular praise. Among the other worthy participants were Judge Albert Tate, Jr., of the Fifth United States Court of Appeals, Consul General Enrique Iranzo of Spain; Dean Cecil Morgan and David Combe, Tulane University School of Law; Lawrence N. Powell and Sylvia Frey, Tulane University History Department; Joseph Logsdon, University of New Orleans History Department; Stanley M. Hordes of the New Mexico State Records Center and Archives; William Forman of New Orleans; David J. Bodenhamer, University of Southern Mississippi Department of History; and Robert D. Bush, Director of the Wyoming State Archives, Museums and Historical Department. Shael Herman of the Tulane University School of Law also contributed a fine commentary.

William S. Coker and Hazel P. Coker of The Perdido Bay Press shepherded this publication through each essential step. Polly Coker, however, merits particular praise for her diligence and persistence with the legal citations.

Director Robert R. Macdonald of the Louisiana State Museum, creator of *Studies in Louisiana Culture*, also deserves special applause. He conceived the plan for the interpretive exhibition and provided important encouragement and guidance throughout the entire project.

Edward F. Haas
Louisiana Historical Center
New Orleans, Louisiana

FOREWORD

The association of the Louisiana State Museum with the preservation and study of Louisiana's legal history has continued for more than half a century. In April 1924, Henry Plauche Dart, the President of the Louisiana State Museum Board and noted Louisiana attorney, addressed the Louisiana Bar Association on the topic, "The Law Library of a Louisiana Lawyer in the Eighteenth Century." This study, which outlined Louisiana's colonial legal heritage, was only one of several essays that Dart prepared on the subject between 1911 and 1934. The titles of some of these works reveal the depth and scope of Dart's interest in the history of Louisiana's legal system: "The Sources of the Civil Code in Louisiana," "The Courts and Law in Colonial Louisiana," "The Archives of Louisiana," and "The Colonial Legal Systems of Louisiana, Texas and Arkansas."

Henry Plauche Dart was Louisiana's first legal historian. His work during the early part of this century provided the foundation for "Louisiana's Legal Heritage," a symposium and a later exhibition of the same title that the Louisiana State Museum presented in 1981. A sketch of Dart's career provides insight into the development of this field of Louisiana studies.

Henry Plauche Dart was born in 1857 at Fort St. Philip in Plaquemines Parish along the Mississippi River, south of New Orleans. His parents were of English-Louisiana ancentry. Dart's formal schooling consisted only of an elementary education in New Orleans schools and one year's study at Jefferson City High School. The Civil War and the severity of its aftermath left the Dart family without the means to continue Henry's formal education. The young Dart was necessarily apprenticed as a clerk in the law firm of Cotton and Levy. Henry Dart's abilities were soon demonstrated when, at the age of twenty-two, he was admitted to the Louisiana Bar and established his own practice. In the early 1890s the successful, young lawyer joined with his brother-in-law, Benjamin Kernan, to form the firm of Dart and Kernan. The firm served a wide range of clients including banks, street railway companies, lumber and insurance firms. At the turn of the century, Henry Plauche Dart was recognized as one of Louisiana's leading attorneys and was a major force in the formation of the Louisiana Bar Association.

Dart's interest in the origins of Louisiana's legal system soon led him to the study of history. In 1911 he presented his first paper on the subject, an analysis of the sources of Louisiana's Civil Code. In 1913 he wrote a brief history of the Louisiana Supreme Court. Henry Dart's studies brought him into contact with the records of colonial Louisiana's French Superior Council and Spanish *Cabildo*. These collections of approximately a half a million pages of judicial records dating from 1714 to 1803 were at the time in the custody of the Louisiana Historical Society. Dart soon made the preservation and organization of this collection his major concern. To support his efforts, the attorney obtained a grant of the then sizeable sum of $15,000 from the New Orleans philanthropist, William Radcliff Irby. Dart was appointed to the nonsalaried position of Archivist of the Louisiana Historical Society and later Curator of the Louisiana State Museum. He also became editor of the *Louisiana Historical Quarterly* and in 1922 was elected President of the Louisiana State Museum Board which had been given jurisdiction over the colonial judicial papers. Henry Plauche Dart served as the head of the Louisiana State Museum for twelve years until his death in 1934.

In his 1924 essay on the library of an eighteenth-century Louisiana lawyer, Dart explained his interest in the legal history of the state: "the topic is an absorbing one, not only from the scholastic point of view, but because it is of practical value in the everyday life of the lawyer. The acquisition of the knowledge of the history of our system is the equivalent to the addition of a separate sense to our equipment. To know the sources, to follow the growth and witness the development of procedure, process and law is to be in the position of an architect who plans, and a contractor who erects a building. To have grown up in the presence of each brick, stone, and timber from foundation to roof is surely a practical advantage which no experience can thereafter supplant."

Henry Plauche Dart understood that Louisiana's legal heritage touched all aspects of the state's history. He wrote or sponsored papers on such diverse subjects as the Battle of New Orleans, slavery, biographies of prominent Louisianians and Spain's contribution to the American Revolution. In the years that followed, other historians came to realize that the social, cultural, economic, religious and radical experiences of Louisiana are intertwined with the history of its law. In his impressive work, *Jefferson's Louisiana: Politics and the Clash of Legal Traditions* (1975), historian George Dargo wrote that the ". . . fundamental question of legal change facing Louisiana in the Jeffersonian period was not an esoteric issue which only concerned the professional elites. Rather, it touched upon many questions some of which were rather remote from the strict confines of legal cases and conflicts. For the clash of legal traditions encompassed the interests, the value system, and the very identity of a diverse people who now, for the first time in their history, had to unite in defense of the common elements of their heritage."

The history of law in Louisiana permeates every aspect of Louisiana life past and present. To understand Louisiana one must understand Louisiana's legal heritage. It is hoped that this anthology and the symposium and exhibition that preceded it have made some contribution to this understanding.

Louisiana's Legal Heritage is the second in a series of volumes sponsored by the Louisiana State Museum under the encompassing title, *Studies in Louisiana Culture*. The first volume in the series, *Louisiana's Black Heritage*, was also one part of a broader program that featured a scholarly symposium and an exhibition as well as a publication. Future programs in this historical series will examine diverse subjects such as politics, social structure, economics, cultural development and the history of medicine in Louisiana.

Louisiana's Legal Heritage demonstrates the commitment of the Louisiana State Museum to continue the work of Henry Plauche Dart in the preservation, organization and use of the records of the French Superior Council and the Spanish *Cabildo* that remain an important part of the Museum's collections. In 1976, the State Museum received a $65,000 grant from the National Endowment for the Humanities to prepare calendars and indices for the collection. The judicial papers were recently microfilmed and the Museum has initiated a conservation program to arrest the damage done to this irreplaceable resource through neglect and well-intentioned lamination efforts in the 1930s.

This publication, the exhibition and the symposium from which it derived were made possible by a grant from the Louisiana Committee for the Humanities. The three-phased effort was conducted under the direction of Dr. Edward F. Haas and the staff of the Louisiana Historical Center of the State Museum. The success and quality of this effort reflect the talents of the Louisiana State Museum staff and professional colleagues who have devoted their scholarly energies to give new insight into Louisiana's past. Like Henry Plauche Dart, we recognize the practical and philosophical value of understanding history. The Louisiana State Museum Board continues the tradition of its early leaders to collect, preserve, and disseminate knowledge about Louisiana and its people. On behalf of the Museum Board, I want to thank all who continue to support the Louisiana State Museum in this important work.

May 11, 1983

Robert R. Macdonald
Director
Louisiana State Museum

LOUISIANA'S LEGAL HERITAGE: AN INTRODUCTION

By
Edward F. Haas

Law reflects the culture of a people. History, lore, traditions, religion and the various other components that make up the cultural milieu of a society influence the development of the law. In Louisiana, this cultural milieu has a distinctly Latin flavor. So, too, does the law.[1]

Louisiana is the sole solid enclave of civil law in the United States. In a nation that reveres the Anglo-American tradition of common law, Louisiana stands alone. Its unique legal system, based fundamentally upon Roman law, derives from the lengthy colonial rule of France and Spain. Despite the incursions of common law principles and procedure since the Great Purchase of 1803, the civilian tradition remains strong in Louisiana.[2]

The law that France and Spain transmitted to Louisiana in the eighteenth century had its roots in the civil codes of imperial Rome and differed significantly with the English tradition of common law that Great Britain imparted to its thirteen colonies on the Atlantic Coast. Trial by jury and the writ of habeas corpus, mainstays of the common law, did not exist in the civilian tradition. In civil law, the community property system, the principles of forced heirship and implied warranty, the free alienation of property and freedom of contract protected the rights of the family and its members and simplified the laws of property and obligations.[3] During the 1920s, an admirer of Louisiana law contrasted its "simplicity, unity, precision and clearness" with the "intricacy, complexity, uncertainty, and indistinctness" of the law of real property that prevailed in common law America.[4]

In 1712 France formally instituted civil government in Louisiana. At that time, the Custom of Paris, a code of sixteen titles and three hundred sixty-two articles in the Roman tradition, became the law of the new colony. These laws and ordinances, with the addition of the *Code Noir* (Black Code) in 1724, prevailed throughout the period of French rule.[5]

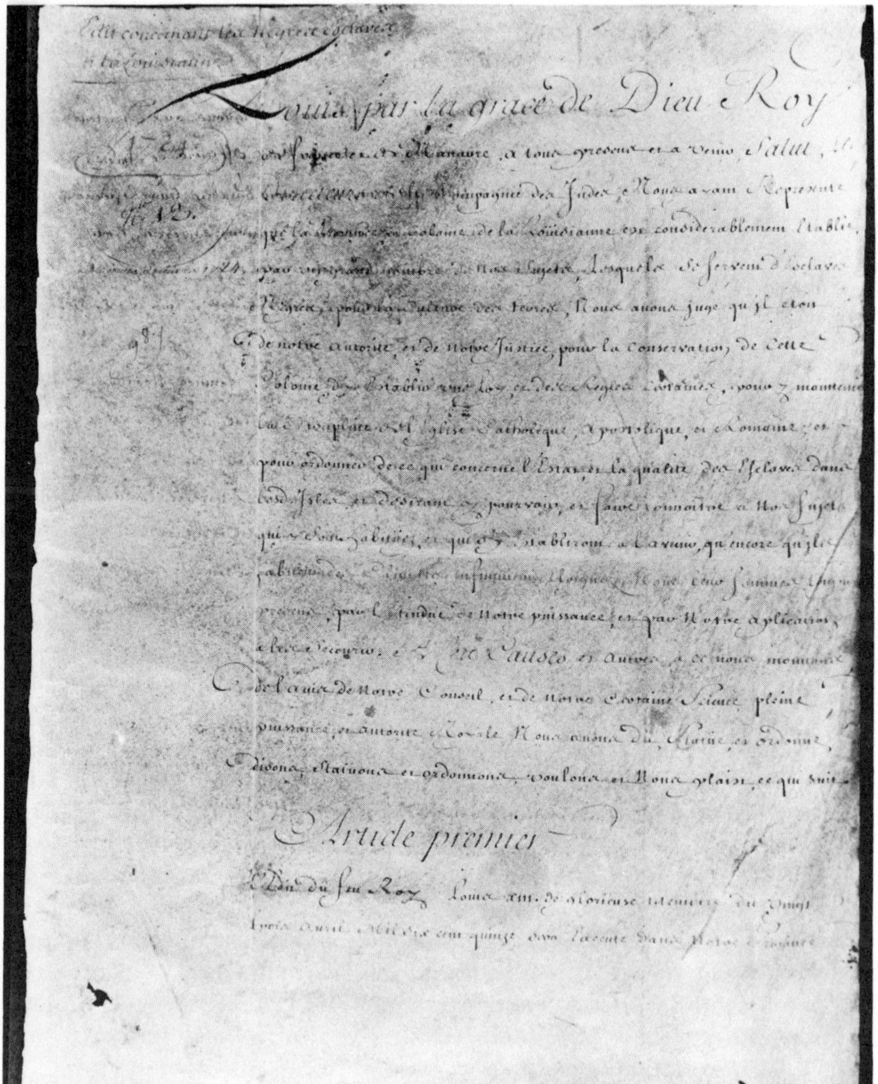
Louis par la grace de Dieu Roy

Article premier

Code Noir, The Louisiana Black Code of 1724. A reproduction of the first page. Louisiana State Museum.

On August 18, 1769, don Alejandro O'Reilly took official and physical possession of Louisiana on behalf of Spain. Among his first acts were the abolition of all French laws and the immediate introduction of the laws of Spain. The regulations that O'Reilly implemented, like the French ones, had their roots in Roman law. The primary sources of law in Spanish Louisiana were the recent laws of Castile (*Nueva Recopilación de Castilla*) and the law of the Spanish colonies (*Recopilación de las Indias*). Additional legal codes included the laws of *Toro*, the *Ordenamento de Alcalá*, the *Fuero Juzgo* and the *Siete Partidas*. In the civilian tradition that favored philosophy and principles over precedent, the Spanish in Louisiana relied heavily upon written works on the law and legal practice in Spain.[6]

Because there was great similarity between the French and the Spanish legal traditions, however, the customs and traditions that had evolved over the years did not succumb to shifts in sovereignty. Although the people of the Louisiana colony lacked a constitutional basis for their law and had no legislative experience in the enactment of the statutes that regulated their lives, they did have a firmly established legal tradition. When the United States took possession of the colony on December 20, 1803, the Americans quickly learned that these legal customs and principles would not be easily cast aside or supplanted.[7]

The coming of the Americans produced a vitriolic clash of legal traditions. William C. C. Claiborne, governor of the Territory of Louisiana, later the Territory of Orleans, had instructions from President Thomas Jefferson to institute American law and practices in the new land to prepare its residents, the "ancien population," for assimilation into the United States.[8] The "ancients," desirous of immediate statehood and fearful of the common law, denounced the "monstrous English code . . . this confused mass of edicts handed down by the most ferocius [*sic.*] despots" as a devilish device to despoil them of their property and to cast them into subordination and slavery.[9] Although the native population eventually accepted trial by jury and the writ of habeas corpus, they remained true to their preference for the civilian tradition.[10]

The presence of numerous great legal minds in territorial Louisiana intensified the conflict. On the scene were Louis Casimir Moreau Lislet, a native of Santo Domingo; Edward Livingston of New York; François Xavier Martin from France and the isle of Martinique; Alexander Porter, a native of Ireland; Etienne Mazureau of France; John R. Grymes from Virginia; Henry Carleton of New Orleans; James Brown of Virginia and

Kentucky; and Pierre Derbigny, another native of France. Governor Claiborne, a native of Virginia, a resident of Tennessee and the former governor of Mississippi Territory, was also a lawyer. Their efforts and their disputes shaped the law of early Louisiana.[11]

Symbolic of the clash of legal traditions was the Batture question. In the thick of the conflict were Governor Claiborne and Edward Livingston who in a series of devastating briefs had successfully defended the rights of John Gravier to the enormously valuable alluvial soil that the Mississippi River deposited between the water's edge and the levee before Faubourg Ste. Marie against the opposing claims of the so-called "front proprietors" who retained title along the old levee line and the city of New Orleans. Because the victory came in the Superior Court, a panel of Anglo-American judges who spoke only English and favored the common law, the outraged "ancien population" viewed the decision as a conspiracy of the common law advocates to subvert their property rights. To preserve public order, Claiborne transferred the city claims to President Jefferson, a fierce political foe of Livingston, and the federal government. Litigation continued for several years afterward.

During this lengthy controversy, Governor Claiborne discovered that most of his support derived from the "ancients." When Aaron Burr's mysterious scheming in the Old Southwest found favor among many of the Americans in the territory, Claiborne gravitated even more into the camp of the loyal French community. These fundamental shifts in political allegiance convinced the governor that the "ancients' " fervid pleas for the continuation of civil law were not unreasonable.[12]

On July 7, 1806, the legislature of Orleans appointed attorneys James Brown and Louis Casimir Moreau Lislet to prepare "a Civil Code for the use of the Territory." These instructions satisfied the clamor of "ancien" residents who wanted a code to clarify the law and to insure them against sudden, chaotic changes in their social and economic condition. They sought familiar law in a usable form.

On March 31, 1808, the legislature approved the *Digest of the Civil Laws Now in Force in the Territory of Orleans*. Divided into three books, "Of Persons," "Of Things or Estates," and "Of the Different Manners of Acquiring the Property of Things," the digest was grounded in French and Spanish law and prepared in the style of the Code Napoleon.[13] According to the legal historian George Dargo, Governor Claiborne, despite his earlier support of common law, signed the authorization with the understanding that the Digest of 1808 was a political compromise which constituted the basis for the "ancien" population's final acceptance of permanent American rule. Claiborne and Thomas Jefferson essentially surrendered their desire for total Americanization in return for a faster and smoother absorption of the territory into the United States.[14] In April 1812 Congress passed an act admitting the Territory of Orleans into the Union as the state of Louisiana.

The first constitution of Louisiana, modeled generally on the fundamental law of Kentucky, preserved the civilian tradition. To prevent the introduction of American common law into the Louisiana legal system, the new constitution stated that the legislature "shall never adopt any system or code of laws, by a general reference to the said system or code, but in all cases, shall specify the several provisions of the laws it may enact." (Article IV, Section II.) Another provision of the document declared that English would be the official language of the state although the original draft of the Constitution of 1812 was in French.[15]

Legal confusion, nonetheless, persisted after the establishment of state government. In 1819 the continuing use of Spanish law caused the Louisiana legislature to approve L. Moreau Lislet and Henry Carleton's translation of *Las Siete Partidas Which Are Still in Force in the State of Louisiana.* This work was completed and published in English in 1820.[16]

On March 14, 1822, the legislature appointed a committee--Edward Livingston, Pierre Derbigny and L. Moreau Lislet--to remodel the Digest of 1808 "in such a manner as they shall deem advisable." Livingston, called "the great jurist of nineteenth-century America and one to rank with Bentham" among English-speaking peoples, was the dominating figure. The result, contends the legal scholar Lawrence M. Friedman, was "one of the most original" of the civil codes, "a learned blend of French, Spanish and common law forms into a skillful, efficient whole." In 1825 the state legislature adopted this code with an accompanying code of procedure. These documents formed the essential foundation for legal practice in Lousiana throughout the nineteenth century.[17]

In the years that followed the adoption of the civil code, Louisiana was a hotbed of legal activity. The development of the Mississippi River and the growth of New Orleans as a trading center led to a variety of commercial conflicts that required legal arbitration. Sectional strife that culminated in the Civil War and its controversial aftermath produced a flurry of legal issues. Numerous disputes that started in Louisiana ultimately established important legal precedents in the United States Supreme Court.

At the core of these later controversies was a new generation of great Louisiana lawyers. Among these noted attorneys were Christian Roselius, Gustavus Schmidt, Judah P. Benjamin, Henry Adams Bullard and Pierre Soule. Frederick Law Olmsted, the famous northern traveler, upon one occasion, proclaimed that "the bar of Louisiana is more talented and respectable than that of any other Southern State, perhaps than that of any State." Another authority has written that "perhaps nowhere else in the United States was there, or has there been since, a more remarkable group of lawyers" than those in New Orleans.[18] These extraordinary jurists, the magnitude of the legal issues and the distinctive system of law that prevailed in the state enhanced Louisiana's unique legal heritage and made a profound contribution to the social and economic growth of the entire nation.

[1]Ferdinand Stone, "The Law with a Difference and How It Came About," in Hodding Carter, ed., *The Past as Prelude: New Orleans, 1718-1968* (New Orleans, 1968), 42-43.

[2]Lawrence M. Friedman, *A History of American Law* (New York, 1973), 155-156; Shael Herman, David Combe and Thomas E. Carbonneau, *The Louisiana Civil Code: A Humanistic Appraisal* (New Orleans, 1981), 3-11.

[3]George Dargo, *Jefferson's Louisiana: Politics and the Clash of Legal Traditions* (Cambridge, 1975), 11-17. See also Herman, *et al.*, *The Louisiana Civil Code*, 31-43.

[4]Quoted in Dargo, *Jefferson's Louisiana*, 14.

[5]Stone, "The Law with a Difference," 43-47; Herman, *et al.*, *The Louisiana Civil Code*, 47.

[6]Stone, "The Law with a Difference," 57; Friedman, *A History of American Law*, 152.

[7]Cecil Morgan, "Commentary," presented on April 24, 1981, at "Louisiana's Legal Heritage: A Symposium," Louisiana State Museum, New Orleans, Louisiana.

[8]Dargo, *Jefferson's Louisiana*, 25-28, 47-50; Friedman, *A History of American Law*, 152.

[9]Quoted in Joseph G. Tregle, Jr., "Louisiana in the Age of Jackson: A Study in Ego Politics" (Ph.D. dissertation: University of Pennsylvania, 1954), 136.

[10]Friedman, *A History of American Law*, 152.

[11]Tregle, "Louisiana in the Age of Jackson," 177-182; Friedman, *A History of American Law*,152-153; Edwin A. Davis, *Louisiana: A Narrative History* (Baton Rouge, 1965), 197.

[12]Dargo, *Jefferson's Louisiana*, 51-101, *passim*. See also Herman, *et al.*, *The Louisiana Civil Code*, 22-24.

[13]Ibid., 24-25.

[14]Dargo, *Jefferson's Louisiana*, 173; Friedman, *A History of American Law*, 152-153.

[15]Cecil Morgan, "Introduction" in *The First Constitution of the State of Louisiana* (Baton Rouge, 1975), 3-14. See also Joe Gray Taylor, *Louisiana: A Bicentennial History* (New York, 1976), 51.

[16]Herman, *et al.*, *The Louisiana Civil Code*, 25-27.

[17]Friedman, *A History of American Law*, 153-154. For the descriptive quotation on Edward Livingston, see Tregle, "Louisiana in the Age of Jackson," 188.

[18]Davis, *Louisiana: A Narrative History*, 196-197.

LE MARI EST SEIGNEUR: *MARITAL LAWS GOVERNING WOMEN IN FRENCH LOUISIANA*

By

Vaughan Baker, Amos Simpson and Mathé Allain

Domestic law is a primary facet of the legal system in any human society. In pre-industrial and early modern societies, the laws governing domestic relationships, along with the laws of inheritance, were the aspects of law that most closely touched the individual member of the community. Regulating the family unit, the foundation of the social structure, these laws generally reflected the most fundamental premises of the social order.

Although the contemporary community property regime has received considerable recent attention and its origins have been the subject of debate by legal historians,[1] few scholars have examined the theoretical bases of the laws governing women and marriage in French colonial Louisiana for understandings concerning the social and economic role of women in early Louisiana society. Such an examination clarifies the role of women in the Louisiana colony and points to important new directions for research into the economic activities of women in the eighteenth century. This essay therefore explores the theory of the marital laws governing women in French colonial Louisiana.

Civil government began in Louisiana in 1712 when Louis XIV ceded the colony to Antoine Crozat. The charter of transfer established the *Coutume de Paris* and the edicts of the King as the fundamental law of Louisiana. Examination of the marital laws governing women must, then, begin with an understanding of the legal status of women according to the provisions of the *Coutume de Paris.*[2]

The fundamental theory of the marital laws contained in the *Coutume de Paris* contradicts modern assumptions concerning the misogynist attitudes of the pre-modern period. While it is true that under the *Coutume de Paris* married women were relegated to an inferior legal status and severely restricted in their rights and prerogatives, the law provided women with economic protections which allowed them an extraordinary measure of economic security and, theoretically at least, accorded them personal dignity and social value. Women's inferior legal status in the

French marital regime was a conclusion rationally derived from the most fundamental premises of the ancient customary law and the eighteenth-century world view. Assumptions governing the role and status of women were rooted in a firmly entrenched hierarchical ideology given new impetus in the seventeenth and eighteenth centuries. In an age which believed strongly in a natural order governed by natural law, every member of society had a place in the orderly scheme of the universe. As the hierarchical conception approached its zenith, symbolically represented in the figure of "*Le Roi Soleil*," women were assigned a rank in what appeared to be a divinely ordained and firmly fixed natural order of society. That position was below the rank of the male.

Eustache Nicholas Pigeau,[3] Professor of Law at the University of Paris and an influential legal commentator of the eighteenth century, served as spokesman for the age when he explained that Providence had gifted men and women differently, endowing men with greater strength. Since the two spouses formed a community which required government, one had to have superior authority. Although women had been given virtues which adorned their sex, their strengths were less conducive to good government than were the male's. The "weakness and febbleness" of the woman made her less able to administer and protect the conjugal community. The *puissance maritale* of the husband was, consequently, necessary to the security of the family and the society. Pigeau stated the theory quite succinctly, ". . . the authority confided to the husband must be considered established in favor of the wife and the conjugal society even as the duties and obedience toward the political power are established to enable the state to fulfill the goal of its institution. They are in favor of the people and not in favor of those who govern."[4]

In the Customary Law of Paris the power of the husband over the wife and the parents over the children prevailed. Resting on fundamental concepts established in the customary laws of the Germanic peoples, the provisions of the law aimed to preserve stability in family institutions and the preservation of family property. Thus preference was given to a system of incontrovertible protection of inheritance, and therefore to the male descendants.[5]

Concerning women, the fundamental premise of the *Coutume de Paris* was "the married women is under the power of husband." "*Le Mari est Seigneur*," said Article 225—the husband is lord.[6] This *puissance du mari* extended to her person and her property. The wife's obligation consisted of dependence and submission, not simple respect, to such extent that married women could perform no valid legal act without the husband's consent, unless she acted as a *marchande publique*, or public merchant, in which case she had independent legal rights. The duty of wifely submission was repeatedly reiterated in legal commentaries. That marital power, stated Robert Joseph Pothier, the most celebrated jurist of the eighteenth century, was based in natural law; the wife owed her husband "all the obligations which are due a superior and his authority extended to her person and possessions."[7]

The wife's duty of submission was not, however, rooted in "the weakness of her reason." Married women who needed their husband's authorization were not rationally inferior to single girls and widows, who did not need legal authorization. But in a society where the concept of descending authority was basic, broad marital powers were a logical extension of the contemporary hierarchical premise.

Despite the eighteenth-century obsession with reason, the justification of the theory of the *puissance marital* seemed, at times, to confound logic. Thus, the husband retained his authority even if he went mad. "When the husband falls into a demented state," Pothier commented, "that state being an infirmity which overcomes him without his fault, it must not deprive him of any of his rights, and, consequently, of the right of power which he has over his wife; it alone must not prevent his exercising [his martial authority].[8] A minor husband had authority over his wife, even if she had attained majority, and separated women were still subject in many ways to the authorization of their husbands. Even if the husband's whereabouts were unknown, the wife could not act legally without authorization, requiring instead a judge's approval. Only if the husband was believed dead could she so act, having then attained the independent status of a widow.[9]

Pothier, reflecting the philosophy of his time and of the legal theorists who preceded him, saw civilized society as a social contract where marriage, "the most excellent and most ancient of all contracts," functioned as the most essential contractual obligation.[10] It was, however, a contract between equals. As such, it imposed mutual obligations on husband and wife. The reciprocal nature of obligations in the areas ruled by French Customary Law limited the husband's marital power. In southern France, where Roman Law prevailed, the husband's power was virtually unbounded; in Potheir's words, "It resembled the power that masters have over their slaves."[11] In contrast, French Customary Law precisely defined the duties of both wife and husband, emphasizing the mutual nature of marital obligations. The wife's place and dignity were protected; in the fundamental theory of contractual organization she yielded sovereignty in the interest of social security, but retained her rights and her responsibilities.

The husband's obligations fell into two major areas. First, the law forbade him to abuse the power that nature and the law itself had given him over his wife and required him to protect and defend her as far as he was able against "insults and injuries and persecutions."[12] Secondly, he had to administer his wife's share of the conjugal property, conserving and augmenting it, in order to insure the economic support he owed her. He was strictly prohibited from frustrating her rightful claims to her share of the community property. The husband was required to love his wife—a term interpreted differently then than it is now—to furnish her with all that was necessary for life to the best of his ability and according to his station, and to bear responsibility for her faults, correcting them in reasonable ways. The law further required that he "have for her a reasonable indulgence, without, however, encouraging her bad habits." Finally, he was obligated to be faithful to her, giving himself to her whenever she demanded it, and abstaining from sexual intercourse with any other woman.[13] Perhaps no provision of eighteenth-century law more clearly revealed the gap between theory and practice than this one.

The community of acquets and gains was a common right in almost all areas of French Customary Law, and a salient aspect of the *Coutume de Paris*. Article 220 of the *Coutume* stated, "Men and women joined together by marriage are common in immovable goods and in the assets acquired during the said marriage."[14] The community began the day of the nuptial benediction; once established, it was immutable and could be neither renounced nor modified by either party. It could, however, be modified or indeed disavowed by mutual contract between afinanced individuals prior to marriage.[15]

The community of goods included antenuptial movables although it did not include immovable property that either party acquired before marriage.[16] Nor did it include property given as gift by marriage contract. Unless renounced by written contract, personal debts fell into the community; the husband as head was held responsible for his wife's debts, even those incurred before marriage, following the ancient adage, "who espouses a woman espouses her debts." The wife, however, was legally responsible for only half her husband's debts.[17] The community remained in existence until the death (natural or civil) of one of the spouses, or until a judicial separation *de corps ou de biens* (of body or of goods). On the dissolution of the community by death of the husband, the wife could accept its continuation or repudiate it, thereby renouncing its debts. The husband did not have the right to renounce the community.[18]

The husband was *seul seigneur* of the community and the goods of which it was composed. As head of the community, he had sole rights of administration with extensive powers of control. Although the law ordered that he administer the property for the good of the conjugal society, legal commentators insisted that his power over the community property was so unrestricted that he could squander it as he pleased without being accountable. A reflection of the growing strength of bourgeois values and bourgeois claims to absolute property rights, Pothier stated of the husband's power of administration, "He can degrade the inheritance, break the moveables, kill through his brutality the horses and other animals belonging to the community without being accountable to his wife for any of these things."[19] The law forbade him, however, to sell, exchange, partition or indebt his wife's personal legacy without her consent. Nor could he contract or obligate her separate property without her consent.[20] Moreover, he could not acquire full rights to her property by marital gift. The law strictly regulated donations between husband and wife, allowing them only when they were mutual gifts. Wives were consequently protected from undue pressure from husbands to bestow by gift their own separate property. At his death, the husband's freedoms to dispose of the community property were sharply curtailed. If there were no children, he could dispose of only half the community property in his will; the other half belonged to his wife. Were there children, his patrimony was divided between his offspring and his widow. His was, then, in essence a usufruct responsibility.[21]

For her part, the wife was obliged to love her husband, submit to him and obey him in everything that was not contrary to God's law. She should work with all her might for the good of the household. She was required to gain her husband's good favor "by her mildness and her pleasing ways," and if, even doing all in her power, she could not please him, she could only oppose her patience to his bad manners and even his bad treatment. As he did her, she owed him physical satisfaction whenever he demanded it, and utter fidelity.[22] Her obligations to the community property were simply defined: she must not interfere in the administration which the law entrusted to her husband; she could, however, dispose of her share of the community goods and her own separate property by will, even should she predecease him.[23]

The *puissance maritale* and the wife's duty of submission required her to live wherever the husband chose. Jean Baptiste Denisart stated that obligation most succinctly: "The woman must live and reside with her husband. It is an obligation imposed on her by natural law and civil law."[24] She could under no circumstance refuse to follow him unless he left the kingdom. As a significant reflection of developing values, French jurists asserted that women owed more to *la patrie* than to their husbands and were not, therefore, obliged to abjure the homeland even if their husbands did. If, however, the wife left the husband's domicile by choice, he could sue her and force her to return. Moreover, he could sue anyone who gave her refuge, even her parents.[25]

From the husband's right to determine domicile, Pothier, with magnificent eighteenth-century logic, concluded that polyandry, but not polygamy, violated natural law. "It is the essence of marriage," he said, "that the wife be subject to her husband and obey him, and follow him wherever he elects to live; but a woman with two husbands at the same time could not obey both when they gave her contrary orders. She could not follow both when they wanted to live in different places. Polyandry is therefore contrary to the nature of marriage and to natural law."[26]

Family stability also dictated that the husband's adultery should be treated differently from that of the wife. His adultery was not legal ground for separation. Hers was, being "more contrary to the good order of civil society since it tends to despoil families and to put possession in the hands of adulterous children who are strangers."[27] Although the wife convicted of adultery lost all her dower rights, her matrimonial privileges, even her *dot*, and could be secluded in a convent for two years, her husband could not punish her with death, as he could under Spanish law. Adultery was considered a private and not a public matter; as Denisart said, it troubled "the order of the household where it is committed rather than the public order."[28]

The law unsurprisingly recognized few grounds for separation; given the fundamental premise that marriage was an indissoluble union essential for a stable society, what is remarkable is that any existed at all. A wife could ask for separation on several grounds: if her husband refused to furnish her the necessities of life; if he falsely accused her of a capital crime; if he openly professed heresy; or if he treated her with extreme cruelty. No illness on the part of the husband, however contagious, provided valid grounds, not even venereal disease, despite the fact that the wife might have strong suspicions that he had "acquired it by his debauchery."[29]

Women could, and did, sue for separation on grounds of ill treatment. In dealing with such a claim, of course, judges had to carefully consider the circumstances, because a husband's difficult behavior could and even should be viewed by his wife "as coming on God's order, as a cross sent for the expiation of her sins." Only if the ill treatment threatened "her life, her sanity or her tranquility to such a degree that cohabitation became intolerable," could separation be justified.[30]

In the instance of a woman's second marriage the new husband enjoyed full marital powers over his wife's person, but not over her property. Although the married woman could not "give, alienate, dispose or otherwise contract without the authority of her husband," the property that she brought into the marriage from an earlier union was nevertheless hers by inalienable right.[31] The ownership of separate property gave her a modicum of independence which she could use to manipulate her husband, and undoubtedly frequently did. The protection of women's property rights and the responsibility of the husband for the wife's antenuptial debts meant that the written, legally recorded marriage contract assumed exceptional importance.

Female property rights were not limited to a claim to half of the community property. The *Coutume de Paris*, like most of French Customary Law, prescribed dower rights. The *douaire*, separate from the *dot* which her parents provided her on marriage, was the property claim granted a woman from her husband's personal property for her upkeep and subsistence should she survive him. It gave widows the means of living honorably, according to the station of their dead husbands. As it was an obligatory share of his property, the *douaire* could not be regarded as a donation, which the husband could make of his own violation.[32] It had been originally the price of the bride's virginity; the *Coutume de Normandie* stated bluntly, "The wife earns her dower in bed," and the *Coutume de Paris* said the *douaire* was made by the husband "*in pretium deflorata virginitatis*" (as a price for her deflowered virginity).[33] A case that Pothier cited involved a young Louisiana widow, eleven years and nine months old. Hoping to regain her dower, her deceased husband's heirs challenged the validity of the marriage on the grounds that she was under age. They lost. The young widow proved she was pregnant, the marriage was judged valid, and she was entitled to enjoy her dower and other matrimonial conventions.[34]

According to the *Coutume de Paris* the wife became eligible for a dower as soon as she received the marital blessing, even should her husband fall dead at the door of the church.[35] There were two kinds of dower rights defined by law: the "Conventional," which the contracting parties could themselves negotiate; and the "Customary," which was prescribed. The *Coutume de Paris* defined the customary dower as half the inheritance the husband held the day of the marriage and half of what he might inherit from his parents or other ascendents during the marriage. Lengthy tomes have been written on the *douaire*; its provisions were precisely fixed for second and even third marriages.[36] Its importance underscored the degree to which women were economically protected in French Customary Law.

The economic protections guaranteed women in the *Coutume de Paris* assured, both in France and in the colonies, a shifting basis of female autonomy. Although women were expressly excluded from holding public office, they could wield considerable economic influence. Single women (although few colonial women retained that status for long) could remain legally and financially independent. Widowed women obtained both legal and financial independence and were, like single women, able to administer their property unrestrained by male authority. Even if they remarried, their separate property remained their own and allowed them a considerable psychological measure of freedom from a husband's domination if the woman chose to exercise it. Even married women, while juridically subjected to the *puissance maritale*, could act independently in business (as a *marchande publique*) and retained legal protections which assured them a greater measure of economic security than women of other nationalities enjoyed. The *Coutume de Paris* sanctioned above all the preservation of the patrimony and the preservation of the social order.

The precarious nature of life in eighteenth-century Louisiana meant that the provisions of the law interacted with the exigencies of frontier life to create a society distinct from the mother country and from the English and Spanish colonies. Only a close scrutiny of the surviving records will yield a valid picture of women's experience in the Louisiana colony. Undoubtedly, in a frontier wilderness, the theory which declared the husband *seul seigneur* had less force than a more highly structured, less dangerous milieu. Such a scrutiny will undoubtedly reveal quite a different picture of the economic participation and social influences of women in the colony than has heretofore been portrayed in the Louisiana historical literature.

[1]See, for example, Rodolfo Batiza, "The Louisiana Civil Code of 1808: Its Actual Sources

and Present Relevance," *Tulane Law Review*, Vol. 46, no. 1 (September, 1971), pp. 4-165; and Robert A. Pascal, "Sources of the Digest of 1808: A Reply to Professor Batiza," *Tulane Law Review*, Vol. 46, no. 4 (April, 1972), pp. 603-627. See also "Community Property: Symposium on Equal Rights," *Tulane Law Review*, Vol. 48, no. 3 (April, 1974), pp. 560-617.

[2]Henry Plauche Dart, "The Legal Institutions of Louisiana: French Period," *Louisiana Historical Quarterly*, Vol. II, no. 1 (January, 1919), pp. 72-103.

[3]Eustache Nicholas Pigeau, born at Mont-Leveque near Senlis in 1750, became Professor of Civil and Criminal Procedure at the University of Paris in 1814. The son of simple artisans, Pigeau began the study of law in his early teens as a clerk in the office of a *procureur*. From the age of seventeen he laid the foundations for his classic work, *Practicien du Chatelet de Paris et de toutes les jurisdictions ordinaires du royaume*, published in Paris in 1773, reprinted in 1779-1787 with numerous additions as *La Procedure du Chatelet de Paris et de toutes les jurisdictions du royaume*. Pigeau was the first to study methodically the precedents of practice at the Chatelet de Paris, the most important court of justice in the kingdom next to the *Parlement*. He served as an *avocat* of the *Parlement de Paris* from 1774. Conservative and fiercely dedicated to order in society, he deplored the excesses of the French Revolution and assisted in drafting the Napoleonic Code. He died on December 22, 1818. *Societé de Gens de Lettres et de Savants, Biographie Universelle Ancienne et Moderne* (Paris: Madam C. Desplaces, 1832), Vol. 33, pp. 307-308.

[4]Eustache Nicholas Pigeau, *La Procedure Civile du Chatelet de Paris et de toutes les jurisdictions ordinaires du royaume, demontrée par principes et mises en action par des formules* (Paris: Desaint, 1787), Vol. II, pp. 175-76.

[5]According to Tacitus, Germanic women enjoyed extensive legal, social and frequently military equality with their men, even accompanying them in battle and in the hunt. "The wife . . . is warned . . . that she comes to share hard work and peril; that her fate will be the same as his in peace and in battle, her risks the same." Tacitus, *Germania*, M. Hutton, trans., *Tacitus in Five Volumes* (Cambridge, Mass.: 1970), Vol. I, p. 159. Other sources, however, indicate a considerably more inferior status for women among Germanic tribes. Lombard and Saxon law, for example, viewed women as perpetual minors under male guardianship. Male permission was necessary in any transfer of property. Paradoxically, Roman law, intrinsically harsh in its provisions concerning women, liberalized the laws of some Teutonic tribes. Visigothic law, after exposure to Roman law, allowed joint administration by husband and wife of either's separate property, considered gains acquired after marriage community property, permitted the wife control of the family property and the inheritance of minor children if the husband died, and dictated equal inheritance rights for boys and girls. Frances and Joseph Gies, *Women in the Middle Ages* (New York: Thomas Y. Crowell Co., 1978), pp. 15-18.

[6]M. Charles Giraud, *Precis de L'Ancien Droit Coutumier Francais* (Paris: Durand, 1852), p. 15; Claude de Ferrière, *Commentaire sur la Coutume de la Prévoté et Vicomté de Paris* (Paris: Guillaume Cavelier, 1719), p. 30; Robert Joseph Pothier, *Traité de la Communaute* (Paris: Tardieu-Denesle, 1819), Part II, Art. 1, no., 471, par. 259.

[7]Giraud, *L'Ancien Droit*, pp. 15-16; Pothier, ibid., Part I, Art. 1, no. 1; *Traité des Personnes et des Choses*, Part I, Title VI, Sec. 1, 128, Vol. IX in Robert Joseph Pothier, *Oeuvres de Pothier* (Paris: Cosse et N. Delamotte, 1845-1848), 10 vols.; M. Argou, *Institution au Droit Francais* (Paris: Veuve Savoye Librarie, 1771), p. 201.

[8]Pothier, *Traité de la Puissance du Mari*, Part I, Art. 1, sec. 1, Par. 3; Part I, Art. 1, sec. 2,

par. 23-28, pp. 10-12.

[9]Ibid., Part I, Art. 1, Sec. 2, pp. 7-12.

[10]Pothier, *Traité de Contract du Mariage*, Vol. VI, Part I, p. 337; Pigeau, *Procedure Civile*, p. 236. Jean-Louis Flandrin points out that the family as an institution was seen as a civil or public society and that kinship relationships served as a model for all social and political structures. The king's authority and the father's authority were closely identified. *Families in Former Times: Kingship, Household and Sexuality in Early Modern France* (Cambridge: Cambridge University Press, 1979), pp. 1-8.

[11]Pothier, *Traité des Personnes et des Choses, Oeuvres Complets*, Vol. IX, Part I, Art. 4, Sec. 2, no. 129.

[12]Pigeau, *Procedure Civile*, p. 175.

[13]Pothier, *Traité du Contrat du Mariage*, Vol. VII, p. 176; Pigeau, *Procedure Civile*, p. 176.

[14]La Ferrière, *Commentaire sur la Coutume de Paris*, Art. CCXX, p. 5. Except in the *Coutumes* of Normandy and Riems, the community of goods established between spouses was a common right in all areas of the customary law. Giraud, *L'Ancien Droit Francais*, p. 61; Denes La Brun, *De la communauté entre mari et femme avec un traité des communautés* (Paris: Brunet, 1754), pp. 41-50.

[15]Ibid., pp. 3-5.

[16]"Movables" included debts, rents, and all obligations as well as those goods commonly considered moveable such as furniture, domestic animals, etc. La Ferrière, *Commentaire de la Coutume de Paris*, p. 6; Le Brun, *De la Communauté entre mari et femme*, pp. 57-59.

[17]Article 221, *Coutume de Paris*, in La Ferriére, ibid., p. 9; Giraud, *L'Ancien Droit Francais*, pp. 63-64. The obligations of the community for antenuptial debts and the right to modify the community property system by pre-marriage agreement meant that marriage contracts assumed major importance. Standard form for marriage contracts in pre-revolutionary France included a clause disclaiming antenuptial debts. Virtually all marriage contracts examined in Paris in the eighteenth century contained this disclaimer. In practice, therefore, the matrimonial regimes of eighteenth-century France were more frequently determined by marriage contract than by the precise stipulations of the community property laws. See Hans W. Baade, "Marriage Contracts in French and Spanish Louisiana: A Study in 'Notarial' Jurisprudence," *Tulane Law Review*, Vol. 53, no. 1 (December, 1978), pp. 15-18. Claude La Ferrière stated that the marriage contract was "the most important transaction made between individuals." La Ferrière, *Commentaire de la Coutume de Paris*, p. 13. The marriage contract could not, however, stipulate that a woman could alienate her separate property without the consent of her husband nor could the husband renounce the *puissance maritale*. Denisart stated that "this would be contrary to the dependence of the wife on the husband," contrary to the welfare of the conjugal community, and contrary to "good manners." Jean-Baptist Denisart, *Collections de Decisions Nouvelles et de Notions Relatives a la Jurisprudence* (Paris: Venve Desaint, 1788), p. 708.

[18]Giraud, *L'Ancien Droit Francais*, p. 65; La Ferrière, *Commentaire sur la Coutume de Paris*, p. 62, Art. 237.

[19]Pothier, *Traité de la Communaute*, Part II, Art. 1, Sec. 470, p. 259.

[20]La Ferrière, *Commentaire sur la Coutume de Paris*, Art. 226, p. 33; Art. 228, p. 37; Pothier, *Traité de la Communaute*, Part II, Art. 1, sec. 261; Giraud, *L'Ancien Droit Francais*, p. 64.

[21]Pothier, *Traité de la Communaute*, Vol. VII, p. 261; La Ferrière, *Commentaire sur la*

Coutume de Paris, p. 54.

[22]Pothier, *Traité du Contrat de Mariage*, Vol. VI, p. 175; Vol. VII, p. 235.

[23]Pigeau, *Procedure Civile*, p. 176; La Ferrière, *Commentaire sur la Coutume de Paris*, Art. 228, pp. 24-25.

[24]Denisart, *Decisions Nouvelles*, p. 543.

[25]Pothier, *Traité de la Puissance du Mari*, Part I, Art. 1, par. 1, pp. 1-2; *Traité du Contrat de Mariage*, Vol. VI, p. 175.

[26]Pothier, *Traité du Contrat de Mariage*, Vol. VI, p. 43.

[27]Ibid., Vol. VII, p. 238.

[28]Denisart, *Decisions Nouvelles*, p. 266; M. Fournel, *Traité de Ladultère* (Paris: Demonville, 1783), pp. 10-12.

[29]Pothier, *Traité du Contrat de Mariage*, Vol. VII, p. 237; Giraud, *L'Ancien Droit Francais*, pp. 16-18.

[30]Pothier, *Traité de Personnes et des Choses*, Part I, Title VI, Sec. 2, no. 132, pp. 236-37; Pigeau, *Procedure Civile*, p. 238.

[31]Pothier, *Traité de la Puissance du Mari*, Part I, Art. 1, par. 2, p. 2.

[32]Pothier, *Traité du Douaire*, pp. 318-24.

[33]La Ferrière, *Commentaire sur la Coutume de Paris*, Art. 237, pp. 114-15.

[34]Pothier, *Traité du Douaire*, pp. 39-40.

[35]*Coutume de Paris*, Art. 248, in La Ferrière, *Commentaire sur la Coutume de Paris;* Giraud, *L'Ancien Droit Francais*, p. 70.

[36]*Coutume de Paris*, Art. 237, in La Ferrière, *Commentaire sur la Coutume de Paris*, p. 114. Roman law did not recognize dower rights, which were unguaranteed as well in the areas of southern France where the influence of Roman law prevailed. The tradition of the *douaire* derived from Germanic tribal custom and was limited to the regions regulated by customary law.

DO IT! DON'T DO IT!: SPANISH LAWS ON SEX AND MARRIAGE

By

Sir Jack D. L. Holmes

Sexual morality as regulated by the government has always posed a problem, since one man's morality did not extend to his neighbor. Ernest Hemingway suggested a light-hearted approach to the dilemma: ". . . what is moral is what you feel good after and what is immoral is what you feel bad after."[1] Contrary to popular negative opinion as to the quality of Spanish laws — another example of the *Leyenda Negra!* — the body of laws relating to marriage and the rights of women was, perhaps, the most involved and protective of any nation in the world.[2] Yet, in the studies of Spanish legal history, there has been but disappointing use of these basic sources, as pointed out in two revealing studies by Professor Hans W. Baade of the University of Texas.[3]

Since there is invariably a gap between the laws and the actual practices, it is necessary to examine individual cases to determine whether the laws were being obeyed or ignored. Still, as a point of departure, it is useful to see what the law *said*, and in the case of Spanish Louisiana and, after 1783, West Florida, which Spanish laws attempted to regulate sex and marriage.

On November 25, 1769, General Alexander O'Reilly applied a series of Spanish laws to Louisiana. They were based on the *Recopilación de Castilla*, the 1680 *Recopilación de leyes de los reynos de las Indias*, and, *Mathieu de criminali contraversia.*[4]

Rape was treated in the first decree: "He who shall ravish a girl, a married woman, or a widow of reputable character, shall suffer death, and his property shall be confiscated to the use of the person injured, but if the said person be not of reputable character, the judge shall inflict such punishment as he may think suitable to the case."[5]

O'Reilly's Code also addressed the problem of adultery,[6] that crime "which a man commits knowingly (*á sabiendas*) by having intercourse with a married woman, or one betrothed (*deposado*) to another man."[7] As for the punishment for such offense, O'Reilly declared, "The married woman, convicted of adultery, and he who may have committed the same with her, shall be delivered up to the will of the husband; with the reservation, however, that he may not put the one to death without inflicting the same punishment on the other."[8] Apparently, O'Reilly was unaware of the liberalization of Spanish laws regarding punishment for this offense. "The woman who commits [adultery] ought to be whipped publicly, and shut up in a monastery with the loss of her [dowry] . . . The man ought to be banished, for the punishment of death imposed by Ley 15, Título 17, p. 7, has been mitigated. At present, the laws which permitted relations to kill the adulterer are obsolete."[9] As a matter of fact, this is the *only* section of O'Reilly's Code which was negated by the Council of the Indies because it was "objectionable."[10]

Pimps and panderers "who entrap women, inducing them by cunning arts, or procuring them to prostitute their bodies," were, by Spanish law, divided into five types.[11] Punishment for the first offense was set at a hundred lashes and ten years hard labor in the royal galleys. A second conviction brought the same whipping plus "perpetual condemnation" to the galleys, "although they may be under twenty years of age." How a pimp condemned to a life of hard labor in the galleys could exercise a third offense is not explained, but the penalty was set at death.[12]

O'Reilly condemned husbands who consented that their wives lived in concubinage with another man "or who shall have induced her to commit the crime of adultery." For the first offense he decreed ten years at hard labor in "some fortress," and for a second conviction, a hundred lashes and imprisonment for life.[13] The same punishment was meted to "those who carry on the infamous trade of enticing women to prostitution, by procuring them the means of accomplishing the same."[14]

Spanish law provided that those guilty of incest would be punished the same as adulterers plus "the confiscation of half his property."[15] O'Reilly's code provided that "he who shall be guilty of fornicating with a relation in the fourth degree shall forfeit half his property to the profit of the public treasury, and shall, moreover, be punished corporally, or banished, or in some other manner, according to the rank of the person and degree of the kindred. If the said crime be committee between parents and their offspring, or with a professed nun, the same shall be punished with death."[16]

Spanish law also frowned on that "detestable crime" (*pecado nefando*) or sodomy. Such "sodomites who commit an abominable sin, having connection with one other contrary to nature or natural custom,"[17] were, if convicted, to be burned and the property confiscated.[18] The *Novísima recopilación* (Ley 1, Título 30, Libro 12) stated, "it is not necessary that the perfection or consummation of the crime should be proved, but the proof of acts approaching to, or very near its conclusion, will be sufficient to produce the punishment mentioned in the text."[19] O'Reilly's code stated, "He who shall commit the detestable crime against nature shall suffer death and his body shall afterwards be burned, and his property shall be confiscated to the profit of the public and royal treasuries."[20]

O'Reilly also forbade illicit sexual liaisons between members of the clergy and female members of the flock: "The woman who shall be publicly (!) the concubine of an ecclesiastic shall be sentenced for the first time to a fine of a mark of silver, and to banishment for one year from the city or from the place where the offence may have been committed. The second time she shall be fined another mark of silver, and banished for two years, and in case of a relapse, she shall be punished by one hundred lashes, in addition to the penalties aforesaid."[21]

Finally, O'Reilly considered what should be done to boys and girls who persisted in "doing their thing." He warned, "If fornication be committed between bachelors and girls, they shall be admonished by the judge to discontinue every kind of intercourse with each other, under the penalty of banishment of the man, and confinement of the girl, for such time as may be necessary to operate a reformation. If this menace have not the desired effect, the judge shall put the same into execution, unless the rank of the parties requires a different procedure; and in which case the said offence shall be submitted to the consideration of the judges, collectively, to apply the remedy which their prudence and zeal for the repression of such disorders may suggest. They shall punish all other libidinous offences in proportion to their extent, and to the injury occasioned thereby."[22]

Of course, theory and practice are not always identical in law, as Blackstone's *Commentaries on the English Law*, and Solórzano Pereira's critique of the *Recopilación de leyes de los reinos de las Indias* in *Política Indiana*, suggest.[23] The relative permissiveness during the French dominion during the first half of the eighteenth century continued under the Spanish domination from 1766 until final expulsion of the Spanish officials in 1806. Moreover, there was little change in evidence following American occupation after 1803. New Orleans, it seems, would take no second-class ranking among American cities of sin!

French attitudes toward sex were conditioned by the frontier situation, and French marital laws were little changed following Spanish occupation.[24] When Bishop Luis Peñalver y Cárdenas arrived in New Orleans in 1795, he wrote reports concerning the prevalence of prostitution, adultery, miscegenation, bastardy, and other results of lascivious conduct among the populace.[25]

While there is a danger in making sweeping generalizations based on a relatively small number of incidents, after two decades of research in the primary sources I have concluded that the people of Louisiana in the colonial period favored sexual permissiveness. Governor Carondelet tried to explain the character of the Louisiana population to Bishop Luis. He described the great liberty and "total independence" of the young men. By the time they reached the age of ten they had learned to hunt, fish, ride and ramble. Between the ages of 15 and 20 they were usually married.[26]

Toward the end of Spanish rule, French Préfect Pierre Clément de Laussat met a "pretty, slender young lady riding a horse," whom he compared to a wood nymph with youth, elegance and beauty. He was astonished to learn she was barely fourteen years old and had already been married for six months! Laussat explained that she was a creole and that among those folks and the Acadians, early marriages and large families were quite common: "eighteen to twenty [children] astonished no one."[27]

Although marriage *was* the socially-approved channel through which sexual passion might be expended, the age-old alternatives kept pace in Spanish Louisiana, notwithstanding O'Reilly's admonition to the judges to keep a watchful eye upon fornication. Gossip, then as now, commonly centered on the promiscuous activities of the famous and not-so-famous.[28]

The regular non-married sexual alliances—"shacking up" or *concubinato*—were common during the colonial period, and for several generations thereafter. Spanish law provided that "the married man who lives in concubinage with a single woman" was obliged to give her a dowry equal to a fifth of his property, but if she were married, he lost one-half of his property.[29] Certainly, this was preferable to an early law of the *Recopilación de leyes de Indias*, which specified the punishment of a branding, double in the Indies to that inflicted in Spain![30]

Unfortunately, the laws against the practice were not administered uniformly. Mons. Labussière of Opelousas, who maintained a mistress named Chenet, was arrested and sent to New Orleans.[31] During a heated debate of the New Orleans *Cabildo* on May 2, 1788, prosecutors urged the application of royal decrees against the practice, all of which urged prosecution of those guilty of concubinage.[32]

In 1766 Father Clements de Saldaña wrote that keeping a mistress in Louisiana was such a common practice that no one bothered to comment on it: it was *not* a source of scandal![33] Auxiliar Bishop Cirilo de Barcelona claimed in 1772 that Louisiana women were generally more honest than the women in Spain, but they still suffered from "small sins in morals which might be remedied in time."[34] Governor Esteban Miró in 1786 condemned the practice, particularly among the free blacks, mulattoes and quadroons, who felt no compulsion to work as long as they were supported by their "*maris.*" Miró even condemned bizarre and garish dress by these women as evidence of their "misconduct."[35]

Inter-racial alliances had existed from the earliest European occupation of Louisiana, and the products of miscegenation were a common sight in French and Spanish Louisiana.[36] An early careful observer of Louisiana customs, the Pennsylvania historian, John Fanning Watson, described the "beautiful yellow women" who had no more ambition "than to become the concubine of a while gentleman." Watson felt they were "a good race of women; they are faithful ones who never desert their *maris* (or supporters) in any case of adversity," but he also noted they never married, and their children "however rich . . . must do as their predecessors—the daughters can at most *settle* as their mothers before them. . . . I do not know of a single case of a white gentleman marrying any one of the concubines, but I know those who deplored their position."[37]

Watson may not have known anyone who married his black or colored mistress, but there are cases when it happened. Moreover, in one case, a high-ranking white official, who kept a mulatto mistress, left his entire estate to his natural, mixed-blood daughters. Dr. Nicolás María Vidal was *Auditor de Guerra*, or military legal counselor to the governor, whose advice was sought on various points of law.[38] As a young man in Cartagena de Indias (present-day Colombia), Vidal had lived with a mulatto and a negress, by each of whom he had natural daughters. Upon his arrival in New Orleans in 1791, he took as his mistress Eufrosina Hisnard, a free mulattress, by whom he sired two quadroon daughters. María de las Mercedes (Merced in some records) caused an international incident in Pensacola when she appealed to Andrew Jackson as territorial governor to intercede with Spanish officials to recover documents regarding her late father's estate. When Spanish Governor José María Callava demurred, Jackson jailed the outraged official and obtained the documents himself. Merced Vidal did not live up to Watson's dire predictions for women of her class. She was married to another mixed-blood creole and had two children and was accepted in her social circles in Pensacola and New Orleans.[39]

Dr. Vidal's experience was hardly an exceptional one. A glimpse at the Spanish census for 1820 in Pensacola revealed a large number of unmarried mothers—Negro and mulatto "seamstresses" for the most part—who lived openly with their white *maris.* At least thirty-nine mothers of illegitimate children in such a small population indicates that such liaisons at the military garrison-town were common.[40]

And so it was in the Spanish Mobile District, wrested from the British in 1780. During 1788 an Irish priest named Father Michael Lamport spent a good portion of his parish duties for Nuestra Señora de la Purísima Concepción in marrying such interesting couples as Richard Bailey, a white English Protestant, and an un-identified Indian "heretic woman," while at the same time baptizing their two children, María and Martha.[41] Dr. John Chastang, the patriarch of a large mixed-blood family in the Mobile District—"Master of Harigay Hall"—married his black mistress, who had formerly been his slave but subsequently he had freed. Their many children became prominent land and cattle barons in early Alabama. Apparently, Dr. Chastang's sexual and racial choices did not damage the family's reputation in the St. Stephens area where they all lived.[42]

Racism was rare, but it did exist, particularly where such inter-racial couples were concerned. Lieutenant Domingo Bouligny, an important Spanish military officer and son of one-time acting governor-general Francisco Bouligny, condemned the Chevalier d'Anemours when he presented his mulatto mistress to the Ouachita Post settlers and expected them to shower her with honors. "The commandant here," Bouligny wrote, "so forgetful of his duty, received this whore publicly as his house guest and included her among the invitations to parties and dances which were given by the most prominent people in town." When the girl died, her grieving *mari* held an elaborate funeral to which the leading officials and military officers were requested to attend with their wives. Such intermingling, opined Bouligny, would surely lead to wide-spread revolts among the black slaves.[43]

It was a rare officer in the Spanish line regiment, the Louisiana Infantry Regiment, who did not maintain a "*casa chica*" or mistress. Bishop Luis noted the practice in a 1799 report: "They do not blush at carrying the illegitimate issue they have by them to be recorded in the parochial registries as their natural children."[44] Certain it is, that a large number of names appear in the records which show that this practice was, indeed, prevalent.

Of course, the sexual connections between black and white were responsbile for the mulatto population of the Gulf Coast. Problems which arose during the American dominion seem not to have affected the colonial settlers. Thus, Garret E. Pendagrast [Pendergast?], a white settler from the Tensaw River section near Mobile, joined his free mulattress mistress Isabel in having their free quadroon daughter Sophia baptized at

Harigay Hall on November 8, 1801.[45] Such events were a common occurrence, particularly in the Spanish Mobile District and Pensacola.

Notwithstanding the prevalence of unmarried couples living together, the church attempted to convince "by friendly persuasion" those living in sin to have their relationship sanctified by marriage. Thus, when Jacobo Herman, a Lutheran who had been living with a Catholic widow named Waible, asked for government permission to marry her, Governor-general Carondelet recommended to Bishop Luis that the ceremony be performed either in Natchez or Opelousas.[46]

On the other hand, the government sometimes disapproved to the point where love matches were deliberately broken up. Antonio Panis, son of a prominent Sainte Genèviéve settler, faced government opposition to his continued illicit relationship with María Luisa, a mulattress slave belonging to Vidal Beauvais. Although Panis and his paramour were the parents of two children, María Luisa's master broke up the union by sending the girl to his son-in-law who lived some thirty leagues away and across the river at San Carlos. Stubborn Antonio then fled to the American side of the river, borrowed money to purchase his mistress's freedom, and unsuccessfully pleaded with the Spanish government to intercede on his behalf. Not only had the couple lived together "without legal or moral sanction," but Antonio's presence in American territory was an additional impediment. Apparently, not everyone loved a lover![47]

Miscegenation also occurred between white men and Indian women, as it had since the initial contacts of the races in the fifteenth century. French trappers and British traders often took pride in their mixed offspring, and the names Colbert and McGillivray suggest such mestizo children played an important historical role in the southeast.[48] During the Spanish dominion, the practice continued. Samuel Martin deserted his white family and took up with an Indian mistress in the Chickasaw Nation because, as he claimed, "my debts drove me to it."[49]

Benjamin Payatt, one of the more notorious mean frontier ruffians, took an Indian girl as his mistress and, when her father objected, he killed him and fled from Alabama to the Natchez District, now a fugitive for murder as well as counterfeiting. Apprehended by a constable in the Natchez District, Payatt slipped his bonds, killed the law officer and escaped once more.[50] Lieutenant-governor Athánase de Mézières reported that white deserters from Spanish regiments frequently found refuge among the Arkansas villages where they purchased captive Indian women. They paid them no wages, other than "the promise of quieting their lascivious passions."[51]

As unfortunate as such behavior was in Louisiana and West Florida, it was an improvement over New Mexico, where Father Pedro Serrano wrote in 1761 that the Comanches introduced "X-rated" shows at the Taos Fairs. After the public deflowering of young slave girls, they turned their unfortunate victims over to the new owners with the leering phrase, "Now you can take her; now she is good.!"[52] American agent among the Creeks, Benjamin Hawkins, claimed all Indian women were sensuous and showed "the temper of the mule, except when they are amorous, and then they exhibit all the amiable and gentle qualities of the cat."[53]

When the records cite "mixed marriages," they are not referring to a racial mixture, but rather to the union where one of the partners was a Roman Catholic, and the other was not. During the 1790's in Natchez, for example, Father Francis Lennan maintained separate records in the Parish of Our Savior of the World concerning such "mixed marriages."[54]

Although the *Recopilación de Leyes de los Reinos de las Indias* contains a number of regulations governing marriages in general,[55] they were only loosely followed along the Spanish-American frontier. There seems to be but little difference in the modifications forced on metropolis institutions by the frontier whether we discuss the Spaniards, the French or the English. What the English common law called informal marriages without benefit of documents, licenses, blood tests, or other trappings of the metropolis, the Spaniards considered "clandestine marriages," and in 1791, Captain-general Luis de las Casas warned against permitting them in Spanish Louisiana and West Florida.[56]

A Royal Order in 1792 banned the *More Anglicano* which sanctioned such loose marriages: "Protestants of whatever sect they may profess," were still free to marry each other, or even Catholics, but the ceremony was to be performed by a Catholic priest before two witnesses and with the approval of the local commandant. Such a formula had been established at the Council of Trent. Such marriages as the alleged one between Andrew Jackson and Rachel Donelson Robards, said to have been performed by a justice-of-the-peace in Bayou Pierre, were declared null and void.[57] Those Protestant ministers still in Spanish Louisiana and West Florida were warned against performing marriage ceremonies, even for members of their own flock. Adam Cloud, an Episcopalean minister in the Natchez District, reported that several couples had applied to him to marry them, but Cloud asked government permission to do so.[58]

Cloud's subsequent violation of the law resulted in his expulsion from the district, and continued complaints from the Irish priests in Natchez indicated that the Protestants were flaunting the government ban on such marriages.[59] Still, a number of Protestants did abjure "their errors" of faith and joined the Catholic church, which was the designed purpose of the easy pressure adopted in West Florida. In the Mobile District, Father Michael Lamport married Protestants and "heretics" and baptized their children as well.[60]

Even more controversial were the laws concerning marriage among the Negro slaves. On the one hand their planter-owners urged them to cohabit for the purpose of increasing their wealth with the resulting children. According to C. C. Robin, some planters even forced their female slaves to spend their "free time" in paid prostitution.[61] Yet, official government attitudes as expressed in the laws, whether referring to the *Code Noir* of 1724 or subsequent Spanish codes, were opposed to the sexual exploitation of Negro slaves.[62] One official report noted that between 1777 and mid-August 1791, there had been only 54 marriages of Negro or mulatto slaves, yet the baptism of their children reached 205. The custom followed by these blacks was described as "*maries en face pieux*," or "*a la faz de las Estacas, ó por detrás de la Iglesia.*" That is, they merely announced before their friends at the fort gate and, with an English-style "common-law marriage," proceeded to live together as man and wife.[63]

Double standards of justice seemed to prevail regarding whites and blacks, if the Natchitoches experience is any indication. Lieutenant-governor Athánase de Mézières in 1770 ordered that any *black* woman "whose profligacy shall become scandalous," should be "exposed on a wooden horse and subsequently flogged." As for *white* women guilty of prostitution, they would be punished "to the full extent of the royal ordinances pertaining to the matter." Since O'Reilly's 1769 ordinance made distinctions based on the *class* standing of the guilty culprits, it may be assumed that few white women were exposed on the wooden horse![64]

A Spanish royal decree of May 31, 1789, called upon slave-owners to foment the marriage of their own slaves within the plantation compound so as to avoid the difficulty inherent when slaves of one master sought to marry those of another. Should the distance between plantations be such that married slaves belonging to different owners could not get together with their mates, then the wife was to follow the husband. To compensate the owner of the wife, *peritos*, or expert appraisers, would establish a monetary value for her, which the owner of the husband's slave should then pay to the wife's master. Should the husband's master decline to buy the new wife, the Spanish decree allowed the wife's owner to buy the slave husband, again at the price set by the appraisers.[65]

Spanish laws protecting the rights of the couple, as well as the State, were elaborate and eminently fair by modern standards. Permission from the parents, or if they were deceased, from other responsible family members, was a prevailing requirement seldom waived.[66] For government employees, especially military personnel, express permission from the Ministry of War was also required, and the dossiers used to petition for such approval are a valuable genealogical source. Lieutenant-colonel Enrique de Ocerin, a military engineer and knight in the Royal Corps of *Hijosdalgo de la Nobleza de Madrid*, furnishes a guide to these *expedientes matrimoniales*, along with a valuable analysis of Spanish legal theory concerning marriages.[67]

Ocerin cites Juan Martínez de la Vega's study of military marriages to prove that Spain was probably the first European nation to regulate military marriages and set the pattern which other countries followed.[68] In 1632, for example, Philip IV addressed the problem concerning the failure of Spanish troops marrying in Italy to obtain a dowry.[69] The crown modified military marriages in 1701, 1716 and 1760 before setting up the pension fund known as the *Montepío Militar* on April 20, 1761. This set forth the basic requirements for brides-to-be: daughters of noble fathers, or at least of "good citizens" whose *limpieza de sangre* showed no tainted ancestors (meaning blacks, Moors or Jews); girls with a dowry of at least 20,000 *reales de vellón* (roughly $2,500 in eighteenth century funds or property) for daughters of noble fathers, or 50,000 *reales de vellón* from less "distinguished" girls; and permission from the parents or legal guardians/relatives. The law stated that any officer marrying without first securing such military permission under the *Monte Pío* could be dismissed from the service and, if he died first, his widow would receive no pension.[70]

These requirements remained in effect until the Army Organic Code of June 9, 1821.[71] At various times, the rules were amended to fit certain needs, as with the March 23, 1776 decree, which required permission from parents or guardians of *both* bride and groom prior to receiving the war ministry's approval.[72] When some officers attempted to speed up the procedure by claiming they had given their "word of honor" to their fiancées, and had promptly set up housekeeping with them, Carlos III declared that henceforth any such miscreants would be promptly separated from the service.[73]

If an *expediente matrimonial* or marriage dossier lacked certain documents, a widow might be excluded from benefits unless these requisite papers were supplied. Lieutenant Juan Mier y Terán received approval from the *Consejo de Guerra* on October 6, 1804, to marry María

Gertrudis Armand de Courville, but with the proviso she *not* be entitled to draw her pension because the dossier lacked a key document, unless her husband died in action. Five days later, when the document was supplied, the Minister of War, Josef Cavallero, granted her full rights under the *Monte Pío*.[74]

In 1773 the Crown approved the application of Alexandro Cousot, a captain of grenadiers in the Louisiana Infantry Regiment, to marry Doña Francisca Paget, but without her *Monte Pío* protection unless she produced a dowry of 50,000 *reales de vellón* and justified her nobility, "as required in Article 5, Chapter 6" of the pension regulation.[75]

How generous were such military pensions to army widows? In the case of Doña Genoveva Damarrón, the widow of Captain Juan Trudeau of the Louisiana Batallion (predecessor of the Louisiana Infantry Regiment), his salary while on duty was $62 per month. Following his death on June 10, 1772, her pension began the next day at the rate of 3,000 *reales de vellón* per year. Converting the currency, she got about $250 per year as opposed to his salary of about $750 per year — ⅓.[76]

Although dower rights were carefully guarded under Spanish law, a wife was able to sell property and renounce her rights. Thus, Celeste Lasausale, wife of Henry Caller in the Mobile District, sold his lot on Conception Street in 1799, and in the sale ageed to renounce "the laws which protect the dowry, *senatus consultus*, New Constitutions, the Laws of Foro, the [*Siete*] *Partidas*, and of Madrid."[77]

As in so many laws, Louisiana and West Florida did not follow exactly the Spanish laws covering the other provinces in America. This is particularly true when we consider the law forbidding government employees and high-ranking officials from marrying women from their districts in America.[78] Cecilio Odouardo, chief military counselor and tax assessor for Louisiana, was given permission to marry Louisiana native Doña María Boucher de Grand-Pré in 1773.[79] It was a usual practice in Spanish Louisiana for unmarried governors to choose for their wives the creole (Louisiana-born) ladies whose family connections facilitated wide acceptance of Spanish rule. Two examples show how this was done.

When Bernardo de Gálvez (interim-governor from January 1, 1777; governor "*en propiedad*" from 1779) lay on what he thought was his "death bed in 1777," he was married to Doña Felicité de St. Maxent, widow of Juan Bautista Honorato d'Estrehan. In his capacity as vicar general and priest of St. Louis Parish in New Orleans, Fray Cirilo de Barcelona blessed the secret marriage because the governor-general had *not* obtained the required permission from the Ministry of War. Four years later, after the 1781 campaign against Pensacola, Havana's bishop blessed the marriage once more in a public ceremony. Royal permission had finally arrived![80]

Governor-general Manuel Gayoso de Lemos apparently ignored the prior-permission requirement when he married Elizabeth Watts on April 23, 1782, but she died within three months, and official records are silent on this marriage. On January 14, 1796, however, Gayoso signed a marriage contract with his deceased wife's sister, Margaret Cyrilla Watts, promising "to celebrate their nuptials according to the rites of the church as soon as the royal license is obtained." The couple then began housekeeping together, and their son Fernando was born July 14, 1797. When Gayoso took over as governor-general in New Orleans, he arranged for Bishop Luis to baptize young Fernando and to marry the parents the same day—December 10, 1797. War Ministry permission had finally arrived. Such irregularity in the procedures did not prevent the widow Margaret from drawing her *Monte Pío* pension following the death of Gayoso in 1799.[81]

With successive changes from French to Spanish in Louisiana, and from English to Spanish in West Florida, the *meum et tuum* of private law continued to govern such relationships as marriage. Thus, when Étienne Ferland died at Natchez in 1794, he left a young widow with nursing infant twins. She bore his name, "but as she said, only under contract of marriage." The Spanish government accepted the legality of her marriage.[82]

During his pastoral visit to West Florida in 1791, Auxiliar Bishop Cyrillo de Barcelona baptized a number of children and wed their parents at the same time.[83] It was not that the rural folks deliberately flouted the institutional procedures of metropolis marriages, but rather, that the expediency dictated by frontier conditions obviated such things as marriage licenses, publication of the banns, or tuxedo rentals! There was little difference whether they were Protestant, Catholic or non-professing; whether they were French, English or Spanish. They all did it at times.

Martínez de la Vega argued that man by nature was a social being whose heart was formed by affection, and that marriage was "the basic cell in society for the foundation of its sustenance."[84] Joseph Villars Dubreüil, a prominent Louisiana creole, wrote moralistic essays on the conduct among married persons and urged the Louisiana legislature to regulate marriage and inheritance rights.[85]

If the marriage did not work out, there was a type of permanent separation or divorce provided for under Spanish dominion. American

Louisiana discussed the desirability of divorce in 1806,[86] but as Professor Baade noted, under Spanish dominion, there was a provision for divorce under the jurisdiction of an ecclesiastical tribunal.[87] As with many aspects of church law, however, the government also played an important role. Henrique Henriquez wrote from Havana on November 29, 1791, regarding "divorce cases (*causas de divorcio*) the couple should proceed with strict compliance to what His Majesty has disposed in his Royal *Pragmática.*"[88] A Texas case involving the divorce of Josefa Castañeda and the Marqués de Casacastillo defined the power of ecclesiastical judges in divorce cases.[89]

The divorce of Juan José D'Orquigny resulted in his being jailed and an appeal as far as the *Consejo de Indias.* On July 24, 1786, the *Consejo* ordered him released, but to appear in Havana within five months to rejoin his estranged wife or to follow divorce proceedings as decreed. In either case, he was forbidden to return to Louisiana under any pretext.[90]

The Natchez District, which had been under English control from 1763 to 1780, had a long experience with Protestant divorces. In 1786, a longtime resident of Natchez, Anthony Hutchins, explained to the court what relationship a divorce had to a subsequent marriage.[91] A do-it-yourself type of divorce existed in the case of James Smith and his wife Sarah. "For divers causes and mutual consent, we, from this time forward, are to remain and live apart and separate each from the other, having no dependence on each other for livelihood or things of this world." Apparently Sarah had reason to regret her signing, which she claimed she only did to satisfy her husband, and she petitioned for justice from Governor Gayoso in 1792.

Gayoso ordered a local sheriff to examine the situation and act according to justice. On June 19, 1794, James Smith testified as to the rectitude of his position. He claimed she was an orphan on whom he bestowed money, "a suit of clothes," paid her debts, and lavished affection upon her. For three years all went well, but, according to James, "my wife grew sullen and abusive and on the most trifling occasions called me dirty names." James discovered the source of this change in disposition: "she had engaged in an intrigue with a neighbor who had seduced her and to whom I believe she prostituted herself." Finally, James said, they divided up their property and he left her. Sarah Smith then had her chance to testify.

They were "only tolerably happy" for three years, she declared: "their tempers did not suit." She claimed she did not separate from him willingly although "they lived in great dispute." She lived dependent on her brother-in-law, William Joyner, with her two children. Joseph Miller then testified he heard Sarah brag that she would leave her husband and follow William Collins (the "other man") "over the world." Upon hearing the testimony of the couple and the witness, Gayoso decreed on July 1, 1794, that they were to be permanently separated with an equal division of the community property.[92]

Another divorce was rendered at the Baton Rouge post by Captain Josef Vázquez Vahamonde, the commandant, in the presence of parish priest Carlos Burke and Miguel Mahier. Leonora Mullen had petitioned for justice at Pointe Coupée or *Punta Cortada* on August 9, 1794, complaining James Mullin, her husband, abused her badly and tore her clothes off her back, sold her property and deserted her, leaving her penniless. Anselme Blanchard reported to Vázquez Vahamonde from New Feliciana that the wife had always behaved herself and gave her husband nothing of which to complain. James Mullin then testified and showed an April 22, 1792, agreement signed by "Nelly Mullen" and him which stated, "James Mullen has delivered to Nelley Mullen all her property, debts, dues and demands from the beginning of the World to this day, and they have both agrede [*sic.*] never to have aney demands or clames against each other." Based on the proper settlement of finances, James Mullen gave Leonora his note-on-demand for $58 and the post commandant signed the divorce agreement on September 26, 1794, as witnessed by Father Carlos Burke and others.[93]

Not even prominent government employees were free from marital break-ups. *Guarda-almacén* (royal quartermaster and supply officer) Miguel Eslava at Mobile had been married to Hypolite Alexandre since July 10, 1794, and they had several children.[94] On November 24, 1803, however, Hypolite petitioned Mobile Commandant Cayetano Pérez for separate maintenance for herself and children while the Ecclesiastical Tribunal considered the evidence, took testimony from witnesses, and rendered a decision in her divorce request. It seems that her husband had abused her and thrown her out of the house.[95] Eslava refused to give his wife any financial aid whatever because, he maintained, he was a treasury official and outside the jurisdiction of the Mobile commandant.[96]

The entire question was submitted to Dr. Nicolás María Vidal, the *auditor de guerra*, or military and legal advisor for Louisiana and West Florida, for his opinion, which he gave on December 14, 1803. Since the acting-commandant of Mobile (Pérez) took over the treasury functions as well as the political and military ones, whatever Pérez had decided in the Eslava-Alexandre matter should prevail. As for Hypolite's request for financial assistance during the pending divorce, Vidal felt that the $20 per month decreed by Pérez sounded reasonable, providing Eslava had that much money, but if not, he should still be required to give his wife as much as he could afford. In this divorce case, Fathers Juan Francisco Vaugeois of Mobile and James Coleman of Pensacola intervened when Eslava attempted to sell three of his slaves in 1807 before the divorce was final.[97] What these various divorce cases illustrate is that the rights of the contracting parties in marriage dissolution were protected by a benevolent government, acting in concert with the church.

If marriage was the accepted channel for releasing sexual energy, and divorce was the approved solution of non-functional marriages, we must not ignore the pre-marital and extra-marital sexual liaisons which seemed to flourish. Seduction of the "helpless" female by the "predatory" male is a tale often told in the archival records. In the Mobile District, for example, Juana (Jane, nicknamed Jabota) Chastang yielded to the promises of Dr. Thomas Blair, became pregnant, and then suffered the indignity of seeing her lover flee the district before he could be sued for breach of promise.[98]

As Juana (Jabota) saw her slender figure increasing in girth, her sister, Goton, came up with a possible solution to her "problem." She had been approached by Agustín Rochon, scion of another noted Mobile family, who was trying to seduce her. With a ploy as old as the hills, Agustín suggested that his friend Benjamin Dubroca, son of another "in-family" of the district, might be persuaded to marry the pregnant Juana if Goton yielded to his pleas. Goton did, but Benjamin and Agustín did not! They had fled before the wrath of an outraged Chastang father, who promptly appealed to the parish priest for justice and won a $2,000 judgement against the Rochon family for breach-of-promise and seduction.[99]

A husband whose wife was seduced by another man might also appeal for justice from the government. John Barcley, the successful pioneer builder of a cotton gin in Natchez in 1795,[100] had entrusted his wife and child to his "good friend and neighbor," James Todd, while he journeyed to the United States. When he returned to Natchez with the bluprints for Whitney's gin in his mind, he discovered his family had been increased by one, although he had been absent for more than a year. He discovered that his firend Todd had taken his stewardship too seriously, and in the lawsuit filed against him, Barcley won an award of $300 in damages.[101]

Another Natchez scandal affected Elizabeth Denham and her father, Reuben. Benjamin Kimball induced and seduced Elizabeth and she was soon with child. When Kimball aided in performing a frontier-style abortion, the rogue added insult to injury by spreading a rumor that the girl's own father had impregnated her and then had aborted the resulting "problem." Reuben promptly filed suit against Kimball for "making false statements and debauching Elizabeth." The errant Kimball was subsequently ordered out of the Natchez District.[102]

No one, it seems, was immune to having his wife or fiancée seduced. Mobile's commandant, Vicente Folch y Juan, offered the hospitality of his home and board to Ensign Lorenzo de Rigolene, not aware that the visitor would add bed to the deal! After all, he had letters from Folch's friends in Spain, and he was a noted officer in the Flanders Walloon Guards. The young ensign sat at Folch's table, borrowed money at no interest, and took too seriously the old Spanish welcome, "*mi casa es suya.*" While Folch was on duty inspecting the district, Rigolene was amusing his evenings in bed with María de la Merced Bernardina Rodríguez Junco. Folch learned of the "affair" from a loyal slave and determined to catch the pair *in flagrante delicto.*

With several officers and witnesses, his alleged trip to the far points of his command was cut short as the group sneaked back into the fort and exposed the naked couple with lights and an outraged husband. "I left my musket and retired to my room to feel the pain of my disgrace," Folch wrote Governor-general Esteban Miró, his uncle. "This is the way an ungrateful officer, whom I had received in my home as a brother, has repaid me!"[103]

Folch quizzed his tearful wife about the incident, only to learn she had been forced to submit—several times at that! In consideration of his sons and daughters, Folch said he would not take vengeance, but until the truth of the matter might be resolved, he would keep her and her lover in jail "until it appears for sure that she did not give in willingly." In concluding his complaint, Folch said that in Spain a man's wife would be protected by kin, but on the frontier of Louisiana and West Florida, "the vile seducers who always direct their attacks against the most vulnerable women," were not checked by such *dueñas.*[104]

On the other hand, there was reason for wives to complain about their husbands who left them in Spain and went to America, only to "fool around." Spain's official policy was to frown on such behavior and to threaten dishonorable discharge to military personnel who took mistresses in America while legally married to wives in Spain. A rotation plan sought to being husbands back to their spouses after a reasonable tour of duty.[105] Husbands who were found guilty of living with strange women in the Indies while their wives remained in Spain, were to be punished and returned to the homeland.[106] The clergy was urged to investigate such incidents and try to persuade such errant husbands to eschew their evil ways and return to their wives in Spain and "resume their husbandly duties with their legitimate wives."[107]

Tomás and Ventura Villaró were two brothers who came afoul of this proscription in 1796. Both had mistresses in Louisiana while their legitimate wives were still living in Cataluña, Spain. Bishop Luis condemned such profligate behavior and warned such men set a bad example for the moral Christian climate in Louisiana. Two days later, Governor-general Carondelet gave orders for sending the Villaró brothers back to Spain.[108]

Doctor-patient relationships often led to fornication, as our non-medical charts seem to indicate. Dr. Blair seduced Juana Chastang, as noted above. In Opelousas, Dr. Carnotte prescribed sexual therapy to one settler's wife when her outraged husband broke in and caught them in bed. Mons. Despau promptly filed suit against the doctor in what must be one of the earliest examples of "malpractice" in Louisiana, but the "sensuous doctor" had fled the district before being brought to trial.[109]

In Pensacola, two physicians came to blows over the attention paid by Dr. Juan Ruby to the wife of Dr. Eugenio Antonio Sierra. Dr. Ruby felt that Mrs. Sierra would be cared for better if she were moved to his home so that he might minister to her needs around the clock. Dr. Sierra labelled Ruby a "dirty, old-man," and hit him with a stick. Dr. Ruby promptly filed suit for assault and battery.[110]

Bigamy was a double-edged problem for the government and church. According to a royal decree of February 18, 1754 and subsequent *real cédula* of March 19, 1754, the "crime" of bigamy was a "*mixto fuero*," that is, it belonged both to the Inquisition and the Royal Justice. The Royal Council discussed the problem during 1757 and 1766 and agreed to leave the "said crime" to the Inquisition.[111] In 1770, however, bigamy and polygamy were crimes under the jurisdiction of the civil authorities, and the Inquisition no longer was involved.[112] Those folks who were married at one time to two women were in the seventh rank of those who "caused public scandal," according to White, who noted the punishment for this crime was 200 lashes and ten years in the galleys.[113]

Buenaventura Collell should have been relaxed. His father was acting-governor during the American Revolutionary campaigns of Bernardo de Gálvez, and commander of an *isleño* settlement near Baton Rouge. Unfortunately, not even a prominent father could save a son from such errant behavior as bigamy! Francisca Esteves was "Ventura's " wife in Barcelona. He had married in 1788 Constance Condé while at St. Louis, but when the bigamy was discovered, Governor-general Carondelet ordered the young Collell jailed and his property confiscated.[114]

Rumor was not sufficient to condemn a person for bigamy, however, and Dr. Juan Josef D'Orquiny, the French surgeon sited above, was charged by his first father-in-law, Antonio Marmillón, with bigamy and attempted murder. The investigation revealed that d'Orquiny had actually divorced his first wife in Philadelphia, and he was subsequently cleared of all charges.[115] Various cases in the Natchez District illustrate that the practice of bigamy was widespread along the Spanish-American frontier, and indeed, in established areas as well.[116]

Incest also existed in these colonial areas as elsewhere, but the abuse does not seem to have gone to such extremes as in New Mexico, where the documents illustrate numerous cases of criminal action brought against fathers whose affection for their daughters exceeded permissible bounds.[117] There is an instance, however, in 1778, where the Rome Tribunal waived a second-degree of consanguine relationship so that Santiago Larcheveque might marry his niece, Doña María Gervais.[118]

We could extend our historical query on sexual customs into such nooks and corners of misbehavior as bastardy, homosexuality, or any of the infinite variety of sexual expressions of man-(and woman!)-kind! Yet for our purpose here, it is sufficient to examine some of the sexual practices concerning marriage, divorce and extra-curricular activities. We might, with some justice, agree with George Bernard Shaw, "A lifetime of happiness! No man alive could bear it: it would be hell on earth."[119]

Spain's protection of its vassals in and out of marriage certainly puts a dent in the old hackneyed "*leyenda negra.*" Here was a sovereign anxious to provide his subjects with channels of expression not inconsistent with the aims of society. As White quotes from the Spanish laws, "Marriage being so advantageous to the welfare of the state, our laws favor it in various ways."[120]

Naturally, frontier conditions worked their modification on marital institutions just as the frontier changed all manner of metropolis conditions. That sex and marriage continued to defy the accepted norms of approved behavior should not be construed as unique on the Spanish-Ameican frontier in Louisiana and West Florida. After all, as Alfonse Kerr properly observed, "the more things change, the more they remain the same."

[1]Ernest Hemingway, *Death in the Afternoon*, Chapter I.

[2]See, for example, Joseph M. White, *A New Collection of Laws . . .* (2 vols.; Philadelphia: T. and J.W. Johnson, 1839); and Gustavus Schmidt, *The Civil Law of Spain and Mexico* (New Orleans: Printed for the author by Thomas Rea, 1851).

[3]Hans W. Baade, "The Form of Marriage in Spanish North America," *Cornell Law Review*, LXI, No. 1 (November, 1975), 1-89; "Marriage Contracts in French and Spanish Louisiana: a Study in 'Notarial' Jurisprudence," *Tulane Law Review*, LIII, No. 1 (December, 1979), 1-92.

[4]A copy of O'Reilly's regulations is in the Parsons Collection, Humanities Research Center, University of Texas at Austin. It has been translated in Lawrence Kinnaird, *The Revolutionary Period, 1765-1781*, Part I, *Spain in the Mississippi Valley, 1765-1794* (3 parts; vols. II-IV), American Historical Association *Annual Report for 1945* (Washington, 1946-1959), 114 *et seq.* It is also in "Digest of the Laws of Louisiana," in *Annals of Congress*, 8th Cong., 2nd Sess., 1804-1805 (Washington, 1852), 1550-1551. Referred to hereafter as Code O'Reilly.

[5]Code O'Reilly, Section V, Par. 5. Should a victim's relations not accuse a rapist, "any of the people' might do so: White, *New Collection of Laws*, I, 116.

[6]Code O'Reilly, Section V, Par. 6, citing *Recopilación de Castilla, Libro* VIII, *Título* 20, *Ley* 1.

[7]White, *New Collection of Laws*, I, 228.

[8]Code O'Reilly, Section V, Par. 6.

[9]White, *New Collection of Laws*, I, 240-241.

[10]Marqués de Grimaldi to Luis de Unzaga, No. 24, El Pardo, March 24, 1770, *Archivo General de Indias (Sevilla)*, *Papeles procedentes de la Isla de Cuba* (hereafter cited as *AGI, PC*), *legajo 174.*

[11]White, *New Collection of Laws*, I, 225. The Spanish word for pimp is *alcahuete.*

[12]Ibid., I, 241-242.

[13]Code O'Reilly, Section V, Par. 7, citing *Recopilación de Castilla, Libro* VIII,*Título* 21, *Ley* 5.

[14]Code O'Reilly, Section V, Par. 8, citing *Recopilación de Castilla, Libro* VIII, *Título* 21, *Ley* 5.

[15]White, *New Collection of Laws*, I, 249.

[16]Code O'Reilly, Section V, Par. 9, citing *Recopilación de Castilla, Libro* VII, *Título* 18, *Ley* 3; and *Libro* VIII, *Título* 10, *Ley* 7.

[17]White, *New Collection of Laws*, I, 225.

[18]Ibid., I, 252.

[19]Ibid.

[20]Code O'Reilly, Section V, Par. 10, citing *Recopilación de Castilla, Libro* VIII, *Título* 21, *Ley* 1.

[21]Code O'Reilly, Section V, Par. 11, citing *Recopilación de Castilla, Libro* VIII, *Título* 19, *Ley* 1.

[22]Code O'Reilly, Section V, Par. 12, citing *Mathieu de re criminali contraversia*, 59.

[23]Juan de Solórzano Pereira, *Política Indiana* (Madrid, 1648).

[24]Rodolfo Batiza, "*La unidad del derecho privado en Luisiana durante el régimen español,*" *Interamerican Law Review* (*Revista Jurídica Interamericana*), IV, No. 1 (January-June, 1962), 121-137 (Spanish) and 139-156 (English). A popular "study" of sexual mores in colonial Louisiana is Herbert Asbury, *The French Quarter, an Informal History of the New Orleans Underworld* (New York, 1936), 11-13, 47-50.

[25]Luis Peñalver y Cárdenas (Bishop of Louisiana) to Eugenio Llaguno y Amirola (Minister of Grace and Justice), New Orleans, November 1, 1795, *Biblioteca Nacional* (Madrid), Ms vol. 19,509, folios 24-27, cited in Jack D. L. Holmes, *Gayoso, the Life of a Spanish Governor*

in the Mississippi Valley, 1789-1799 (Baton Rouge, 1965), 224-225.

[26]Baron de Carondelet (Governor-general of Louisiana and West Florida) to Bishop Luis, New Orleans, June 9, 1796, *AGI, PC, leg. 2354.*

[27]Pierre Clément de Laussat, *Memoirs of My Life* . . . translated by Sister Agnes-Josephine Pastwa; edited by Robert D. Bush (Baton Rouge, 1978), 63-65.

[28]For example, Anthony Hutchins of Natchez, spread the rumor that American boundary commissioner Andrew Ellicott and his son were sharing the sexual favors of their housekeeper, although the story was probably false: Stephen Minor to Manuel Gayoso de Lemos, Natchez, October 21, 1797, *AGI, PC, leg. 2371.*

[29]White, *New Collection of Laws*, I, 242.

[30]*Recopilación de leyes de los reinos de Indias, Libro* VII, *Título* 8, *Ley* V.

[31]Carondelet to Luis Andry, New Orleans, October 20, 1795, *AGI, PC, leg. 22.*

[32]Minutes of the New Orleans *Cabildo*, May 2, 1788, manuscript originals in the New Orleans Public Library Archives. Cited were laws of November 19, 1771, February 20, 1777, and December 21, 1787.

[33]Father Clements de Saldaña to Joseph Antonio de Armona, New Orleans, March 30, 1766, *Biblioteca Nacional* (Madrid), Ms vol. 18,745-29, quoted in Vicente Rodríquez Casado, "*Costumbres de los habitantes de Nueva Orleáns en el comienzo de la dominación española,*" *Miscelánea, Revista de Indias* (Madrid), II (Octubre-diciembre, 1941), 174, 177.

[34]Charles E. A. Gayarré, *History of Louisiana, The Spanish Dominion* (New York, 1854), 57.

[35]Ibid., 179. The original is in the Minutes of the New Orleans *Cabildo* for the 1786 sessions.

[36]H. E. Sterkx, *The Free Negro in Ante-Bellum Louisiana* (Rutherford, NJ), 60, 66.

[37]John F. Watson, "*Notitia* of Incidents at New Orleans in 1804 and 1805," *American Pioneer*, II, No. 5 (May, 1843), 233-236.

[38]Jack D. L. Holmes, "*Dramatis Personae* in Spanish Louisiana," *Louisiana Studies*, VI, No. 2 (Summer, 1967), 152-155.

[39]Vidal's will, New Orleans, April 25, 1798, New Orleans Notarial Archives, Notary Pedro Pedesclaux, fol. 288-292, cited in Jack D. L. Holmes, "Merced Vidal: A Remarkable Black Woman in Spanish West Florida," unpublished paper read to the Florida Historical Society, Orlando, May, 1980.

[40]Duvon C. Corbitt, "The Last Spanish Census of Pensacola, 1820," *Florida Historical Quarterly*, XXIV, No. 1 (July, 1945), 30-38. For a complete study of the census, see William S. Coker and G. Douglas Inglis, *Spanish Censuses of Pensacola, 1784-1820: A Genealogical Guide to Spanish Pensacola* (Pensacola, 1980).

[41]Baptismal books, Parish of *Nuestra Señora de la Purísima Concepción*, Mobile Chancellor's Office, I, fol. 22.

[42]Marriage records in ibid., I, fol. 72. See Jack D. L. Holmes, "The Role of Blacks in Spanish Alabama: The Mobile District, 1780-1813," *Alabama Historical Quarterly*, XXXVII, No. 1 (Spring, 1975), 5-18.

[43]Domingo Bouligny to Marqués de Casa-Calvo, Ouachitá, April 7, 1800, *AGI, PC, leg. 70-B.*

[44]Louis Houck (ed.), *The Spanish Régime in Missouri* (2 vols.; Chicago, 1909), II, 221.

[45]Baptismal book, Parish of *Nuestra Señora de la Purísima Concepción*, Mobile Chancellor's Office, I.

[46]Bishop Luis to Carondelet, New Orleans, January 2, 1797, *AGI, PC, leg. 102.*

[47]Carondelet to Zenón Trudeau, New Orleans, January 16, 1796, *AGI, PC, leg. 23.*

[48]John W. Caughey (ed.), *McGillivray of the Creeks* (Norman, Oklahoma, 1938).

[49]Manuel Gayoso de Lemos to Esteban Miró, No. 126, Natchez, June 10, 1791, *AGI, PC, leg. 41.*

[50]Gayoso to Carondelet, Natchez, July 9, 1792, in ibid.

[51]Athánase de Mézières to Luis de Unzaga y Amézaga, Natchitoches, May 20, 1770, in *Athánase de Mézières and the Louisiana-Texas Frontier, 1768-1780*, edited by Herbert Eugene Bolton (2 vols.; Cleveland, 1914), I, 166. My thanks to Professor Russell Magnaghi of Northern Michigan University for sharing this and the subsequent reference with me in 1974.

[52]Fray Pedro Serrano to Viceroy Marqués de Cruillas, 1761, cited in Charles W. Hackett (ed.), *Historical Documents Relating to New Mexico, Nueva Vizcaya and Approaches Thereto, to 1773* (3 vols.; Washington, 1923-1927), III, 486.

[53]Benjamin Hawkins to Mrs. Eliza Trist, Cusseta in the Creek Nation, November 25, 1797, in *Letters of Benjamin Hawkins, 1796-1806*, Vol. IX, *Collections of the Georgia Historical Society* (Savannah, 1916), 256.

[54]Many of Father Lennan's entries for such "mixed" marriages are in the archives of St. Joseph's Cathedral, Baton Rouge. A brief guide is Elizabeth Becker Gianelloni, "Miscellaneous Records of St. Joseph Cathedral, Baton Rouge," *Louisiana Genealogical Register*, XVI, No. 3 (June, 1969), 121-125. For an example in the Mobile District, see permission given by Commandant Cayetano Pérez, on July 26, 1810, to a Protestant, Elias Morben [Morgan?] to marry a Catholic girl, Anna Parna, in Parish of *Nuestra Señora de la Purísima Concepción* of Mobile Marriage Records, Vol. I, fol. 37.

[55]See *Libro* VII, *Título* II, *Leyes* i-ix.

[56]Luis de las Casas to Juan Nepomuceno de Quesdada [Governor of East Florida], Havana, October 29, 1791, cited in Quesdada to Marqués de Bajamar, No. 8, *San Agustín de la Florida*, April 20, 1792, *AGI, Audiencia de Santo Domingo, legajo 2588.*

[57]Ibid., being an "*expediente sobre el modo de contraher válidamente sus matrimonios los anglo-americanos y demás Protestants domiciliados en la Luisiana y Floridas y instrucción sobre el particular*" (dossier concerning the method by which Anglo-Americans and other Protestants living in Louisiana and the two Floridas may contract matrimony together with instructions and orders concerning the same). A copy is also in the archives of the Parish of *Nuestra Señora de la Purísima Concepción*, Mobile, Marriages, miscellaneous documents.

[58]Holmes, *Gayoso*, 81-83. Stephen Minor to Gayoso, Natches, October 29, 1791, *AGI, PC, leg. 46.*

[59]Ibid.; Jack D. L. Holmes, "Spanish Religious Policy in West Florida: Enlightened or Expedient?" *Journal of Church and State* XV, No. 2 (Spring, 1973), 259-260.

[60]Marriage and baptismal records, Parish of *Nuestra Señora de la Purísima Concepción*, Mobile Chancellor's Office, *passim.*

[61]C. C. Robin, *Voyage to Louisiana . . .*, translated by Stuart Landry (New Orleans, 1966), 246-247.

[62]Carl A. Brasseaux, "The Administration of Slave Regulations in French Louisiana, 1724-1766," *Louisiana History*, XXI, No. 2 (Spring, 1980), 141.

[63]Auto, New Orleans, August 16, 1792, repeating Theodoro Thyrzo. Henrique Henríquez, Havana, November 29, 1791, *Artículo* 30, in Parish of *la Purísima Concepción*, Mobile, Marriages, I.

[64]Athánase de Mézières, Proclamation, Natchitoches, January 21, 1770, translated in Carl A. Brasseaux, "Official Correspondence of Spanish Louisiana (1770-1803)," *Revue de Louisiane/Louisiana Review*, VII, No. 2 (Winter, 1978), 177.

[65]"*Real cédula de su magestad sobre la educación, trato y ocupaciones de los esclavos en todos sus dominios de Indias, é Islas Filipinas, baxo las reglas que se expresan*," Aranjuez, May 31, 1789, and printed at Madrid, 1789. Chapter VII concerns "*matrimonio de esclavos*." A copy is in the *Archivo General de la Nación* (México), *Reales Cédulas*, CXLIV, fol. 34. See also, *Recopilación de leyes de los reinos de Indias, Libro* VII, *Tomo* 5, *Ley* 5; and White, *New Collection of Laws*, I, 23.

[66]*Pragmática* of March 23, 1776, in Santos Sánchez, *Cédulas de Carlos III* (Madrid, 1792), Vol. I, 424-438, *Leyes* 1-19.

[67]Enrique de Ocerin, *Índice de los expedientes matrimoniales de militares y marinos que se conservan en el Archivo General Militar (de Segovia) (1761-1865)* (Madrid, 1959), I, lv.

[68]Ibid., I, lvii, citing Juan Martínez de la Vega, *Matrimonios militares.*

[69]Ocerin, *Índice de los expedientes matrimoniales*, lvii-lix.

[70]Ibid., lix-lx. The April 20, 1761 decree is in ibid., *Apéndice* No. 1, 662-669.

[71]Ibid., lx.

[72]Cited in *Expediente matrimonial* of Juan Barnó y Ferrusola, in *Archivo General Militar de Segovia.*

[73]Julián de Arriaga to Governor of Louisiana [Unzaga], No. 171, San Lorenzo, October 15, 1774, *AGI, PC, leg. 174-A.*

[74]*Expediente matrimonial* of Juan Mier y Terán, October 6, 1804, *Archivo General Militar de Segovia.*

[75]Julián de Arriaga to Governor of Louisiana [Unzaga], Madrid, July 15, 1773, *AGI, PC, leg. 174-A.*

[76]Royal Order, El Pardo, March 20, 1773, sent in Arriaga to Unzaga, same date, No. 116, in ibid.

[77]Translated Spanish Records, Mobile Probate Court, I, 246-247.

[78]*Recopilación de leyes de los reinos de las Indias, Libro* V, *Título* 2, *Ley* 44; Richard Konetzke, "*La prohibición de casarse los oidores o sus hijos é hijas con natuarles del distrito de la Audiencia*," in *Homenaje a Don José María de la Peña y Cámara* (Madrid, 1969), 105-120.

[79]Julián de Arriaga to Governor of Louisiana [Unzaga], Aranjuez, May 26, 1773, *AGI, PC, leg. 174-A.*

[80]María del Carmen Galbis Díez, "Bernardo de Gálvez," in *Los virreyes de Nueva Espaã en el reinado de Carlos III*, edited by José Antonio Calderón Quijano (2 vols.; *Sevilla*, 1967-1968), II, 329-330; Eric Beerman, "The French Ancestors of Felicité de St. Maxent," *Revue de Louisiane/Louisiana Review*, VI, No. 1 (Summer/*Ét,́* 1977), 69-75.

[81]Holmes, *Gayoso*, 122-124.

[82]May Wilson McBee (trans. & comp.), *Natchez Court Records, 1767-1805, Abstracts of Early Records*, Vol. II, *The May Wilson McBee Collection* (Greenwood, MS., 1953), 154.

[83]Confirmation records, baptismal, and marriage registers for the Parish of *Nuestra Señora de la Purísima Concepción*, Mobile Chancellor's Office. An *expediente* on the pastoral visit is in *AGI, Audiencia de Santo Domingo, legajo 2531.*

[84]Martínez de la Vega, *Matrimonios militares*, quoted in Ocerin, *Índice de los expedientes matrimoniales*, lvi.

[85]"*Princips de conduit pour les personnes maries.* . . ." undated essay; and translation of a bill drawn up by Joseph Villaré Dubreüil, no date [1806?], William R. Perkins Library, Duke University, Flowers Collection.

[86]Samuel S. Mahon, "A Discourse on Divorce: Orleans Territorial Legislature, 1806," *Louisiana History*, XXII, No. 4 (Fall, 1981), 434-437.

[87]Hans W. Baade, "The Form of Marriage in Spanish North America," *Cornell Law Review*, LXI, No. 1 (November, 1975), 45n205.

[88]Auto, New Orleans, August 16, 1792, quoting from Theodoro Thyrzo, Henrique Henríquez, Havana, November 29, 1791, Parish of *Nuestra Señora de la Purísima Concepción*, Mobile Chancellor's Office, Misc. Marriages.

[89]*Castañeda* vs. *Marqués de Casacastillo*, March 12, 1787, Bexar Archives, University of Texas at Austin, No. 0092.

[90]*Catálogo de los fondos cubanos del Archivo General de Indias, Tomo* I, Vol. II: *Consultas y decretos, 1784-1820* (Madrid, 1930), 49.

[91]Statement of Anthony Hutchins and Isaac Johnson, Natchez, April 3, 1786, in McBee, *Natchez Court Records*, 178.

[92]*Sarah Smith* vs. *James Smith*, in ibid., 194-196.

[93]*Expediente* (dossier), 1792-1794, *Mullen* vs. *Mullen*, *AGI, PC, leg. 30.*

[94]Marriage record in Parish of *Nuestra Señora de la Purísima Concepción*, Mobile Chancellor's Office, Marriages, fol. 11; Baptismal records for Miguel [Jr.], May 1, 1798 [born May 20, 1797] and Getrudis Francisca, May 19 [born May 6, 1795], in Baptismal records, ibid., fols. 49, 61.

[95]Her petition, November 24, 1803, *AGI, PC, leg. 587.*

[96]Cayetano Pérez to Juan Ventura Morales, Mobila, December 1, 1803, *AGI, PC, leg. 587.*

[97]Vidal's opinion, sent to Morales, New Orleans, December 14, 1803, in ibid.; Father Juan Francisco Vaugeois to Francisco Maximiliano de San Maxent, Mobile, April 8, June 16, 1807, *AGI, PC, leg. 75.*

[98]Carondelet to Manuel de Lanzós, New Orleans, March 25, 1795, *AGI, PC, leg. 22.*

[99]The case is in the first volume of marriage records for the Parish of *Nuestra Señora de la Purísima Concepción*, Mobile Chancellor's Office. It is summarized in Jack D. L. Holmes, "Alabama's Forgotten Settlers,: Notes on the Spanish Mobile District, 1780-1813," *Alabama Historical Quarterly*, XXXIII, No. 2 (Summer, 1971), 97. Apparently Dr. Blair did marry Juana, for his son, Tomás Bler [Blair?] was born in New Orleans, although no mention is made of his legitimacy! See marriage record of Tomás Bler to Eufracia Lami, Mobile, June 21, 1815, Mobile Parish Records, fol. 45.

[100]Jack D. L. Holmes, "Cotton Gins in the Spanish Natchez District, 1795-1800," *Journal of Mississippi History*, XXXI, No. 3 (August, 1969), 161-166.

[101]*Barcley* vs. *Todd*, June, 1796, in McBee, *Natchez Court Records*, 281.

[102]Holmes, *Gayoso*, 64-65.

[103]Folch to Miró, Mobile, July 7, 1788, *AGI, PC, leg. 52.* On Folch, see Jack D. L. Holmes, "Three Early Memphis Commandants: Beauregard, DeVille DeGoutin, and Folch," *Papers of the West Tennessee Historical Society*, XVIII (l964), 14-26.

[104]Folch to Miró, July 7, 1788. According to his petition, Madrid, January 24, 1787, *AGI, Audiencia de Santo Domingo, legajo 2657*, Rigolene served seven years in the Royal Flemis

Guard before transferring to the Louisiana Infantry Regiment at lower pay!

[105]*Recopilación de leyes de los reinos de Indias, Libro* VII, *Título* 3, *Ley* 1.

[106]Ibid., *Ley* 3.

[107]Ibid., *Libro* I, *Título* VII, *Ley* xiv.

[108]Bishop Luis to Carondelet, New Orleans, March 9, 1796; and Carondelet to Bishop Luis, New Orleans, March 11, 1796 (draft), both in *AGI, PC, leg. 102.*

[109]*Despau* vs. *Carrière*, June 26, 1799, Opelousas [St. Landry Parish Archives], now in Louisiana State Archives, Baton Rouge.

[110]The suit is in *AGI, PC, leg. 268.* Dr. Sierra was also involved in another suit caused by a different wife! See the *sumaria* and *petición, San Marcos de Apalache,* January 8, 1800, *AGI, PC, leg. 134-A.*

[111]Royal Decree, San Ildefonso, September 8, 1766, copy in *AGN, México, Reales Cédulas,* Vol. 89, fols. 96-97.

[112]*Real Cédula*, February 5, 1770, in Santos Sánchez, *Cédulas de Carlos III* (Madrid, 1792), I, 159-160.

[113]White, *New Collection of Laws*, I, 226, 242.

[114]Collell to Carondelet, St. Louis, October 20, 1794, Louisiana Collection, Bancroft Library, Berkeley, CA.; Carondelet to Zenón Trudeau, New Orleans, January 27, 1795, *AGI, PC, leg. 22*; *Crown* vs. *Buenaventura Collell, AGI, PC, leg. 172-B*; Carondelet to Bishop Luis, New Orleans, January 16, 1796, *AGI, PC, leg. 102*; Carondelet to Zenón Trudeau, New Orleans, January 20, 1796, ibid., *leg. 23.*

[115]*Expediente* on d'Orquiny, July 24, 1796, *AGI, Audiencia de Santo Domingo, legajo 2588*; see also, *supra*, note 90.

[116]MacBee, *Natchez Court Records*, 216, 320-321, and *passim*.

[117]Professor Russell Magnaghi to Jack D. L. Holmes, Marquette, Michigan, March 16, 1974, letter owned by author.

[118]Bernardo de Gálvez to Josef de Gálvez, Nos. 323, 370, New Orleans, October 16, 1779, June 6, 1780, *AGI, PC, leg. 223-B.*

[119]*Man and Superman*, Act I.

[120]White, *New Collection of Lawes*, I, 47.

*THE LAW OF SLAVERY IN SPANISH LUISIANA** *1769-1803*

By
Hans W. Baade

Introduction

There is a tradition in Luisiana that O'Reilly confirmed or perhaps even guaranteed the continued applicability of the French *Code Noir* in 1724[1] under Spanish rule. This tradition is already reflected in the classic nineteenth-century works of Judge Martin and Charles Gayarré.[2] Although squarely contradicted by the Supreme Court of Luisiana as early as 1816, it is still carried forward more or less routinely by authors with ready access to original Spanish-period sources.[3]

Closely allied with the notion that French *slave* law continued to be applied in Luisiana after O'Reilly's 1769 reorganizations[4] is the more general proposition that French *private* law, too, remained in effect. This proposition, as well, has had eminent supporters, from Thomas Jefferson to Gustavus Schmidt and, more recently, Colonel John Tucker.[5] Such a radical "Francophile" view of the legal history of the Spanish Luisiana cannot, however, still be maintained today. The original sources now accessible demonstrate, it is submitted, beyond doubt (1) that O'Reilly was authorized to change the law of the Province if he deemed it advisable to do so;[6] (2) that he did, indeed, introduce the law of Castile and of the Indies;[7] (3) and crucially, that his actions in this respect received the express approval of his Majesty in Council;[8] (4), and finally, that the judicial authorities of Spanish Luisiana routinely applied Spanish rather than French law between 1770 and 1803.[9]

If "Spanish" rather than French *private* law prevailed (and was in fact applied) in Spanish Luisiana after O'Reilly's reorganizations, it seems unlikely that the situation as to slave law was different. For one thing, as the insurgents of 1768 were to find out rather quickly, the public law (including the penal law) of the new sovereign was applied more or less automatically,[10] and slave law tends to be, in the nature of things, more of a public-law than of a private-law character. (Legal restrictions on the freedom to manumit, to take the key factor, are *iuris publici* almost by definition.) Furthermore, even in the realm of "private" slave law, the

*Louisiana is consistently spelled Luisiana in this essay.

two most significant transactions with slaves as objects: their sale and their mortgaging, were subjected to an elaborate set of regulations enacted by O'Reilly and Governor Unzaga in 1770, and reflecting Castilian rather than French legal institutions.[11]

It is reasonably clear, therefore, that the slave law of post-1769 Spanish Luisiana operated in a "Spanish" rather than in a French legal environment, and that at least in part, it reflected the law of Castile and of the Indies rather than French colonial law. The white population of Luisiana, however, remained basically Francophonic and socially as well as culturally oriented towards metropolitan and especially overseas France during Spanish rule. It may be, therefore, that the "living" slave law of the province between 1769 and 1803 was French rather than Spanish in content. That possibility gains further in strength in direct proportion to remoteness from New Orleans, for as I have attempted to show elsewhere, Spanish Luisiana was essentially a "dual state," and the legal folkways at the posts remained French.[12]

The kind of ambivalent coexistence thus envisaged could, however, have existed only to the extent that there were no fundamental differences between French and Spanish slave law as actually enforced by the Spanish judicial authorities of the Province. Wherever there was such a fundamental difference, on the other hand, pertinent Spanish judicial practice in Luisiana will readily inform us whether the Spanish authorities of the Province applied French or Spanish slave law.

The present study therefore seeks, first, to identify the salient differences between Spanish and French prototypes of slave law in the latter part of the eighteenth century. As will be seen presently, this task is greatly facilitated by a lively and ongoing debate among historians of what might be called the comparative "living law" of slavery in the Americas. Secondly, an attempt is made to place O'Reilly's "confirmation" of the *Code Noir* into the general context of his reorganization of the administrative and judicial structure of the province. Thirdly, by examining some thirty judicial records and about three hundred notarial instruments, we will try to determine to what extent (if any) the Spanish authorities in Luisiana actually applied, in their day-to-day practice, those parts of "Spanish" slave law that were *directly contrary* to the *Code Noir* of 1724.

I.
Comparative Views of Eighteenth-Century Slave Law In The Americas

A. Systems of Slave Law Compared

In a famous essay first published in 1946, Frank Tannenbaum drew attention to some fundamental differences between the situations of slaves (and of free persons of color) in Latin and Anglophonic America. English and United States slave law treated the slave, in effect, as a non-person: a chattel without legal rights and spiritual needs. Latin America slave states, on the other hand, recognized the fundamental humanity of slaves, and powerful religious institutions ministered to their spiritual welfare. Most importantly, Latin American legal institutions and social customs favored manumission, while "opposition to manumission and denial of opportunities for it are the primary aspect of slavery in the British West Indies and the United States."[13]

This theme was taken up again, and considerably expanded, by Stanley Elkins in his study of slavery as a problem of American institutional and intellectual life.[14] He agreed with Tannenbaum's basic classification, and attributed the abject legal status of slaves in the United States mainly to the dynamics of "unopposed capitalism" and, in particular, the absence of a powerful established church with a spiritual mission encompassing all of mankind.[15] While noting some differences between various Latin American systems of slavery and, in particular, between Spanish and French slave law,[16] Elkins agreed with Tannenbaum's basic assessment that Brazilian and Spanish slave law favored manumission, and thus made for a "peculiar kind of fluidity . . . that permitted a transition from slavery to freedom that was smooth, organic, and continuing."[17] For those manumitted, color itself posed no great obstacle, social or legal; and free persons of color were a familiar part of the social scene, even in prominent social positions.[18]

That fluidity did not exist in the ante-bellum South, but as Elkins points out in a later chapter, the very notion of an intermediate, transitional stage between chattel slavery and freedom was foreign to the increasingly shrill and sterile debate between abolitionists and defenders of slavery as an institution.[19] He attributes this phenomenon to the lack of national non-governmental institutions to which a reasoned intellectual appeal for gradual emancipation might have been made.[20] While that explanation might not be entirely satisfactory to less charitable students of mid-nineteenth century sectional debate in the United States, few would deny today that this debate was both parochial and unimaginative.

The Tannenbaum-Elkins thesis of a qualitative difference between Anglo-American and Latin American slave law was roundly challenged by David Brion Davis in his now classic work on slavery in Western culture.[21] Professor Davis not only questioned the proposition that Anglo-American slave law failed to recognize the moral personality of slaves, but he also disagreed with the view that Latin American slave law was qualitatively more benign. He disputed, first, that "certain humane laws of the late eighteenth and nineteenth centuries were typical of bondage in Latin America throughout its long history," and secondly, "that the admirable laws of European governments were obeyed by colonical slaveholders."[22]

Especially the former of these assertions as to Latin American slave law is significant for present purposes, as it suggests the possibility of differences between the French and the Spanish systems of slavery in the Americas. Indeed, Professor Davis proceeds to point out that one such difference existed with respect to what he, too, regards as a highly significant feature of Latin American slavery: "the well-known provision allowing a bondsman to purchase his own freedom." That possibility, he observes, was not available in the French colonies.[23] Perhaps even more significantly, it was of obscure origin, and did not exist uniformly even in all Spanish ultramarine possessions.

Coartación, as the right of self-purchase was called, developed on a customary basis in eighteenth-century Cuba, and spread from there to other parts of Spanish America.[24] It was not, Professor Davis notes, practiced in the Spanish part of Santo Domingo. A slave code drafted by the *audiencia* of that island in 1785 permitted manumission only by voluntary act of the master, and then subject to approval by the government.[25] We may add that the legislative history of the Santo Domingo code, as reconstructed by Javier Malagón Bárcelo, shows even more remarkable parallels between the slave law systems of the Spanish and the French parts of that island. The Council of the Indies had directed the *audiencia* to draft a slave code, taking into account the *Code Noir*, and the annotated draft reflects the direct influence of the French model.[26]

Professor Davis points out, however, that the situation as to Luisiana was somewhat different: The royal Governor had opposed the introduction of *coartación* into that province "claiming that what was proper for Cuba was not necessarily suitable for other Spanish possessions," but despite the Governor's opposition, Luisiana courts "upheld slaves' pleas for appraisal and the right to purchase freedom, at least by the 1770's."[27]

This thumbnail description of a key feature of the law of slavery of Spanish Luisiana is, as will be seen below, entirely accurate.[28] It is based on the digests of Spanish decisions prepared by Laura Porteus, and conveniently abstracted from the *Louisiana Historical Quarterly* in Mrs. Catterall's monumental collection of judicial cases concerning slavery and Negroes in the United States.[29]

The Elkins-Davis debate was moved into sharper focus by Herbert Klein's detailed comparison of slavery in Cuba and in Virginia.[30] That study demonstrated the tremendous importance of *coartación* and the hope of eventual freedom for the slave population of Spanish Cuba. It also called attention to the products of *coartación*: the freedmen of color, as indicators of the quality of life in specific slave societies. As Professor Klein stated: "Probably the best indication of a society's attitude toward enslaved peoples within its ranks is the role that the freedman plays within the predominantly slave regime."[31]

This observation is of direct relevance to Luisiana, which had the highest proportion of freedmen to slaves in the ante-bellum South in the first three decades of the last century.[32] Historians had, of course, been aware of this, and had also noted the exceptionally favorable ratio of free *gens de couleur* to slaves in New Orleans.[33] That seemed readily explained, however, the size of the Crescent City, and by the generally favorable ratio of free persons to slaves in urban settings.[34] Moreover, ante-bellum Charleston, too, had a sizeable and socially district free black community, and those who viewed this phenomenon comparatively were tempted to regard it as attributable to French as well as Spanish influence.[35]

Further inquiry into the origins of the free black community of New Orleans showed, however, that such an undifferentiated "other-cultural" explanation was too general. A key study in point, frequently used but not seen in historical context until recently, is Donald E. Everett's unfortunately still unpublished dissertation on "Free Persons of Color in New Orleans, 1803-1865." Dr. Everett discussed the published abstracts of French and Spanish Luisiana slave cases in some detail.[36] Readers with knowledge of the Elkins-Davis dispute could hardly fail to notice the total lack of freedom-purchase cases in the jurisprudence of the *Conseil Supérieur*, and their almost routine appearance and disposition by the Spanish Governor and *Cabildo* sitting judicially.[37]

The direct causal connection between the Spanish Luisiana judicial practice of *coartación* and the emergence of a numerous and socially significant community of free *gens de couleur* was clearly identified by

Laura Foner, whose comparative description of the three-caste societies of Luisiana and Ste. Domingue relies heavily on Dr. Everett's study. Dr. Foner writes:

> When the Spanish took control of the Colony in 1769, they continued a liberal policy toward manumission and even provided a number of additional ways for slaves to gain their freedom. By far the most important of these was self-purchase. A slave was allowed to buy his own freedom, usually with money earned by extra work for his master or someone else. If the master was unwilling to set a price or if the price was thought to be unfair, the slave could petition the Court to appoint a disinterested party to determine a fair value. The free Negro population grew from 165 in 1769 to 1,175 by 1785.[38]

As will be seen presently, the assumption that French Luisiana, too, had a "liberal policy" towards manumission is, to say the least, questionable.[39] Dr. Foner's remarks as to the key change in the law of slavery brought about by the establishment of Spanish rule in Luisiana is, however, quite correct.

B. Self-Purchase in French and Spanish Slave Law

Historians of slavery, we have seen, are agreed today that the right of self-purchase was a key feature of the Spanish law of slavery as applied in some (but not all) Spanish ultramarine possessions in the eighteenth century. What were the sources and particulars of this right, and how did it differ from the French law of slavery then prevailing?

1. French Law

The latter question can be answered with the substantial assurance. The basic source of French slave law is the *Code Noir* for the islands of French America, adopted in 1685.[40] That code started by proclaiming the Catholic faith as the state religion, ordering the expulsion of Jews, and providing for the baptizing of slaves. Slaves were to marry as prescribed in metropolitan France, *i.e.*, in canonical form.[41] Detailed provisions were made for their food and clothing, and these were sanctioned by the possibility of complaint to the public prosecutor. Other than that, however, slaves were without rights. They could not acquire property by work or by donation *inter vivos* or *mortis causa*; their property belonged to their masters. Nor could they be officials, arbitrators, experts, or (subject to or on exception) witnesses in civil or in criminal cases, or parties in civil suits.[42]

There was, on the other hand, at least initially no restriction on the right of slave owners over the age of twenty to manumit their slaves for any reason deemed appropriate by them. The testamentary appointment of a slave as an heir testamentary, an executor, or a guardian of the master's children automatically worked manumission. Once manumitted, free persons of color were assured "*les mêmes droits, privilèges et immunités dont jouissent les personnes libres.*"[43]

Both the freedom of masters to manumit and the legal equality of *gens de couleur* were, however, drastically modified within a few decades after the enactment of the *Code Noir* for the Islands. An ordinance of October 24, 1713, reenacted on June 13, 1736, imposed the requirement of the written permission of the Governor and the Intendant (or where there was none, of the *Commissaire-Ordonnateur*) for all manumissions. Another enactment, dated February 8, 1726, and expressly referring to the *Code Noir* for Luisiana enacted less than two years earlier, invalidated donations by white persons to *free gens de couleur*. By specific reference and operation of law, this ordinance apparently abolished implied-in-law manumission by testamentary appointment as heir.[44]

The *Code Noir* promulgated for Luisiana in March, 1724, is modelled on the 1685 code for the Islands to such an extent that Moreau de Saint-Méry's authoritative collection of French colonial legislation does not reprint the full text but refers, where appropriate, to the corresponding provisions of the prior enactment. In particular, the Luisiana *Code Noir* follows the 1685 code for the Islands in disqualifying slaves as witnesses or parties in civil litigation, and in denying them the right to own property or to contract in their own names.[45] Slaves could only be manumitted by masters at least twenty-five years of age, with the permission of the *Conseil Supérieur* for reasons accepted legitimate by the latter.[46] As already mentioned, free persons of color were expressly rendered incapable of receiving donations *inter vivos* or *mortis causae* from whites, but subject to that exception, they were granted the same rights as French subjects of the white race.[47]

It is readily apparent that the system of slave law just described precluded the development of any judicially enforceable right to self-purchase. Slaves could not own property or funds with which to buy their freedom; and in any event, they could not validly contract on their own behalves. Furthermore, the courts were closed to them not only as witnesses, but also as plaintiffs, so that any *de facto* understanding with their masters lacked the possibility of legal sanction.

This is not to say that self-purchase was not practiced nevertheless. Quite the contrary, article 50 of the Luisiana *Code Noir* made express mention of the possibility of "finding masters sufficiently mercenary to put their slaves at liberty for a price." As there stated, this was apt to lead to theft and to robbery on the part of slaves (presumably to obtain their purchase price).

It was for this specific reason that the 1724 *Code Noir* prohibited the manumission of slaves without the permission of the Superior Council, and stipulated that such permission was to be granted only if the master's motives in manumitting his slave were found to be legitimate by the Council.[48] In sum, the Luisiana *Code Noir* expressly reprobated the practice of self-purchase, and sought to inhibit it by making manumission contingent upon government approval upon a showing of "legitimate" motive, *i.e.*, a non-"mercenary" one.

2. Spanish Law

Several key provisions of the French colonial law of slavery as codified in the late seventeenth and early eighteenth centuries are readily traced to Roman precedent. This applies, in particular, to disqualifications and incapacities of slaves: as witnesses, arbitrators, private litigants, and contracting parties.[49] Given the heritage of the French legal system, the fact of these borrowings is not nearly as remarkable as their one-sided selectivity to the detriment of slaves. No provision was made for the judicial sale of slaves cruelly abused by their masters, recognized in Imperial Rome.[50] *Peculium*, or the Roman-law notion of quasi-property by sufference, was precluded by inference; and self-purchase (widely practiced in the Roman Empire) was inhibited by the *Code Noir* of 1724.[51] This one-sided legislative preference of masters over slaves and of slavery over liberty was further underlined by the speedy supression or restriction of two Roman-law borrowings in the 1685 *Code Noir* that were favorable to slaves: the power of masters twenty years of age to manumit, and implied manumission by testamentary institution.[52]

The Castilian legal system, too, was built in part on Roman foundations, and several provisions of Alfonso el Savio's *Siete Partidas* on the subject of slavery are of Roman origin. The most famous of these is the initial sentence of Title 21 of the fourth *Partida*, which declares slavery to be contrary to natural reason. Law 6 of that title authorized slaves to file complaints of cruelty against their masters, and directed the judicial sale of such slaves when cruelty is established, so as to preclude their return to the same master. A third well-known provision is a law of the fifth *Partida* confirming the validity of guarantees by a slave as a natural obligation, "*por cuanto es ome.*" As interpreted by the authoritative commentary of Gregorio Lopez, this passage reflected the general Roman-law rule expounded by the Glossators and by Bartolus that slaves could contract natural obligations; and by the mid-seventeenth century, it supported standing to enforce self-purchase contracts.[53]

Perhaps even more importantly, until the Bourbon reforms of the late eighteenth century, Castilian secular law was taught almost entirely on the basis of Roman texts and Roman-law treatises, with the *derecho patrio* serving only as an occasional illustration. The university reforms initiated by Charles III ultimately reversed this pattern and made Castilian-language instruction in the laws of the land the rule rather than the exception.[54] These reforms, however, reflected a more pervasive policy reorientation based on the Enlightenment. Thus, when the Council of the Indies undertook to formulate a cohesive policy on the subject of slavery in the last decades of the eighteenth century, it could (and did) resort to those institutions and doctrines of the Roman law of slavery that were supportive of liberty rather than slavery, and that favored slaves rather than masters.

This process is best documented by a lengthy report, or *informe*, filed with the Council of the Indies at its request in January, 1782, and jointly prepared by the former Intendants of Caracas, Havana, and Luisiana.[55] The Council was at that time considering the representations of the inhabitants of these intendancies, and of Santo Domingo, against the local promulgation of the famous *Cédula* of May 31, 1789, on the Education, Treatment, and Employment of Slaves. After a brief summary of the law of slavery since antiquity, the *informe* noted that in modern times, slaves received "incomparably milder" treatment in Spanish overseas possessions than in the American colonies of France, England, or the Netherlands. One of the results of this mild treatment, they pointed out, was the much more favorable ratio of freedmen to slaves in Spanish possessions.[56]

The Intendants attributed the mildness of the Spanish system of slavery as compared with other European slave systems then extant to three factors. These were the protective concern of the Spanish sovereigns for the Indians, which by analogy extended to slaves as well; the constant protection of these disadvantaged castes by judicial and ecclesiastical authorities; and finally, "*la sabiduría de nuestras leyes patrias, que adoptando únicamente la parte benigna de la legislación romana, ciñeron los derechos de la esclavitud a los precisos términos de la necesidad.*"[57]

In particular, the *informe* pointed to three institutions of Spanish law that had "*suavizado la esclavitud hasta un grado desconocido en las demas naciones.*" First, masters did not require official permission for the manumission of their slaves. Secondly, Spanish law enabled slaves to purchase their freedom, and that of their wives and children, by paying their purchase price to their masters. Thirdly, and finally, Spanish tribunals were open to slaves who complained of the cruelty of their masters, and where *mal trato* was established, the judge was empowered to sell the slave to another master.[58]

These conclusions were incorporated into a *consulta* of a plenary session of all three *salas* of the Council of the Indies, dated March 17, 1794.[59] There is little doubt, therefore, that they expressed not only the views of seasoned senior officials with field experience in the Americas (including Luisiana) but also the legal position of the Council of the Indies itself. Nevertheless, a few qualifying remarks seem indicated.

First, the situation described by the Intendants and by the Council was that prevailing at the very end of the eighteenth century. Spanish slave law as actually applied in the Indies had undergone considerable development in the course of that century, and this development had not been uniform. To take an example of the former factor: self-purchase was bitterly resisted by some slave owners in New Granada even in the latter part of the eighteenth century. Their lawyers argued that the *peculium* of slaves belonged in law to the master, who could repossess it at any time, and that in any event, no one could be forced to sell his property if he did not want to. These arguments were, as we have seen, contrary to a benign view of Roman law as received in Castile. They accordingly failed to prevail before the *Audiencia* of Nueva Granada and tribunals subject to it, but the right of self-purchase had to be vindicated, even at that late date, by persistent litigation.[60]

As regards lack of uniformity, it will be recalled that even as late as 1785, the *Audiencia* of Santo Domingo had favored the *Code Noir* over a "libertarian" version of Spanish law.[61] Conversely, Cuba practiced a system of self-purchase (known as *coartación*) even more advanced than that described in general terms by the Intendants. Cuban slaves could purchase their freedom, as it were, on the installment plan, with the double advantage that their purchase price was fixed at the early stage, and more "free time" became available for outside employment to obtain funds for payment of the balance remaining.[62] So far as can be determined, this type of limited self-purchase was not practiced outside of Cuba.

Finally, mention must be made of the self-laudatory tone of the *informe*, which stands in stark contrast with its ultimate recommendations. The question to be answered was, after all, if the *Cédula* of 1789 should be promulgated in places where it had been suspended upon the protests of the local population, *i.e.*, of the slaveholders and their supporters. The Intendants recommended *against* the enforcement of the *Cédula*, arguing that its principles were entrenched in Spanish slave law then prevailing, while the rules as to implementation were too detailed for reasonable accommodation to local circumstances.[63] Given the acknowledged gap between theory and practice in legislation for the protection of slaves against their masters, this was hardly a further step in the direction of "*humano trato.*"[64]

Nevertheless, it seems abundantly clear that eighteenth-century Spanish slave law was qualitatively different from the French law of slavery then prevailing. France had, as it were, codified those parts of the Roman law of slavery that were to the advantage of slaveholders: lack of legal capacity, of power to contract, and of property rights. To these, it had added the requirement of official approval for manumissions. Spanish law, on the other hand, had received, implemented, and expanded the rules and notions of Roman slave law favoring the well-being and the ultimate freedom of slaves: *peculium*, self-purchase, and judicial protection. Additionally, it had always favored rather than restricted voluntary manumission.

The results were there, for all to see. The proportion of freedmen to slaves was highest in the Spanish ultramarine possessions. Slaves fled from the French to the Spanish part of St. Domingue, not in the opposite direction,[65] and even foreign observers opposed to the institution of slavery praised the mildness of Spanish slave law in comparison to other Western systems of slavery in America.[66]

II.

O'Reilly's "Reenactment" of the *Code Noir* and the Reorganizations of 1769-70

A. The "Reenactment"

By royal *Cédula* of April 16, 1769, General Alexandro O'Reilly was commissioned to proceed to Luisiana with a force of arms to take formal possession of that colony. He was authorized to appoint an *asesor*, or legal adviser, and a *fiscal*, or prosecutor. With the assistance of these two *letrado* (university-educated) lawyers, he was directed to "institute prosecutions, and to punish in conformity with the Laws, the instigators and accomplices of the uprising" against Governor Ulloa, and to set up, "in the military as well as the political establishments, the administration of justice and the management of my royal *hacienda*, the form of government, dependency and subordination which may be advisable according to the instructions you bear and those which may be issued to you later."[67]

On August 18, 1769, General O'Reilly took formal possession of New Orleans on behalf of Spain. He quickly moved to accomplish the legal and political objectives of his mission. His activities in this regard can be divided chronologically into three phases: the establishment and consolidation of Spanish power, the punishment of those responsible for the expulsion of Governor Ulloa in 1768, and the basic reorganization of the judicial and administrative system of Spanish Luisiana.[68] His "reenactment" of the *Code Noir* falls into the first of these three phases.

On August 27, 1769, or less than two weeks after having taken formal possession of Luisiana, O'Reilly issued a proclamation on the subject of the administration of justice.[69] After stating that nothing was more essential for good order than the observation of laws, and expressing admiration for the "wisdom and piety" of the *Code Noir* of 1724, O'Reilly directed that this code be "observed with exactitude." He then announced that his "other occupations" did not permit him to attend to litigation in person, and appointed two individuals, Sieurs Fleurieu and Ducros, to "*administrer la Justice dans cette Partie.*" The proclamation then directed that the judgments to be rendered by Fleurieu and Ducros be followed and executed, and concluded by ordering all "officers and others" to lend all the aid and forceful support to this end that might be required of them.

O'Reilly's motives in making this proclamation (along with some others) are further explained in his report to the Marquess of Grimaldi, dated August 31, 1769, on the taking of possession of New Orleans and acts connected therewith.[70] He wrote that these initial *providencias* had-been received with much favor locally, and had been of good effect. As a general preposition, he stated, no change was to be made unless it was "*necesaria y muy reflexionada.*" The next step, he continued, was the banishment of evil elements and the punishment of the ringleaders of the uprising. After that, provision would have to be made for the future government of the colony. O'Reilly expressed assurance that in four months, Royal authority would be solidly established, and that he would then be able to return to Havana.

B. The Reorganizations

The "other occupations" referred to in the proclamation of August 27, 1769, we see, were the need to deal with subversives and to punish the ringleaders of the rebellion. This second phase of O'Reilly's activities in Luisiana was concluded with his judgment in the treason trials, dated October 24, 1769. That judgment imposed severe penalties, including sentences of death, on the principal ringleaders. It was expressly based on "*nuestras leyes*,"[71] thus giving a strong indication as to the nature of the legal system to be established in the third and ultimate phase of O'Reilly's activities in Luisiana.

That phase began on November 25, 1769, when O'Reilly issued a proclamation reciting the role of the Superior Council in the late insurrection, and stating that

> with a view to prevent hereafter evils of such magnitude, it is indispensable to abolish the said council, and to establish in their stead that form of political Government and administration of justice prescribed by our wise laws, and by which all the states of His Majesty in America have been maintained in the most perfect tranquility, content, and subordination.[72]

This policy was implemented by two sets of texts that are of decisive significance for the subsequent development of Luisiana law under Spanish rule.

The first set consists of two documents: Ordinances of the *Ayuntamien-*

to of New Orleans, and Instructions for adjudicating civil and criminal cases in Luisiana. These documents are collectively known today as "O'Reilly's Laws"; they are both dated November 25, 1769 and form the basis of the organization of the *Cabildo* and the central administration of justice.[73] The Ordinances regulate the organization and functions, including the judicial functions, of the *Ayuntamiento* or secular *Cabildo* of New Orleans, which replaced the Superior Council. The Instructions set forth the rules of civil and criminal procedure to be applied by the governor and the *Cabildo*, sitting judicially, but they also contain substantive rules, especially on criminal law and the law of both testate and intestate succession.

The second set of legal texts consists of a series of instructions issued to the two lieutenant governors at St. Louis and at Natchitoches on January 26, 1770, and on February 12, 1770, to the "lieutenants" or, in subsequent parlance, the commandants, of the nine original posts. They are, in substance, adaptations of the Instructions of November 25, 1769 to the needs of judicial administration and legal recording outside New Orleans, and they incorporate these Instructions by reference where appropriate.[74]

In addition to these two sets of major texts, O'Reilly also promulgated a regulation on the subject of mortgages, dated February 12, 1770. Soon thereafter, on November 9 of that year, his successor, Governor Unzaga, enacted an ordinance regulating the sale of slaves, immovables, and ships.[75]

C. Courts and Lawyers

As described in greater detail elsewhere, Spanish Luisiana was a "dual state" so far as the administration of justice is concerned. There was a highly sophisticated Spanish-type judicial system at the capital, paralleling those of municipalities of similar size and importance elsewhere in Spanish America.[76] The posts, on the other hand, were administered by commandants with limited judicial powers comparable to those of justices of the peace. The judicial powers of the two territorial Lieutenant Governors at Natchitoches and St. Louis were somewhat more extensive but still limited, in civil matters, to controversies under one hundred *pesos*.[77]

In New Orleans and its immediate environs, the *alcaldes* of the *Cabildo* exercised general civil jurisdiction, subject only to immunities conferred by the military and ecclesiastical *fueros*. The Governor had exclusive jurisdiction in litigation where members of the military were defendants, and in cases arising outside of New Orleans where the object in controversy exceeded the jurisdictional powers of the Commandants or Lieutenant Governors of the posts. As a practical matter, this included all slave cases arising outside of the New Orleans metropolitan area. Clerics with faculties as ecclesiastical judges and later, the Bishop, had exclusive-jurisdiction over civil actions against members of the clergy, but no freedom-purchase case in the *fuero ecclesiastico* has come to our attention.

The judicial decisions of the Governor of Luisiana and of the *alcaldes* of New Orleans were subject to review by a special Tribunal of Appeals at Havana, composed of high officials of the Spanish administration of Cuba and convoked on an *ad hoc* basis as occasion arose.[78] While there were a number of appeals to that Tribunal from Luisiana,[79] none of these, apparently, involved a freedom-purchase question. Decisions of the Havana Tribunal of Appeals could be appealed, in theory, to the Council of the Indies sitting judicially, but diligent search has yielded only one Luisiana case which reached that Council in this manner.[80] At the turn of the century, the *ad hoc* appellate tribunal at Havana was replaced by the *Audiencia* of Santo Domingo, which had been evacuated from Hispaniola to Cuba.[81] There is, however, no known instance of a Luisiana appeal to that *audiencia*.

The slave-law jurisprudence of Luisiana, then, consists of decisions of the Governor or one of the *alcaldes* of the *Cabildo* of New Orleans sitting judicially. These officials were almost invariably not law-trained.[82] In most instances, however, they had the benefit of the advice of the *auditor de guerra*, or judge advocate, who also acted *ex officio* as the *asesor letrado*, or law officer, of the courts at New Orleans. Under the customary law of Castile and of the Indies codified by *Cédula* late in the eighteenth century, lay judges were not liable for negligence in the exercise of their judicial functions if they conformed their decisions to the legal advice (*or dictamen*) of an *asesor letrado* holding a Royal appointment.[83]

Records of judicial proceedings were kept by the appropriate *escribano*, or notary, who also issued citations to the parties and to witnesses, and received proof documentary and deposition testimony. Pleadings had to be in Spanish, and had to be filed through a *procuradores del numero*, or pleaders. Initially, there were two *escribanos* and two *procuradores* in New Orleans, but this number was increased to three at a later date.[84] These notaries and pleaders were licensed after being examined as to the skills of their crafts,[85] but unlike the *asesor letrado*, they were not university-trained lawyers. Costs were taxed pursuant to a detailed fee schedule.[86] This made the legal system essentially self-financing.

Perhaps the most remarkable feature of the judicial system just described is the complete lack of law-trained counsel to litigants. Whether this was deliberate is difficult to determine. Apparently the only non-official author of legal briefs in Spanish Luisiana was Hermengildo Ruiz de Molina, a Spaniard who had at one time been majordomo of the military hospital of Pensacola after its conquest by Gálvez. He was expelled from the Province for "fomenting litigation and discord," but part of the charge was that he had done so without being a duly qualified *letrado* lawyer.[87] Ruiz de Molina was later licensed to practice by the *Audiencia* of New Spain, having obtained special dispensations on the representation that he intended to return to his "home" in Luisiana which suffered under the total lack of advocates.[88] This endeavor was frustrated at least in part by the changes in sovereignty, but it seems also clear that the Governor of Luisiana would not have admitted *Lic.* Ruiz de Molina back into the Province.[89] Again, it is difficult to distinguish between objections to the person and to the exercise of his profession, but whatever the prevailing motive, the tendering of learned legal counsel remained an official monopoly in Luisiana until the end of the Spanish era.

The need for professional legal advice varied, of course, in proportion to the complexity of the legal question presented. When it is recalled, however, that eighteenth-century Spanish slave law was essentially a humanitarian doctrinal adaptation of Roman-law sources,[90] it will be realized that in purchase-of-freedom cases, in particular, the role of the *asesor letrado* could well be crucial.

III.

Jurisprudence, Policy, and Notarial Practice, 1770-1803

A. The Impact of the Reorganization on the Law of Slavery.

We have seen further above that on August 27, 1769, General O'Reilly made provisional arrangements for the administration of justice, and directed the observance of the 1724 *Code Noir*. On October 24 of the same year, he passed sentence on the 1768 insurgents pursuant to *Spanish* law; and one month later, he abolished the *Conseil Supérieur*. Within a year thereafter, he and his successor completely revised the judicial and administrative system of Luisiana, which became, in essence, a Spanish

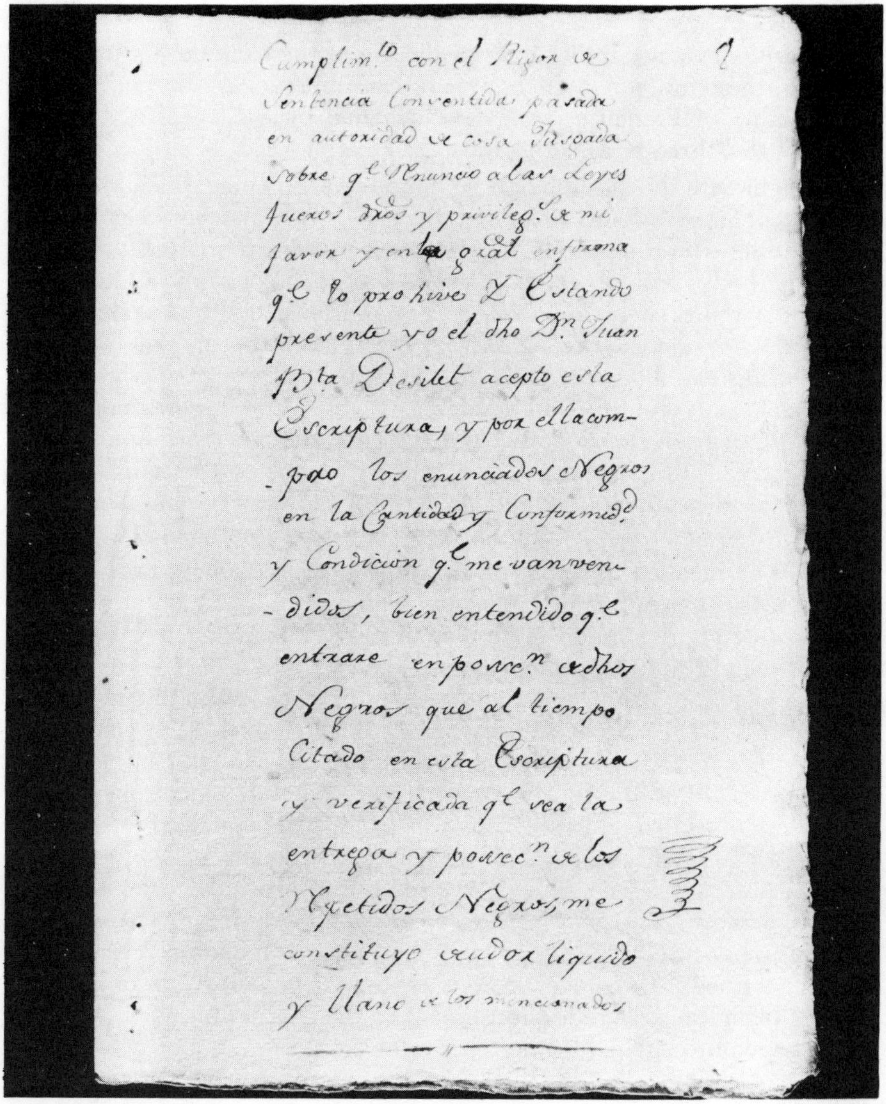

Cumplim.to con el Rigor de
Sentencia Conventida pasada
en autoridad de cosa Juzgada
sobre q.e Renuncio a las Leyes
fueros dros y privileg.s de mi
favor y en la gral en forma
q.e lo prohive Y Estando
presente yo el dho D.n Juan
Bta Desilet acepto esta
Escriptura, y por ella com-
-pro los enunciados Negros
en la Cantidad y Conformid.d
y Condicion q.e me van ven-
-didos, bien entendido q.e
entrare en posec.n de dhos
Negros que al tiempo
Citado en esta Escriptura
y verificada q.e sea la
entrega y posec.n de los
Repetidos Negros, me
constituyo deudor liquido
y llano de los mencionados

A bill of sale for 15 slaves sold by Daniel Clark to Jean-Baptiste Desillest and Charlotte de Lhommer, 1778, a reproduction of the first page. Louisiana State Museum.

ultramarine province under the jurisdiction of the Council of the Indies. How did these fundamental changes in Luisiana's legal system affect the applicability of French slave law, which had been decreed at the very outset of this three-phase process?

To begin with the most obvious and immediate change, the abolition of the *Conseil Supérieur* did away with the necessity or indeed the possibility of obtaining a finding of "legitimate cause" and a manumission license from that body, both of which were necessary prerequisites for manumission under the French *Code Noir.*[91] As readily verified by the numerous *cartas de libertad* in the Spanish notarial archives of New Orleans, Spanish Luisiana did not continue the French requirement of government approval for voluntary manumissions. In 1775, for instance, the *escribania* of Juan (Jean) Garic passed 24 notarial acts of manumission, and that of Andrés Almonastér, nineteen.[92] None of these instruments refer to a governmental or judicial approval, and the minutes of the *Cabildo* of New Orleans contain no reference to manumission petitions.[93]

It will be recalled that the slavery *informe* of 1792 was later to single out three features of Spanish slave law which, in the opinion of the three former Intendants, made it "incomparably milder" than other slave systems then extant, including that of France. These were the freedom of voluntary manumission, the right of self-purchase, and judicial protection against the cruelty of slave owners.[94] The first of these humanitarian features, we just saw, became part of Luisiana law almost immediately with the abolition of the *Conseil Supérieur.* The third-mentioned of the key humanitarian features of Spanish slave law, remarkably, was introduced by O'Reilly's *Instructions.* These provided that slaves could ordinarily initiate proceedings only with the approval of their masters. Where, however, a master had exceeded the bounds prescribed by law in exercising his authority over a slave (*i.e.*, where he had acted cruelly as legally defined), the slave could secure judicial approval to proceed against his master. Upon establishment of the charge, the slave was "entitled to require either his liberty or to be sold."[95]

Thus, two of the three main humanitarian features of late eighteenth century Spanish slave law, both of them directly contrary to the *Code Noir* of 1724, became effective in Luisiana as a result of O'Reilly's legislation. Another change, of a lesser nature, was brought about by the Spanish Luisiana mortgage and conveyance ordinances of 1770. This legislation classified slaves as immovables for purposes of sale and hypothecation; the *Code Noir* had provided that they were movables.[96]

There can be no doubt that these changes in the law of Luisiana brought about by positive enactment of the Spanish authorities displaced preexisting French slave law at least *pro tanto*, for whatever the legal significance of O'Reilly's "reenactment," of the *Code Noir*, it could not have stood at a higher level than his subsequent legislation.

There still was the question, however, whether the *Code Noir* remained effective in Luisiana to the extent that its provisions were not abrogated or modified by Spanish legislation applicable to and in Luisiana. As we shall see further below in connection with the purchase-of-freedom jurisprudence of Spanish Luisiana, that was not the case: O'Reilly's reorganizations had introduced the law of Castile and of the Indies in its entirety, and the Spanish judicial authorities applied only that law. The point of the continued applicability of the *Code Noir* was, so far as our research indicates, specifically raised in only one of these cases.[97] There is, however, at least one Spanish Luisiana decision in a case not involving the purchase of freedom where that point was also put in issue.

In *Angelica* v. *Juan Perret Estate*, a free person of color sought to enforce a testamentary bequest to her by the decedent. Two of the heirs favored compliance with this bequest, but a third one objected. Acting on her behalf, her husband Luis Ranson argued that the testamentary bequest was void because O'Reilly had "ordered that the Edict of the King that serves as the Regulation for the Negroes be preserved, observed, and complied with." He then textually recited, in Spanish, article 52 of the *Code Noir*, which as we saw invalidated donations *mortis causa* or *inter vivos* from white persons to persons of color.[98] The objector concluded by requesting that the court accordingly declare the bequest to Angelica to be invalid. *Alcalde* Forstal ruled, with the assistance of *Lic.* Odoardo as *asesor*, that despite this *contradicción* by Luis Ranson, the movables of the decedent be handled over to Angelica as provided in his will.[99]

Exactly eleven months earlier, *Lic.* Odoardo had assisted the Governor sitting judicially in a purchase-of-freedom case. This was the petition of *Catalina*, a mulatress thirty-six years of age, for freedom for herself and her five-year old daughter from the estate of J. B. Destrehan. Initially, the estate objected to the petition, but at a later stage, the dispute was over the price. On October 14, 1773, Governor Unzaga, with the advice of *Lic.* Odoardo, ordered the appointment of Santiago Beauregard as the official estimator, and his valuation of 320 *pesos* was paid by the petitioner. Thereupon, Estevan Boré as executor of the estate issued a letter of manumission to the petitioner and her daughter.[100]

It thus seems clear that when professionally advised, the courts of Spanish Luisiana did *not* apply the *Code Noir* even where there was no contrary Spanish legislation directly in point, and that they *did* apply the Spanish law of freedom-purchase which had not been expressly extended to Luisiana. On the other hand, as *Angelica's* case illustrates, O'Reilly's initial preservation of the *Code Noir* was well remembered under Spanish rule, and its text continued to be accessible. It should come as no great surprise, therefore, that a determined effort was made to return to the *Code Noir* as soon as opportunity presented itself.

B. Governor Gálvez and the Slaveholders' *Fronde*

Let us recall at this point the astute observation by Professor Davis that a Spanish governor of Luisiana had opposed the introduction of freedom-purchase into that Province, claiming that "what was proper for Cuba was not necessarily suitable for other Spanish possessions."[101] This refers to the judgment of Governor Gálvez in *Suriray* v. *Jenkins*,[102] an epic case which will require detailed attention here.

The key figure in that case was María Juana, a slave of Juan Suriray. She had filed a purchase-of-freedom petition in Governor Unzaga's court, and the appropriate initiating order had been made. In a new proceeding in the Governor's court, she alleged that thereupon, she had been removed by her master to Juan Dubourg's plantation, inhibited in her efforts to secure her freedom, and treated with cruelty. She had fled to the city, and now sought to obtain her freedom. She asserted that her claim was unopposed by secular law, and supported by Divine law.[103]

When ordered to reply on penality of suffering judgment by default, Juan Suriray argued, first, that in the laws of Spain, there was no obligation for the master to free or to sell a slave, or to destroy his property. He also called attention to General O'Reilly's confirmation of the *Code Noir*, which recognized the absolute right of masters to dispose of their slave property at their own free will. As to the facts, he alleged that María Juana was trying to enter the possession of an Englishman, with whom she was in collusion.[104]

When Governor Unzaga came to rule on these submissions, Suriray had already filed proceedings against Jenkins, the master of a British vessel then in port, charging him with enticement and harboring a fugutive slave. For this reason, and on the supposition that María Juana's (second) petition was a smoke screen in the enticement case, Governor Unzaga revoked his prior dispositions in the petition-for-freedom case, and joined this matter to *Suriray* v. *Jenkins*.[105] In so doing, he had the benefit of advice from the *asesor letrado, Lic.* Odoardo.[106]

The litigation between Suriray and the British captain was fairly protracted and apparently somewhat lurid. When all proofs had been taken and the matter was ripe for adjudication, *Lic.* Odoardo was absent from the province and had not been replaced. Governor Unzaga, expressing his inability to arrive at a just decision without professional consultation, thereupon decided to refer the case for advice to a member of the Havana bar.[107] The advice tendered in due course by *Lic.* Veranes, a Cuban advocate, was to the effect that the plaintiff had not made out his case, and that the action should be dismissed with costs to be taxed against him. As regards María Juana, he advised that she be given her *carta de libertad* upon payment of the price of her acquisition by her master, as was customary in Cuba in like cases pursuant to a royal *Cédula* of June 21, 1768. If the slave did not have the price of her redemption, on the other hand, her owner was to be compelled to sell her to another master.[108]

When this consultation reached New Orleans, Governor Unzaga had been replaced by Bernardo de Gálvez, but the new *asesor letrado* had not as yet arrived. On May 23, 1777, Governor Gálvez, again without the aid of a legal adviser, disposed of *Suriray* v. *Jenkins* in accordance with the advice tendered by *Lic.* Veranes. In the *María Juana* case, however, he ruled differently. The Governor assigned two reasons for departing from the *dictamen* of the Havana *letrado*. First, he said, the *Cédula* relied on (described by Gálvez as a *Real Ordén*) was addressed to Cuba, and thus not effective in the other domains of his Majesty, which as provided were governed by "*las leyes Generales del Reyno*." Secondly, he added, customs and usages locally prevailing should not be changed without grave reasons known to the King.[109]

This ruling seemingly comes close to accepting the plaintiff's twin submissions that the general law of Spain did not recognize a right to self-purchase, and that such a right had no place in Luisiana in view of O'Reilly's confirmation of the *Code Noir*.[110] It overlooked, however, that the *Siete Partidas* provided, and that O'Reilly's Instructions had expressly spelled out, the right of slaves to be sold to new masters or obtain their freedom upon establishing cruelty, which had been very much at issue in the instant case. Moreover, it failed to reflect the local custom of Spanish Luisiana, which had already recognized an enforceable right to self-purchase.[111]

The error of Governor Gálvez in these respects may have been simply due to the lack of competent professional legal advice in New Orleans at the time. There is, however, another possibility. While in Luisiana, Bernardo de Gálvez contracted marriage with Feliciana de Saint-Maxent, a daughter of Gilberto de Saint-Maxent, who was one of the wealthiest merchants of New Orleans and owned 200 slaves. Some of these slaves were included in Feliciana's *dote.*[112]

Even in the absence of such a direct interest, the Governor does not seem to have been immune to the charge of familial bias. His recommendations or trade policy, in particular, are said to have carried the "strong flavor of nepotism."[113] It is not unlikely, therefore, that the views of Governor Gálvez as to the slave law and policy appropriate for Luisiana were influenced to some considerable extent by his family connection to French slave-holding New Orleans society, if not more directly by his own interests as a local slave owner.

That may also serve to explain the Governor's participation in a contemporaneous attempt of the *Cabildo* of New Orleans to secure the enactment of a slave code at utter variance with Royal enactments of eighteenth-century Spanish slave law, and reflective of the most repressive features of the French *Code Noir.* This endeavor was initiated on October 10, 1777, when Governor Gálvez presented a Royal communiction relating to compensation for runaway slaves executed pursuant to judicial sentence.[114] Some time later, on February 13, 1778, the *Cabildo* charged two of its officials, F. M. de Reggio and Joseph Ducros, with the task of preparing the regulations requisite for implementing the Royal communication. Some eight months after that, the two commissioners submitted a draft "*reglamento dirigido por los negros mulatos y pardos,*" which the *Cabildo* ordered to be communicated to the principal inhabitants of the Province before its submission "*a los pies de Su Majestad.*"[115]

The *Cabildo* minutes and records do not contain the text of the de Reggio-Ducros draft, but the printed text as communicated to the posts has survived. It is entitled, in full, *CODE NOIR OU LOI MUNICIPALE, SERVANT DE REGLEMENT POUR LE Gouvernement & l'administration de la Justice, Police, Discipline & le Commerce des Esclaves Négres, dans la Province de la Louisianne, entreprit par Délidération* [*sic.*] *du CABILDO en vertu des Ordres du* **Roi**, *que Dieu garde, consignés dans sa Lettre faite à Aranjuez le 14 de Mai 1777.*[116] Since Ducros knew no Spanish,[117] it is highly likely that this is the version submitted by the two commissioners on October 16, 1778.

Ducros, it will be recalled, had been one of the two provisional judges appointed by O'Reilly's proclamation "confirming" the *Code Noir*. It is hardly surprising, therefore, that the de Reggio-Ducros draft *Code Noir* of 1778 closely follows the slave code enacted by Louis XV for French Luisiana in 1724.[118] Many of its 73 provisions reflect literally, or substantially, those of the French *Code Noir*, which obviously served as the model.[119] The proliferation of sections is due, in the main, to three causes. First, a number of provisions of the French prototype were divided into individual sections. Secondly, the rules dealing with runaway slaves and their abettors were considerably expanded. Thirdly, and more significantly, there were a few substantive innovations, which may serve as indicators of the spirit inspiring this draft.

Most remarkable about these proposed innovations was the endorsement of racial discrimination of free persons of color as a guiding principle. Subject to a relatively minor exception, it had been a basic rule of French colonial law that lawfully manumitted freedmen enjoyed "*les mêmes Droits, Privilèges et Immunités dont jouissent les personnes nées libres*."[120] This rule was now to be converted into its exact opposite: the *affranchis* were admonished not to insult, injure, or beat white persons, "*ni pretendre s'égaler à eux*," but to the contrary, to yield and to be respectful, on penalty of twice the punishment inflicted on white persons for like offenses.[121] For good measure, the final article of the de Reggio-Ducros draft provided that free Negresses and mulatresses were not to wear show pieces, nor garments ornamented with gold or silver, nor silk clothes, on pain of confiscation of these effects.[122]

Given this general orientation, it comes as little surprise that the 1778 *projet* of a black code for Luisiana faithfully reflected the major repressive features of the 1724 *Code Noir*. Thus, slaves were to be incapable of holding property, of contracting, and of receiving inheritance; subject to one exception, they were to be disqualified as witnesses; and they were generally deprived of standing in civil litigation.[123] Even the proscription of donations from whites to *free* blacks, which we saw had been held inapplicable in Spanish Luisiana, was to be re-introduced.[124]

Under the French slave code of 1724, we have seen, slaves could be manumitted only with license of the *Conseil Superiéur* upon a showing of legitimate cause.[125] This provision now had to be revised, if only because the Council had been abolished in 1769.[126] The 1778 draft provided, accordingly, that manumissions were to be effective only if approved judicially. Before granting his approval, the judge was to take testimony from four inhabitants of good repute, both as to life and morals of the slave and as to the legitimacy and truth of the master's motives. Manumissions made without observation of these formalities were to be void even if passed in notarial form, and the notaries were admonished to decline "absolutely" to pass such acts.[127] An explanatory footnote to this provision added: "*Quand il s'agit de faire un Citoyen d'un Esclave, on doit prendre toutes les précautions possibles pour s'assurer de la Régularité de ses moeurs, de la docilité de son caractère & de sa disposition au travail.*"[128] For the selection of those destined to be second-class citizens forever, this was surely a wise precaution.

As already mentioned, a printed text of the de Reggio-Ducros draft *Code Noir* was communicated to the post commandants, with directions to ascertain the actions of local inhabitants. In February, 1779, the *Cabildo*, with Governor Gálvez in attendance, devoted two full sessions to the reading of the *projet* and of the comments thereon. It thereupon decided to convoke an extraordinary session, to be attended by "*los mas notables habitantes y los mas distinguidos de esta Jurisdiccion*," for the purpose of finalizing the text for submission to the Crown for appropriate action.[129] The extraordinary *Cabildo* as thus augmented met in due course on March 1, 1779, and unanimously resolved to petition his Majesty for approval of the draft *Code Noir*. A large number of local notables signed this petition along with Governor Gálvez and the *Cabildo*.[130]

The subsequent fate of the de Reggio-Ducros *projet* is somewhat obscure. The matter came up again before the *Cabildo* more than five years later, on June 11, 1784, when Leonardo Mazange reported, in his capacity of *sindico procurador* (or city attorney) on the prosecution of runaway slaves and their accomplices then awaiting trial. The exemplary penalties required for the occasion, he stated, were not available, because the *codigo negro* prepared by the *Cabildo* in cooperation with Gálvez and the notables had not been submitted to his Majesty for approval. The *Cabildo* thereupon decided to charge the *alcalde* with the task of preparing the prosecution of the culprits and their accomplices "*con arreglo a las Leyes de estos reinos de Indias.*"[131]

Whether the decision not to submit the draft *Code Noir* of 1778-79 for royal approval was due to the arrival of the new *asesor letrado* in May, 1779, or to the cooling of relations between Gálvez and the *Cabildo*, or to yet other causes, seems difficult to determine. Whatever the reasons, the *fronde* was over before it began. The episode just described is nevertheless of considerable significance, as it illustrates the enduring attachment of Francophonic notables (including both rural squirarchy and New Orleans officialdom) to a slave law system as well as a biological racism totally at variance with the eighteenth-century Enlightenment. We will see further below that these attitudes, expressed in virtually identical language, were to come to the fore again some two decades later, when Spanish authority was no longer there to protect the subject races.[132]

C. Spanish Freedom-Purchase Law in Operation

Pursuant to a decree issued by Governor Unzaga on November 9, 1770, all sales and donations of slaves had to be in notarial form, and the schedule of fees promulgated by General O'Reilly in 1769 prescribed a charge of twelve *reales* [1.5 *pesos*] for the passing of slave sale contracts by Luisiana *escribanos*.[133] While neither of these enactments dealt directly with the formal requisites of manumissions, it seems to have been assumed quite generally that these, too, should be in notarial form. Freedom-purchase cases decided for the plaintiff uniformly ordered the master to execute a notarial *carta de libertad*.[134]

Where freedom was purchased by bargain transaction, the buyer appears to have insisted regularly on the execution of such a notarial instrument. Random examination of the notarial archives shows several instances of the subsequent formalization of emancipations initially executed by private writing.[135] As a self-authenticating public document, the *carta de libertad* both perpetuated and facilitated the proof of freedom. Furthermore, it routinely contained boilerplate warranties and jurisdictional submissions by the master-vendor, including language as to the actual payment or waiver of the *exceptio non numeratae pecuniae* so as to preclude future claims by the vendor on the ground that the purchase price had not in fact been paid.[136]

The following figures might give some idea as to the frequency of manumissions in notarial form. In 1775, Garic passed twenty-four *cartas de libertad*, and Almonaster, nineteen, for a total of forty-three.[137] Twenty-five years later, the three *escribanos* then in practice executed a total of fifty-four such documents, and in 1803, that figure had risen to ninety.[138] On the average, there appear to have been about twenty acts of manumission per *escribano* per year. Thus, Garic's successor, Mazange, passed twenty-one *cartas de libertad* in 1780, and his successor, Pedesclaux, passed twenty-eight such acts in 1790.[139] Even without the benefit of a comprehensive calculation, it seems reasonable to assume that considerably more than one thousand instruments of manumission were executed by the New Orleans *escribanos* in the thirty-three years of direct Spanish rule.

More importantly for present purposes, the notarial acts of manumission regularly recite the objectives of the parties. It is possible, therefore, to determine the statistical incidence of freedom-purchase bargain transactions (both voluntary and judicially sanctioned) in relation to unilateral acts of manumission motivated by family considerations, charity, or desire to reward loyal services. Of the twenty-four instruments of manumission passed by Garic in 1775, for instance, eight evidence transactions in which the slave bought his or her freedom at a price agreed upon with the master.[140] Of the fifty-four *cartas de libertad* recorded by the three New Orleans *escribanos* in 1800, twelve were self-purchase agreements.[141] Another twenty-five were third-party transactions, in which a free person (typically a close family relation) bought the liberty of a slave or of a slave family.[142] Only one of the manumission acts passed by New Orleans *escribanos* in 1800 was executed pursuant to a judgment in a purchase-of-freedom case.[143]. Of the ninety *cartas de libertad* passed by the same three *escribanos* in 1803, fifty-seven evidenced freedom-purchase transactions (27 self-purchase; 30 third-party), but there were only two notarial manumissions pursuant to judicial decree.[144]

This numerical disparity between purchase-of-freedom litigation and voluntary manumissions seems fairly representative for the last quarter of the eighteenth century in Luisiana. In 1780, for instance, there were only two purchase-of-freedom cases, but Mazange alone passed twenty-one acts of manumission.[145] Of the twenty-eight *cartas de libertad* recorded by Pedesclaux in 1790, only one was passed in compliance with judicial mandate.[146] Our own examination of the judicial archives indicates that in the sixteen years between June, 1773 and August, 1791, a total of seventeen freedom-purchase cases were filed; and Dr. Burson states in her carefully researched study that the total of such cases for the entire Spanish period is fifty-two.[147] On the cautious estimate of a rate of slightly less than two freedom-purchase cases and forty notarial manumissions including about fifteen to twenty freedom-purchase transactions per year during this period, it seems reasonably certain that in about nine cases out of ten, freedom did not have to be vindicated by litigation but was purchased at a price agreed upon by the parties.

That should serve to put into proper focus the function of freedom-purchase litigation in Spanish Luisiana. The law of Castile and of the Indies as there in effect, we have seen, permitted slaves to purchase their freedom at their appraised value, irrespective of the master's determination not to manumit.[148] Given a ready market for slaves, this meant in practice that the parties could negotiate with full assurance of the outcome and reasonable assurance as to its cost. The primary function of litigation was not to force the master to manumit the slave, but to determine the price at which he had to do so. All of the freedom-purchase actions examined in connection with this study[149] are, in essence, disputes over the monetary price of freedom—*i.e.*, the current market value of the slave.

Two cases, chosen more or less at random, illustrate the operation of this system. In 1780, *Nicolas*,[150] a slave of Mme. Prevost, petitioned for his freedom. The estimates of the experts nominated by the parties differed, 1,200 to 800 *pesos*. The expert appointed by the court agreed with the latter figure, and freedom was decreed at that price. Costs were assessed against the petitioner, as was customary. They came to 27.5 *pesos*, or 220 *reales*, of which 107 went to the *escribano*, and 32, to the *asesor* (*Lic.* Postigo). Early in 1789, Tonton, a *parda*, successfully petitioned to purchase the freedom of his sister *Feliciana*, a slave of Gravier Beltran.[151] The parties' experts came in at 600 to 1,200 *pesos*. Manumission was decreed by Governor Miró, with *Lic.* Postigo as *asesor*, at 800 *pesos*, the valuation of the court-appointed *tasador*.

Only one instance of attempted slaveholder resistance to manumission at the judicially-approved appraisal value of a slave has been found. This is the 1789 case of *Josefa*,[152] a mulatto slave of Mme. Brazeau. The petitioner demonstrated substantial resourcefulness, starting by an inquiry as to her estimated value in the inventory of M. Brazeau's will. The widow objected to valuation at this sum (350 *pesos*), and appointed her own expert. She listed all the virtues of the slave, whom she described as a good cook, washerwoman, ironer, and pastry maker. The widow's expert, obligingly, came in at 1,000 *pesos*, and the petitioner's expert, at 600. The officially appointed expert's figure was 700 *pesos*, and Josefa now sought her freedom from that amount.

What followed then is highly instructive for present purposes. Governor Miró, sitting with *Lic.* Postigo, ordered the respondent to issue a letter of manumission upon payment of the 700 *pesos*. The widow Brazeau responded to this judicial order by stating that she should not manumit Josefa at such a price. Upon re-application and deposit of the 700 *pesos* in court, Mme. Brazeau was ordered by Governor Miró to issue a letter of manumission to Josefa within three days.[153]

Further description and analysis of freedom-purchase cases would be repetitive at this point. It should, however, be pointed out that the system as just outlined could operate efficiently only if a number of rules of Spanish slave law directly contrary to the *Code Noir* were routinely enforced. First, slaves had to possess judicial standing to bring freedom-purchase petitions against their masters. This right was never in doubt in Spanish Luisiana.[154] Secondly, again contrary to the *Code Noir* and its abortive 1778-79 offspring, slaves had to have the right to accumulate some property, or *peculium*. This, too, was recognized, as illustrated by the 1788 case of *Juan Francisco Mangloar*,[155] who petitioned to purchase his freedom from his owner, Carlos Olivares. The petitioner (a slave) was willing and able to purchase his freedom in cash at his estimated value of 1,050 *pesos*. Governor Miró, with *Lic.* Postigo as *asesor*, promptly inquired as to the source of the funds. It was established to the satisfaction of the court that Mangloar had made substantial savings in his business activities, and the execution of a letter of manumission was ordered.

Finally, freedom-purchase by relatives, which appears to have become the prevailing method by the end of the eighteenth century, would have been hampered seriously if persons of color had been legally incapacitated from receiving donations from whites as provided by the French *Code Noir*. We have already noted that in the 1774 case of *Angelica* v. *Juan Perret Estate*,[156] the validity of such donations had been upheld. Rather unsurprisingly, this jurisprudence, too, was folowed in subsequent cases.[157]

IV.

Legacy and Restoration

A. The French Interlude

On November 30, 1803, Pierre Clément de Laussat took possession of Luisiana for France; on December 20, he surrendered the colony to the United States.[158] The twenty days of his *interregnum* as Colonial Prefect of the French Republic are generally regarded to be of little significance in the legal history of Luisiana, and are, in any event, outside the time focus of the present study. Nevertheless, this brief period of French rule in early nineteenth-century Luisiana deserves consideration here, if only because a bare three days before the second change of sovereignty,

Laussat issued a proclamation reenacting the *Code Noir* of 1724.[159]

That proclamation was dated the 24th of Frimaire of the Year XII, or December 17, 1803, and consisted of a broadside printed page in five columns. It started by reciting that on the previous day, *i.e.*, December 16, the Municipal Government of New Orleans had submitted to the Prefect for provisional enactment a set of draft regulations for the Police of Negroes, extracted from the *Code Noir* of 1724. That draft, however, contained modifications of, as well as additions to, the 1724 code, which the Prefect felt unable to examine in the time remaining and unable to enact without further authority.

Nevertheless, he continued, he had the greatest confidence in the wisdom of the members of the Municipal Council, chosen (by himself, incidentally[160]) from among the leading property owners and merchants of the country, and nine months' prior residence there had convinced him of the insufficiency, relaxation and virtual absence of any police regulation of Negroes. Even more sinister consequences could follow if the current state of affairs were allowed to continue, and it would be some time before the Territorial Legislature of the future sovereign could act in the premises.

Laussat noted that the property-owning inhabitants of Luisiana were much disquieted by this situation, and recalled that at the commencement of Spanish government thereat, its chief had, by ordinance of August 27, 1769, ordered the strict observance of the *Code Noir*. He then stated that the events of the last years had added memorable lessons to the experience gained in times past. Referring to his instructions, he observed that these empowered him to reenact (*remettre en vigueur*) the *Code Noir*. The two operative paragraphs of Laussat's arrêté of December 17, 1803, ordered the execution of the Luisiana *Code Noir* of March, 1724 as originally enacted, with the exception of the provisions thereof that dealt with state religion or the slave trade or were otherwise contrary to the Constitution of the United States.

In his memoirs, Laussat supplies the following additional information:

> The members of the local government tormented me to sanction yet one more decree relative to the regulation of the Negroes. They pointed out that they daily felt an extreme need for it. They came back to the charge several times. I kept refusing on the grounds that this was on the eve of my laying down my ephemeral power. Finally, I

> gave in. I explained the motives for my conduct in the preamble of a decree that I drew up for the purpose. A good deal of trouble was taken to hasten printing and publication [on December 17, 1803] of this decree. It will be my testament, in the name of the French Republic, on behalf of this dear Louisiana.[161]

B. The Interregnum (1804-1807)

Laussat's reenactment of the *Code Noir* of 1724 has remained virtually unnoticed until recently.[162] This may be due, in part, to the persistent disregard of that legislation in contemporaneous practice. The French *Code Noir*, we will recall, prohibited the manumission of slaves without the permission of the Superior Council, and stipulated that such permission was to be granted only if the master's motives in manumitting his slave were found to be legitimate by the Council. It specifically condemned freedom-purchase as "mercenary," and as likely to lead to theft and to robbery on the part of slaves (presumably to obtain their purchase price).[163] Additionally, there were the disqualification of slaves as witnesses or parties in civil litigation and their incapacity to hold property or to contract in their own rights.[164] These latter seemed to preclude at least self-purchase, even by voluntary agreement.

The requirement of government approval for manumission appears to have been ignored entirely, probably for the simple and by now familiar reason that the *Conseil Supérieur* referred to in the 1724 enactment had ceased to exist in 1769 and had not been revived.[165] Thus, we find Pierre Pedesclaux alone passing twenty-one acts of manumission in 1804, twenty-three in 1805, and no less than 40 and 39 in 1806 and 1807, respectively.[166] Narcise Broutin executed over fifty acts of manumission in those four years; Estevan de Quiñones, fifteen,[167] and John Lynd, nine,[168] for a grand total of almost two hundred, or an average of about fifty per year. It is quite clear from the language of the instruments, and from the subsequent practice of some of the same notaries,[169] that governmental approval had not been solicited for any of these manumissions.

Even more surprisingly, self-purchase continued to be practiced extensively between 1804 and 1807. No less than nine of the twenty-one acts of manumission passed by Pedesclaux in 1804 were self-purchase transactions.[170] These would have been both void and impossible under the 1724 *Code Noir* because slaves could neither contract nor own property.[171] Only in four of fifteen acts of manumission passed by Quiñones in 1806 and 1807 is the motive stated to be gratitude and reward for faithful service. Five were self-purchase transactions—four of them being dated as late as August 29, 1807.[172]

The manumission practice just described suggests a contemporaneous prevailing opinion to the effect that Spanish slave law continued to be in force in Orleans Territory under United States rule unless and until repealed by local or federal enactment. That impression is strengthened by two additional factors. First, while the Francophonic former *escribanos* were quick to change to the French language for a variety of notarial acts almost immediately after November 30, 1803,[173] the use of the Spanish-language and Spanish-form *carta de libertad* persisted for some considerable time. Only two of the twenty-one manumission acts passed by Pierre (as he now called himself) Pedesclaux in 1804 are in French.[174] Secondly, Judge Prevost of the Superior Court of the Territory of Orleans ruled in November, 1805, that Spanish rather than French law was then in effect in what is now Louisiana,[175] and this apparently included Spanish slave law.

That seems to be precisely what Judge Prevost decided in the unreported case of *Paul* v. *Succession of Carriere* (March 22, 1806). Diligent search has failed to unearth a record of that case,[176] but its existence and purport are established by a notarial act passed that very day. That act evidences a transaction by which G. Mombrun, as executor of the Gerard Carriere estate, granted the slave Paul his freedom for the sum of 450 *piastres* "*en vertu d'une ordre de la Cour Superieur* [*sic.*] *de ce territoire en datte de ce jour.*"[177]

As will be seen presently, the basic features of French slave law were restored almost immediately thereafter through legislative action.[178] Before proceeding to a brief discussion of that legislation, however, it should be noted that freedom-purchase was in all likelihood not viewed at that time with disfavor by all elements of Luisiana French society. Merchants, in particular, regarded the buying and selling of slaves as a legitimate business activity, and it was at least as profitable to sell a slave his freedom as it was to sell the slave.[179] In 1807, for instance, Salomon Prevost was engaged in no less than six freedom-sale transactions, for a total of 2,800 *pesos*.[180] This trade was a mere fraction of slave sales, but it was still trade. Louis XV (or, more accurately, his advisers) might have viewed freedom-sale transactions as "mercenary" in 1724,[181] but eighty years later, the French merchant community of New Orleans could hardly be expected to regard that as a term of opprobrium.

C. The Reenactment of the French Model, 1806-1808

As we have just seen, Laussat's attempt to reenact the *Code Noir* of 1724 remained without consequence. His prediction that it would be some time before the Territorial Legislature could act, on the other hand, proved to be accurate. Nevertheless, slave law figured importantly in the initial legislative agenda of Orleans Territory. A Black Code with forty articles was enacted on June 7, 1806.[182] It seems a fair inference that this action was prompted in good part by Judge Prevost's decision in *Paul's Case*[183] less than three months earlier.

The *Code Noir* of 1806 deals mainly with the maintenance, discipline, and punishment of slaves. It was followed, on March 9, 1807, by an "Act to regulate the conditions and forms of the emancipation of slaves."[184]

These two enactments, adopted within less than one year, demolished the two main freedoms of Spanish slave law. The Black Code deprived slaves of the capacity to own property without the consent of their masters, and disqualified them as parties to civil suits and as witnesses against white persons.[185] The manumission law of 1807 started with the provision that "no person shall be compelled either directly or indirectly, to emancipate his or her slaves." It then proceeded to make manumission contingent upon judicial approval, conditioned upon a showing of requisite age (30) and four years' previous good conduct.[186] These provisions put an end both to judicially enforceable compulsory freedom-purchase and to the freedom of voluntary manumission. Their effect was a drastic decline in the volume of notarial instruments of manumission. Pedesclaux, for instance, passed twelve such acts in 1808, as against thirty-nine in the previous year, and Quiñones, a bare two against a previous record of ten.[187]

The Civil Code of 1808, finally, reiterated the legal disqualifications of slaves, enlarging them to include incapacity to contract and to transmit by succession.[188] It also repeated the rule that masters could not be "compelled either directly or indirectly to enfranchise" any of their slaves, adding, however, that where a master stood convicted of cruel treatment of his slave, the slave was to be sold at public auction "in order to place him out of the reach of the power which his master has abused."[189] Thus, at least one of the "three freedoms" of Spanish slave law survived, if only in substantially weakened form.

By 1808, then, Luisiana slave law had basically reverted to the guiding principles of the *Code Noir*[190] enacted more than eight decades earlier. The humanitarian traces of the Century of Enlightenment had all but been effaced. There was even a further retrogression, as demonstrated by the final article of the *Code Noir* of 1806, which provided that "free people of colour ought never to insult or strike white people, nor presume to conceive themselves equal to the white; but on the contrary that they ought to yield to them in every occasion, and never speak or answer to them but with respect under the penalty of imprisonment according to the nature of the offence."[191] The French text of that provision is borrowed almost word for word from the abortive Ducros-de Reggio *projet* of 1778-79.[192]

Summary and Conclusion

The purpose of this study was to determine to what extent (if any) French slave law survived the introduction of the law of Castile and of the Indies in Luisiana after O'Reilly's reorganizations of November, 1769. That question presented itself because O'Reilly had, on August 27, 1769, reconfirmed the applicability of the *Code Noir* enacted in 1724 by Louis XV for French Luisiana. In view of that action, it more or less had become conventional wisdom that French slave law continued in force in Spanish Luisiana.[193]

A survey of the ongoing debate about the "living law" of slavery in the Americas showed that eighteenth-century French and Spanish slave law differed in three essential respects. Under Spanish law, the master could manumit his slaves without official or judicial license. The slave, if cruelly treated, could institute judicial proceedings for sale to another master, and much more importantly, his freedom could be compulsorily purchased by himself or by a third party at his judicially appraised market value. French slave law, on the other hand, denied the slave standing in court, capacity to contract, and capacity to own property. It also condemned the sale of freedom to slaves, and required an official license based on a finding of "legitimate motive" as a prerequisite for the validity of manumissions.[194]

In Luisiana, the requirement of official permission for manumissions was abolished with the suppression of the Superior Council in November, 1769. "O'Reilly's Laws" also expressly codified the right of slaves to seek new masters after a judicial determination of cruel treatment, but no legislative provision was made for a judicially enforceable right to purchase one's freedom.[195] That right was recognized and enforced, nevertheless, in a steady stream of judicial decisions, averaging somewhat less than two cases per year for the thirty-three year period of direct Spanish rule.[196]

Since claims to freedom at the assessed current market value of slaves were judicially enforceable, there was a substantial volume of voluntary freedom-purchase transactions. A cautious estimate is that nine out of ten paid-for manumissions were obtained by agreement rather than litigation, and that 500 or more manumissions in the Spanish period were obtained by these two devices in combination.[197] It seems well established, therefore, that there is a direct causal relation between the legacy of Spanish slave law and the exceptionally high ratio of freedmen to slaves in early nineteenth-century Luisiana.

On the whole, the Francophonic population of Luisiana does not appear to have opposed the law of compulsory freedom purchase, since it was at least as profitable to sell a slave his freedom as it was to sell a slave. In 1778-79, however, an attempt was made by the *Cabildo* of New Orleans (with the support of Governor Gálvez) to seek Royal sanction for the restoration of French slave law and, as a new element, the codification of "white supremacy." For reasons not entirely apparent today, that effort proved to be abortive.[198]

Remarkably enough, the freedom-purchase features of Spanish slave law survived for the first four years of United States rule, although Laussat had been prevailed upon by the Francophonic notables to "reenact" the 1724 *Code Noir* during the brief interlude of French sovereignty. This was probably so because freedom purchase was viewed by that time as a profitable if minor branch of the slave trade.[199]

Our general conclusion, then, is that Spanish slave law completely replaced the *Code Noir* of 1724 during the period of direct Spanish rule lasting from late 1769 to November, 1803; Judge Derbigny's decision in *Beard* v. *Poydras*[200] has stood the test of time. It has not been our purpose to pass judgment on the past, or to identify villains. We have, however, encountered some genuine heroes and (not to forget) heroines. These are the countless *gens de couleur* who literally slaved for their freedom or who, at the bottom of "free" society, hoarded their hard-earned *reales* to buy liberty for a loved one still in captivity. Their loyalty and industry were monumental, and deserve remembrance as well as admiration.

[1]*Louis XV's Edit concernant las Nègres Esclaves à la Louisiane*, of March, 1724, reprinted in 4 *La. Hist. Soc. Publications* 75-90 (1908).

[2]F. X. Martin, *The History of Louisiana from Earliest Period*, ch. 15 (first published in 1827; p. 214 of the 1963 reprint); 3 C. Gayarré, *History of Louisiana: The Spanish Domination* 37 (1854).

[3]Compare *Beard* v. *Poydras*, *4 Mart.* (O.S.) 348 (1816) with, *e.g.*, J. D. L. Holmes, *A Guide to Spanish Louisiana 1762-1806* at 4 (1970).

[4]These are described *infra*, text at notes 71-75.

[5]Thomas Jefferson, Opinion in the *Batture* case, Mar. 7, 1808, in 2 *American State Papers, Public Lands* 59, 65-66 (1834); Schmidt, "The Batture Question," 1 *La. L. J.*, Aug., 1841, at 84, 98-99; "Exchange of Correspondence with Julien Seghers," 1 *La. L. J.*, Apr., 1842, at 22, 27-38; J. Tucker, *Effect on the Civil Law of Louisiana Brought About by the Change in Its Sovereignty* 2-42 (Soc'y of Bartolus, Juridical Stud., no. 1, 1975).

[6]Royal *Cédula* of April 16, 1769, discussed and quoted *infra*, at note 67.

[7]See *infra*, text at note 72.

[8]Royal *Cédulas* of August 17, 1772, *AGI, Cuba, leg. 180A*, first bundle, items 1-12.

[9]See *infra*, text at note 131, and *e.g.*, *Landreux* v. *Cochrane & Rhea*, 43 N. Broutin 127, 267 at 268-69 (Forstall, *alcalde*, J. Martínez de la Pedrera, *asesor*, 1800) (New Orleans Notarial Archives), citing *Partida* 3, 28, §§ 4 & 9. Further instances of citation to Spanish legal sources are listed in C. M. Burson, *The Stewardship of Esteban Miró 1782-1792* at 204-205 (1940).

[10]The insurgents were convicted, and some of them were executed, pursuant to Spanish law, see *infra*, text at note 71.

[11]These are discussed in Baade, "The formalities of Private Real Estate Transactions in Spanish North America," 38 *La. L. Res.* 655, 686-99 (1978).

[12]See Baade, "Marriage Contracts in French and Spanish Louisiana: A Study in 'Notarial' Jurisprudence," 53 *Tulane L. Rev.* 1, 55-79 (1979).

[13]F. Tannenbaum, *Slave and Citizen. The Negro in the Americas* 43 *et seq.*, 69 (1946); E. Williams, *British Historians and the West Indies*, 224-32 (1966, summarizing an unpublished review written in 1946), while extremely critical, conceded the validity of the Tannenbaum thesis as long as Latin American slavery was geared to small-scale production. Id., at 228.

[14]S. M. Elkins, *Slavery. A Problem in American Institutional and Intellectual Life* 25 (2d ed., 1968).

[15]Id., at 27-62.

[16]Id., at 77 note 112.

[17]Id., at 79.

[18]Id., at 79-80.

[19]Id., at 193-201.

[20]Id., at 201-222.

[21]D. B. Davis, *The Problem of Slavery in Western Culture* ch. 8 (paperback ed., 1970 reprint).

[22]Id., at 224-25 note 1.

[23]Id., at 265-66.

[24]Id., at 266-67; see especially Aimes, "*Coartación*: A Spanish Institution for the Advancement of Slaves into Freedom," 17 *Yale Rev.* 412 (1909).

[25]Davis, *supra* note 21, at 267. A contemporary observer stated, however, that freedom-

purchase was enforceable in Santo Domingo. 1 M. L. E. Moreau de Saint-Méry, *Description topographique et politique de la partie espagnole de l'Isle de Saint-Domingue* 58 & 59-60 (1796).

[26]J. Malagon Barcelo, *Codigo Negro Carolino* (1784) at 81 and 155-240 (1974). The Code is reproduced id., at 269-76.

[27]Davis, *supra* note 21, at 267 with note 6 thereat.

[28]See *infra*, text at notes 100-153.

[29]3 H. T. Catterall, *Judicial Cases concerning American Slavery and the Negro* 422-45 (1932; 1968 reprint).

[30]H. S. Klein, *Slavery in the Americas. A Comparative Study of Virginia and Cuba* 194-227 (1967).

[31]Id., at 194. Professor Klein's conclusions have been challenged by G. M. Hall, *Social Control in Slave Plantation Societies. A Comparison of St. Domingue and Cuba* 2 & 89-92 (1971). This criticism is answered in part by K. F. Kiple, *Blacks in Colonial Cuba 1744-1899* (1976).

[32]See Department of Commerce, Bureau of the Census, *Negro Population 1790-1915* at 57, Table 6 (1918; reprint 1968). The ratio of free persons of color to slaves was 7,585 to 34,660 in 1810; 10,476 to 69,064 in 1820; and 25,502 to 109,588 in 1830. Thereafter, the slave population increased dramatically, reaching 331,726 in 1860, and the population of free persons of color declined (1850: 17,462; 1860: 18,647). In these latter two decades, the ratio of free persons of color to slaves was more favorable in Virginia than it was in Louisiana.

[33]D. C. Rankin, "The Forgotten People: Free People of Color in New Orleans, 1850-1870" (Ph.D. dissertation, Johns Hopkins, 1976) has compiled detailed statistics, see especially id. Table A-2, p. 291. The ratio of slaves to free persons of color to whites in New Orleans was 1,589:862:2,065 in 1791, and 3,105:1,566:3,551 in 1805.

[34]R. C. Wade, *Slavery in the Cities, The South 1820-1860* at 11 & 248 (1964).

[35]Genovese, "The Slave States of North America," in D. W. Cohen & Jack P. Greene, eds., *Neither Slave Nor Free, The Freedman of African Descent in the Slave Societies of the New World* 258, 270 (1972).

[36]D. E. Everett, "Free Persons of Color in New Orleans, 1803-1865" (Ph.D. dissertation, Tulane, 1952). Dr. Everett, now a professor of history at Trinity University, San Antonio, has kindly supplied me with a copy of this seminal work.

[37]Id., at 16-21 and 46-49. See also Everett, "Free Persons of Color in Colonial Louisiana," 7 *La. History* 21, 24-27 & 43-45 (1966).

[38]Foner, "The Free People of Color in Louisiana and St. Domingue, A Comparative Study of Two Three-Caste Societies," 3 *J. Social Hist.* 406, 410 (1970) (footnotes omitted).

[39]*Infra*, text at notes 46 & 48.

[40]*Code Noir, touchant la police des Iles de l'Amérique*, 19 Isambert, *Recueil Général des Anciennes Lois Françaises* 494 (Louis XIV, March, 1685).

[41]Articles 1-3 & 10, id., 494-95; 496. As regards the French law of marriage formalities then in effect, see Baade, "The Form of Marriage in Spanish North America," *Cornell L. Rev.* 1, 20-21 & 49 (1975).

[42]*Code Noir, supra* note 40, articles 22-26; 28-31, id., 496-99.

[43]Articles 56-57 & 59, id., 502-503.

[44]Ordinance of June 13, 1736, reciting and reenacting the Ordinance of October 13, 1713, 3 M. Moreau de Saint-Méry, *Loix et Constitutions des Colonies Françoises de l'Amérique Sous le Vent* 453; Decree of February 8, 1726, id., 159. The latter enactment expressly refers to the

Louisiana *Code Noir* of 1724.

[45]*Edit servant de Reglement pour la Gouvernement et l'Administration de la Justice, Police, Discipline et le Commerce des Esclaves Nègres, dans le Province de la Louisiane*, 3 Moreau de Saint Méry 88. The full French text of the Code is reprinted in 4 *Publ. La. Hist. Soc'y* 75 (1908). The references in the text are to articles 24 and 25; 22, id., at 81-83.

[46]Article 50, id., at 88-89. The jurisprudence of the *Conseil Supérieur* in this respect is summarized by Everett, *supra* note 37, at 29-33 (second citation).

[47]Article 52, id., at 89.

[48]Article 50, *supra* note 46 and text thereat: the Superior Council was not to give its approval only "*lorsque les motifs qui auront esté exposez par les Maistres paroistront légitimes.*" See *supra*, note 46.

[49]Louisiana *Code Noir*, articles 22, 24 & 25; W. W. Buckland, *The Roman Law of Slavery* 82-87 (1908; 1969 reprint).

[50]In Imperial Rome, a slave complaining of ill treatment could seek sanctuary. The complaint had to be inquired into, and if it was found to be true, the slave had to be sold so as not to be returned to his old master. Id., 37-38; Inst. 1, 8, 2 & Dig. 1, 6, pr. (Ulpian).

[51]Under the *Code Noir* of 1685 (article 28) as well as that of 1724 (article 22) *all* of a slave's property belonged to his master. As to *peculium* under Roman law, see Buckland, *supra* note 49, at 187 *et seg.* Freedom purchase was proscribed by article 50 of the Louisiana *Code Noir*, *supra*, text at notes 46 & 48; as to its practice in Roman law, see Buckland at 636-46.

[52]See *supra*, text at notes 44 & 46; Buckland, *supra* note 49, at 537 & 462-64; C. 6, 27, 5, § 1 (Justianian, 531).

[53]Part. 4, 21, § 1, corresponding to Inst. 1, 3, § 2 & Dig. 1, 5, 4, § 1 (Florentinus); id., § 6, Part. 5, 12, § 5, with note 6 by Gregorio López. For a concise statement of the contractual capacity and legal standing of slaves, especially regarding the enforcement of self-purchase contracts, see 2 A. Gomez, *Variae Resolutiones Juris Civilis, Communis, et Regii* ch. 1, no. 3, with add. no. 4 (pp. 427 & 430 of the 1794 edition; the additions, by J. de Ayllon Laynez, are dated 1653). The addition cites, among others, Gregorio López. Most of the pertinent laws of the *Partidas* on slavery and manumission are translated into English in 1 L. Moreau Lislet & H. Carleton, *The Laws of the Siete Partidas which are still in Force in the State of Louisiana* 580-597 (1820). Roman law sources on these subjects are listed id., at 580 & 597.

[54]See generally Peset Reig, *Derecho Romano y derecho patrio en las universidades del siglo XVIII*, 45 *Anuario de Historia de Derecho Español* 273, 325-39 (1975).

[55]*Informe del Consejo de Indias acerca de la observancia de la Real Cédula de 31 de Mayo de 1789 sobre la educación, trato y ocupaciones de los esclavos*, reprinted in 3 J.A. Saco, *Historia de la Esclavitud de la Raza Africana en el Nuevo Mundo y en especial en los Paises Americo-Hispanos* 247-78 (1938). We have failed to locate the original in Seville but the *consulta* corresponding to it is in *AGI, Indiferente General leg. 802.* The signature of the former Intendant of Luisiana, consulted on that occasion, Martín Navarro, is lacking in Saco, see id., 278, but it is clear from the *consulta* that he was one of the three authors of the *informe.*

[56]*Informe, supra* note 55, at 257-58. The *Cédula* of May 31, 1789 is reproduced in Malagon Barcelo, *supra* note 26, at 269-76. It was duly received in Texas, and publicly proclaimed there on September 14, 1790. Bexar Archives, General Printed Series, 5/31/1789.

[57]*Informe, supra* note 55, at 258.

[58]*Informe, supra* note 55, at 258. A Royal *Cédula* of February 8, 1790, which was received in New Orleans, specified that freedom purchases by slaves, whether by agreement or by

operation of law, were not subject to the *alcabala. AGI, Cuba, leg. 180B.*

[59]*AGI, Indiferente General, leg. 802, ff.* 5-7.

[60]Meiklejohn, "The Implementation of Slave Legislation in Eighteenth-Century New Granada," in R. B. Toplin, ed., *Slavery and Race Relations in Latin America* 176, 183-88 (1974).

[61]*Supra*, text at notes 25-26.

[62]This practice is described by Aimes, *supra* note 24, and by Klein, *supra* note 30, at 196-200.

[63]*Informe, supra* note 55, at 266-78.

[64]Id., at 257. The three former Intendants readily acknowledged that there was a gap between legal norms and their application in practice, id., at 256-57, and that Spaniards were not free of sin in this respect. They were of the opinion, however, that Spain's faults in this connection were much smaller than those of other nations. Id., at 276-77.

[65]Moreau de Saint-Méry, *supra* note 25, at 171-72, and most recently, 2 C. E. Deive, *La Esclavitud del Negro en Santo Domingo (1492-1844)* at 502 (1980). The latter author discusses, in considerable detail, French diplomatic attempts to obtain the return of runaway slaves from Santo Domingo, id., at 501-543.

[66]Most prominent among these was A. Von Humbolt, *Ensayo Politico sobre la Isla de Cuba* ch. 3, pp. 179-80 (first written in 1807; Spanish ed. 1826; our citation is to the reprint in *Publicaciones del Archivo Nacional de Cuba*, vol. 50 (1960). The "ameliatory measures" preceding the abolition of slavery in the British Empire were first implemented in Trinidad because the Spanish law there in force was "far milder" than the French *Code Noir* then still in effect in St. Lucia, see L. J. Ragatz, *The Fall of the Planter Class in the British Caribbean, 1763-1833* at 415 with further references (1928).

[67]*AGI, Santo Domingo, leg. 2594, f. 58* (available on microfilm at Loyola University, New Orleans.)

[68]For details, see Baade, "Marriage Contracts in French and Spanish Louisiana: A Study in 'Notarial' Jurisprudence," 53 *Tulane L. Rev.* 3, 34-39 (1979).

[69]*AGI, Santo Domingo, leg. 2543, f. 195* (available on microfilm at Loyola University, New Orleans).

[70]Id., *ff.* 171 *et seq.*, 184.

[71]*AHN (Madrid), Consejos, leg. 20*, 854, at 595-96. For details, see Baade, *supra* note 68, at 35-36, and sources there cited.

[72]English translation reprinted in 1 *La. L. J.* no. 2. at 1, 1-2 (1841).

[73]English translation reprinted id., at 3-27 & 27-55.

[74]*AGI, Cuba, leg. 188A*. For details, see Baade, *supra* note 68, at 37-39; Baade, "The Administrative and Judicial Functions of the Lieutenant Governors and Post Commandants of Spanish Luisiana" (unpublished paper presented at the 22nd Annual Meeting of the Louisiana Historical Association, New Orleans, March 21, 1980).

[75]These two enactments are discussed in Baade, "The Formalities of Private Real Estate Transactions in Spanish North America," 38 *La. L. Rev.* 655, 686-99 (1978).

[76]See generally Baade, *supra* note 68, at 37-39 & 51-53. We have failed so far in our efforts to find a direct parallel in Spanish North America. Puebla is a good prototype of a non-*Audiencia* city, well described by R. Liehr, *Stadtrat und städtische Oberschicht von Puebla am Ende der Kolonialzeit (1787-1810)* (1971). It was, however, entirely Hispanic, much larger, and much more prosperous. Vera Cruz might furnish a better example for comparison, but apparently still awaits in-depth description. For an excellent contemporaneous

description of the legal and administrative system of Santo Domingo, see 2 Moreau de Saint-Méry, *supra* note 25, at 3-99.

[77]See the sources cited, *supra* note 74; Lieutenant Governors' Instructions, §§ 1 & 2; Post Commandants' Instructions, § 1. See also the descriptions of the Louisiana court system in the letters of Governor Claiborne to the President, August 24, 1803, 9 *The Territorial Papers of the United States*, 16, 20-21 (C. E. Carter, ed., 1940) and of Daniel Clark to the Secretary of State, n.d., 1803, id., 29, 36-37. Especially the latter report must be regarded as a major achievement, since it was written by a layman apparently without access to any of the sources here used.

[78]This tribunal was set up pursuant to O'Reilly's recommendations by a Royal *Cédula* of August 17, 1772, *AGI, Cuba, leg. 180A.*

[79]See, *e.g.*, *Aragon de Villega* v. *Perdomo*, May 28, 1788 (Gov. Miró, J.), Spanish Judicial Archives, Louisiana State Museum. Laura Porteus called this case "the best example of legal debate found in the Spanish Archives." Laura Porteus Papers, Louisiana State University, Baton Rouge.

[80]*Aragon* v. *Perdomo*, *supra* note 79, was appealed from the Havana Tribunal to the Council of the Indies, which ordered, on March 10, 1790, the sequestration of Perdomo's *escribania* pending the termination of the cause, id., *f.*51v-52v. Unsuccessful searches for further Luisiana appeals to the Council of the Indies have been made of *AHN (Madrid), Consejos, legs. 21696-21705*, containing judgments of the Council of the Indies rendered between 1761 and 1829; the Spanish Judicial Archives in the Luisiana State Museum, through June, 1791, and of the notes made by Miss Porteus (*supra* note 13) for the entire Spanish period, with like results. Luisiana controversies that would presently be classified as legal, but were then regarded as governmental, reached the Council of the Indies routinely, see, *e.g.*, *infra* note 82. Dispositions of the Council regarding Luisiana that are now in the *AGI (Seville)* are accessible through *Colección de documentos inéditos para la historia de Hispano-América*, vols. 7 & 12: *Catálogo de los fondos cubanos del Archivo General de Indias, Tomo I*, vols. I & II (*Consultas y decretos, 1664-1783 & 1784-1820)* (1929 & 1930). This collection, too, has been searched unsuccessfully for appeals to the Council's *Sala de Justicia*.

[81]Royal Order of August 6, 1800, *AGI, Santo Domingo, leg. 2531, f. 579;* Royal *Cédula* of November 13, 1800 , *AGI, Cuba, leg. 1806*; see also *AGI, Santo Domingo, leg. 1146, no. 20* of 1800.

[82]So far as can be determined, there are two exceptions from this. Dr. Vidal, the last *asesor letrado*, sat judicially in his capacity as Acting Governor after the death of Governor Gáyoso and before the arrival of Governor Salcedo. *Lic.* Joseph Ortega served for a time as *alcalde* of the first vote and sat judicially in that capacity. Elections of law officers of the Crown to positions on the *Cabildo* were, however, later held to be irregular. A Royal *Cédula* of December 26, 1798, invalidated the election of Manuel Serrano, then the *asesor letrado* of the Intendant of Luisiana, as *Alcalde ordinario* of New Orleans, holding that office to be incompatible with his duties as a Royal official. *AGI, Cuba, leg. 180C.*

[83]Council of Castile, *Cédula* of September 22, 1793, *recopilada* in N. R. 11, 16, 9, extended to the Indies by *Cédula* of the Council of the Indies, July 2, 1800, *AHN, Consejos, leg. 51690*, with the proviso that in *asuntos gubernativos*, lay Viceroys, *Audiencia* Presidents, and Governors were to be held to the same standards of liability as their *asesores*. This is perhaps the best illustration of the danger of generalizing about the effectiveness of the *Novisíma Recopilación* in Spain's ultramarine dominions.

[84]For details, see Baade, *supra* note 68, at 50-52.

[85]See, *e.g.*, the examination of Pedro Bertonniere, *procurador* candidate, by J. Postigo, New Orleans 1783, 20 *La. Hist. Q.* 1142, 1143-1144 (1937).

[86]The original fee schedule was enacted as an appendix to O'Reilly's Instructions of November 25, 1769, reprinted in English translation in 1 *La. L. J.* No. 2 at 55-60. For application in slave freedom cases, see *infra*, text at note 150.

[87]*AGI, Santo Domingo, leg. 2532, f.* 136-187v.

[88]See H. Ruiz de Molina to Viceroy of New Spain, August 22, 1799, *AGN (Mexico), Escribanos, vol. 22, exp. 4*, pp. 40-50. In a petition dated August 1, 1800, id., 46, 46v, he stated that upon his return to Luisiana, "*será el unico Letrado particular, y en el continente de los Floridas, q[e] requieren de necesidad profesores de jurisprudencia p[ra] evitar el perjuicio de remitir muchas causas à la Havana p[ra] consultarlas con Abogados de ella, lo que ocasiona crecidos costos y atrasos à aquel publico en la saca de testimonios, y riesgos del mar.*" He was listed, five years later, as one of the three advocates in practice in Vera Cruz. *AGN, Escribanos, vol. 22, exp. 10*, at 269v.

[89]In his report to the Secretary of State cited *supra* note 77, Daniel Clark states that "a Counsellor or two (*Abogados*) have at times resided in this place, but they have been found troublesome to the Governors, Intendants & Auditors & Assessors, & on that account have been sent out of the Country on some pretext or other."

[90]See *supra*, text at notes 53-54.

[91]*Supra*, text at notes 46 & 48.

[92]Compiled from Garic, Acts 6 (1775), and Almonaster, Acts 1775, New Orleans Notarial Archives, Civil District Court, New Orleans.

[93]Minutes of the *Cabildo* of New Orleans, Books I & II, in Louisiana Collection, New Orleans Public Library. That collection contains the original, an excellent typed transcription, and an English translation. We have used the Spanish typescript but frequently consulted the holograph original.

[94]*Supra*, text at note 58.

[95]Instructions, *supra* note 73, Sec. I, § 2, 1 *La. L. J.* no. 2 at 27, 28-29. This provision reflects *Partida* 4, 21, § 6, see *supra* note 53.

[96]*Supra*, text at note 75; *Code Noir* of 1685, article 44; *Code Noir* of 1724, article 40.

[97]*Suriray* v. *Jenkins*, discussed *infra* at 102-112.

[98]Louisiana State Museum, New Orleans, Spanish Judicial Records, May 25, 1774, f. 5, also abstracted in Porteus, "Index to the Spanish Judicial Records of Louisiama," XVIII, 10 *La. Hist. Q.* 438, 445 (1927). (All citations to Spanish Luisiana decisions hereinafter are to these two sources; the Spanish originals are arranged chronologically by initial filing date.)

[99]Id., f. 10.

[100]Louisiana State Museum, June 25, 1773; 9 *La. Hist. Q.* 556 (1926).

[101]*Supra*, text at note 27.

[102]Louisiana State Museum, February 28, 1776; 11 *La. Hist. Q.* 314 & 338 (1928).

[103]María Juana, Louisiana State Museum, February 28, 1776, f. 1 & 3; 4, 11 *La. Hist. Q.* at 339.

[104]Id., f. 7; 7v; 11 *La. Hist. Q.* at 339.

[105]Louisiana State Museum, February 18, 1776; 11 *La. Hist. Q.* 340.

[106]*Supra* note 126, f. 9; 11 *La. Hist. Q.* at 339-340.

[107]*Supra* note 128, f. 291v-292; 11 *La. Hist. Q.* at 349.

[108]Id., f. 296-297; 11 *La. Hist. Q.* at 350.

[109]Id., f. 297v-298; 11 *La. Hist. Q.* at 350.

[110]*Supra*, text at note 104.

[111]Part. 4, 21, § 6, *supra*, text at note 53; O'Reilly's Instructions, Sec. I, § 2, *supra*, text at note 95; Catalina's Case, *supra*, text at note 100.

[112]Ezquerra, *Un patricio colonial: Gilberto de Saint-Maxent, teniente de governador de Luisiana*, I *Miscélanea Americanista* 429, 478 & 496-97 (1951).

[113]J. W. Caughey, *Bernardo de Gálvez in Louisiana 1776-1783* at 250 (1934).

[114]*Cabildo* Minutes, *supra* note 93, October 10, 1777, Spanish typescript, vol. I, 136B-137A (B = v; A = r of the Spanish holograph original).

[115]Id., I, 143A & B (February 11, 1778); 149A-150A (October 6, 1778).

[116]The copy here used was located in Parsons Collection, Humanities Research Center, University of Texas, Austin. For a facsimile reproduction of the title and last page thereof, see D. C. McMurtrie, *Louisiana Imprints* at 102-103 (1942).

[117]*Cabildo* Minutes, Spanish Typescript, vol. II at 45A-46 (October 26, 1781). According to the minutes for July 31, 1778, id., I, 147B-148, the *Cabildo* bought the four volumes of the *Recopilación* of the Indies and a one-volume *Curia Philipica* on that day, not having been able to obtain them earlier despite repeated efforts. (This passage was called to my attention by Professor J. D. L. Holmes.)

[118]*Supra*, text at notes 45-48.

[119]The first ten articles of the 1778 draft, for instance, correspond substantially to the first six provisions of the 1724 *Code Noir*. See also *infra*, note 123.

[120]Slave Code of 1685, article 591; Louisiana *Code Noir*, article 52; *supra*, text at notes 43 & 47.

[121]de Reggio-Ducros draft, article 72.

[122]Id., article 73. This provision was taken from the *Recopilación* of the Indies (9, 5, § 28) which had become available locally a few months earlier, see *supra* note 117. It was a sixteenth-century *recopilada*, in desuetude in the eighteenth century, see 1 Moreau de Saint-Méry, *supra* note 25, at 58-59, and readily accessible through the index.

[123]Id., articles 22, 24 & 25. Articles 24 and 25 of the draft correspond almost literally to articles 25 & 26 of the 1724 *Code*.

[124]de Reggio-Ducros draft, article 68(2) = 1724 *Code*, article 52(2); *Angelica* v. *Juan Perret Estate*, *supra* at notes 98 & 99.

[125]*Code Noir*, article 50; *supra*, text at notes 46 & 48.

[126]*Supra*, text at note 72.

[127]de Reggio-Ducros draft, article 70.

[128]Id., note XXX, p. 14 of the printed text (emphasis supplied).

[129]*Cabildo* Minutes, *supra* note 93, I, 155A-155B (February 19, 1779); id., 156A-156B (February 26, 1779).

[130]Id., 156B-157B. Those signing were (left to right and top to bottom), Bernardo de Gálvez, Pedro Piernas, Pierre Deverges, Franco. Ma. de Reggio, Francisco de la Barre, Joseph Ducros, Forstall, Arnoul, Chabert, Manuel Andrés Armesto, Menéndez Portico, Alberto Auvrin de Lamour, L. Vilte Paseur de Lamour, Bevazeur Waetbezuio, Lech Cacarty, Lason Deusouve, Francisco Deulle, Duparet, J. Mezcier, G. Levyroux, Guydo Dufossat, Sossier, J. Lacoste, Francisco Broutin, N. Bernardez, Deverges L. Boidor, Miou Monplaisier, Leonardo Mazange, Joseph Devalliere, Maxente, Lacou Dussouve, G. Leyroux, Delino

Dalnet, and finally, as *escribano* of the *Cabildo*, Juan Bautista Garic.

[131]*Cabildo* Minutes, II, 131A-132B (June 11, 1784).

[132]*Infra*, text at note 191.

[133]See Baade, "The Formalities of Private Real Estate Transactions in Spanish North America," 38 *La. L. Rev.* 655, 693-95 (1978); Fee Schedule, *supra* note 86, 1 *La. L. J.* No. 2 at 58. The fees for appraisers of slaves, incidentally, were 11 *reales*, id., at 59.

[134]See, *e.g.*, Josefa's Case, *infra*, text at note 153.

[135]See, *e.g.*, 9 & 10 Pedesclaux 286 (1790); 43 id., 749 (1803); 15 N. Broutin 11 (1807). 1 J. Lynd 150 (1805) is a transcription of a Maryland manumission dated 1799. (In the following individual notarial acts in the New Orleans Notarial Archives are cited by *escribano* or notary, volume, page, and year.)

[136]For details, see Baade, *supra* note 133, at 715-16.

[137]These figures are compiled from Garic, Acts 6 (1775), and Almonaster, Acts 1775. Unless otherwise noted hereinafter, all *cartas de libertad* ("emancipations") listed in the indices to notarial acts have been examined.

[138]Pedesclaux, Acts 36 & 37 (1800); N. Broutin, Acts 2 (1800); Ximinez, Acts 16 (1800 abstracted only); Pedesclaux, Acts 43, 44 & 45 (1803), N. Broutin, Acts 5 & 6 (1803); Ximinez, Acts 19 (1803 abstracted only).

[139]L. Mazange, Acts 1780; Pedesclaux, Acts 9, 10 & 11 (1769) (index count and spot checks only).

[140]Garic, Acts 6 (1775). At least nine of Almonaster's nineteen *cartas de libertad* evidence freedom sales transactions, but the figure is probably greater, as slaves were also manumitted by those who had recently bought them for that purpose, see 1775 Almonaster 259 & 298.

[141]Sources as *supra* note 138.

[142]Sources as *supra* note 138. In 2 N. Broutin 203 (1800) a slave mother appears to have bought freedom for her two-year old son without obtaining freedom for herself.

[143]36 Pedesclaux 452 (1800).

[144]43 Pedesclaux 102 & 44 id., 364 (1803).

[145]Magloir, Louisiana State Museum, August 12, 1780; 14 *La. Hist. Q.* 619 (1931); Nicolas, Louisiana State Museum, October 27, 1780; 15 *La. Hist. Q.* 164 (1932); Mazange, Acts 1780 (index count).

[146]9 & 10 Pedesclaux 286 (1790).

[147]Burson, *supra* note 9, at 191.

[148]*Supra*, text at notes 58 & 100.

[149]For additional documentation, see Baade, "The Law of Slavery in Spanish Luisiana, 1769-1803," unpublished paper presented at a conference on Louisiana's Legal Heritage, Louisiana State Museum, New Orleans, April 23, 1981, pp. 42-50.

[150]*Supra* note 145.

[151]Louisiana State Museum, January 17, 1789.

[152]Louisiana State Museum, March 6, 1789.

[153]Id., ff. 13v-14; 15-15v. Nevertheless, Josefa was taxed the costs, amounting to 34 *pesos* 4½ *reales.*

[154]Even in María Juana's case, discussed *supra*, text at notes 103-106, the court did not deny the legal standing of the petitioner, although expressly requested to do so by the defendant slave owner.

[155]Louisiana State Museum, August 19, 1788.

[156]Discussed *supra*, text at notes 98 & 99.

[157]See, *e.g.*, *Mariana Dela* v. *Carlota Lalande Estate*, Louisiana State Museum, June 30, 1791; *Andrés Gombot Estate*, id., August 31, 1791. In the latter case, the court gave effect to the will of Andrés Gombot emancipating his slave María and leaving his estate to her.

[158]For a first-hand description of these events, see P. C. de Laussat, *Memoirs of My Life* 78-90 (A-J Pastwa, trans. 1978).

[159]Broadside *Arrêté* of *24 Frimaire*, Year XII = December 17, 1803, reproduced in D. C. McMurtrie, *Louisiana Imprints 1768-1810* at 44 (1942).

[160]Laussat, *supra* note 158, at 74-77.

[161]Id., at 87.

[162]See, however, Yiannopoulos, *The Civil Codes of Louisiana, in Louisiana Civil Code* 1982 at XI, XIII.

[163]*Code Noir*, article 50; *supra*, text at notes 46 & 48.

[164]*Code Noir*, articles 24-25; 22, *supra*, text at note 45.

[165]*Code Noir*, article 50; see *supra*, text at note 72.

[166]Pedesclaux, Acts 46-48 (1804); 49-51 (1805); 52-53 (1806); and 54-55 (1807). The figures for 1805-1807 are based on index counts with spot checks.

[167]N. Broutin, Acts 7 (1804), 9 & 10 (1805); 12 (1806), & 13-17 (1806-1807); Quiñones, Acts 1 (1805-1808).

[168]J. Lynd, Acts 1-3 (1805-1807). Lynd was apparently the first English-speaking notary in New Orleans. His acts deserve independent study and description.

[169]When manumission practice was brought into compliance with the requirement of judicial approval imposed by the Act of March 9, 1807, *infra*, text at notes 184 & 186, notarial acts started reciting that such prior judicial approval had been obtained. 56 Pedesclaux 171 (1808); 1 Quiñones 645 & 658 (1808); 18 Broutin 409 & 489 (1808).

[170]Pedesclaux, Acts 46-48 (1804).

[171]See *supra*, note 164 and accompanying text.

[172]1 Quiñones 355, 385, 387 & 388 (1807). As to the last four of these manumissions, see *infra*, text at note 180.

[173]Especially (but not only) for marriage contracts, see Baade, "Marriage Contracts in French and Spanish Louisiana: A Study in 'Notarial' Jurisprudence," 53 *Tulane L. Rev.* 1, 53-57 (1979) and, in addition to the notarial acts there cited, 1 Lynd 133 (1805); 2 id., 39 (1806), and 3 id., pt. 1, 87, 92 & 138. All of these are in French, and specify the applicability of the Custom of Paris.

[174]Pedesclaux, Acts 46-48 (1804); id., 970 & 1130.

[175]G. Dargo, *Jefferson's Louisiana: Politics and the Clash of Legal Traditions* 435. The style and exact date of Judge Prevost's decision cannot as yet be determined; see note 176 below.

[176]The files of the Superior Court for the Territory of Orleans are in the New Orleans Public Library. There is no judgment book, and no register, calendar, or index. A search has been made of filings well past March 22, 1806, but the case bundles, although in roughly chronological order, are obviously incomplete. Judge Prevost's dispositions are usually penned to the lower face of each file.

[177]12 Broutin 122v (1806). See also 47 Pedesclaux 629 (1804): a Spanish judgment ordering manumission not as yet executed at the time of the transfer of sovereignty was transformed, through the mediation of "impartial persons," into a freedom-purchase transaction effecting the manumission of a slave and her five children.

[178]*Infra*, text at notes 182-186.

[179]Since the plaintiff (slave or third party) invariably had to pay the costs of the legal action, see *supra* note 153 & text at note 151.

[180]1 Quiñones 385, 386, 387 & 388 (1807); 55 Pedesclaux 540 (1807); 3 J. Lynd (pt. 2) 11 (1807).

[181]*Code Noir*, article 50; *supra*, text at notes 46 & 48.

[182]Acts Passed at the First Session of the First Legislature of the Territory of Orleans 150-190 (Black Code).

[183]*Supra*, text at notes 176-177.

[184]Acts Passed at the Second Session of the First Legislature of the Territory of Orleans 82-88.

[185]Black Code of 1806, *supra* note 182, articles 15 & 16.

[186]*Supra* note 184, articles 1 & 2. Compulsory manumission could occur, pursuant to a proviso of article 1, exceptionally "in the name and at the expence of the territory, by virtue of an act of the legislature of the same."

[187]Pedesclaux, Acts 56-57 (1808); 1 Quiñones 645 & 658 (1808). As recited there, L. Moreau Lislet was the parish judge at the time.

[188]Digest of Civil Laws, Terr. of Orleans, Bk. I, tit. 6 articles 17 & 18, p. 40.

[189]Id., article 27, p. 42. That article also provided that slaves could be manumitted by compulsory purchase by act of the Legislature in reward for services to the Territory, as already envisaged by the 1807 enactment, see *supra* note 186.

[190]See *supra*, text at notes 45-48.

[191]Black Code, 1806 (English text), article 40. At the time, legislation in the Territory of Orleans was enacted in French and English, and printed with the texts in the two languages facing each other.

[192]Black Code, 1806 (French text), article 40; de Reggio-Ducros draft, article 71, *supra*, text at note 121.

[193]*Supra*, text at notes 1-12.

[194]*Supra*, text at notes 13-66.

[195]*Supra*, text at notes 91-95.

[196]*Supra*, text at notes 100; 148-153.

[197]*Supra*, text at notes 140-147.

[198]*Supra*, text at notes 114-131.

[199]*Supra*, text at notes 158-181.

[200]4 Mart. (O.S.) 348 (1816).

THE EARLY SOURCES OF LOUISIANA LAW: CRITICAL APPRAISAL OF A CONTROVERSY

By

A. N. Yiannopoulos

The 1981 edition of the Louisiana Civil Code contains a Foreword by John H. Tucker, Jr.[1] The distinguished Louisiana jurist maintains that: at the time of the Purchase, Louisiana was governed by French private law; the principal source of the Louisiana Civil Code of 1808 was the French Civil Code of 1804, that is, the Code Napoléon; most legal historians, relying on "hearsay,"[2] have erroneously assumed that Spanish law prevailed in Louisiana at the time the territory was retroceded to France; and that such erroneous assumptions have been effectively refuted by the work of Professor Batiza of the Tulane law faculty.

The same edition of the Louisiana Civil Code contains also an introductory essay by the current editor that contradicts most of the statements made in the Foreword.[3] This divergence of views concerning the early sources of Louisiana Law reflects a controversy that is older than the State of Louisiana.[4] The purpose of this paper is to take a critical view of the controversy. Such a view requires, in the first place, identification of issues.

The issues are two: Was the law of Louisiana at the time of the Purchase Spanish or French? And were the sources of the Louisiana Civil Code of 1808 French or Spanish? The resolution of the first issue tends to color the approach to, and resolution of, the second issue. There is consensus that the Louisiana Civil Code of 1808 was *not* intended to break definitively with the past. Therefore, if Spanish law prevailed at the time of the Purchase, the sources of the Louisiana Civil Code of 1808 should be essentially Spanish, and if French law prevailed the sources of the Code should be essentially French.

I. The Law of Louisiana at the Time of the Purchase

Determination of the law prevailing in Louisiana at the time of the Purchase requires a brief historical excursus.

The legal history of Louisiana[5] began in 1712 when Louis XIV granted a Charter to Antoine Crozat for the development, administration, and exploitation of the possession. This Charter provided that the territory was to be governed by Edicts, Ordinances, and the Custom of Paris, namely, a collection of customary rules prevailing in the city of Paris and its surrounding areas that had been reduced to writing in the sixteenth century. Louisiana proved a great burden on the purse of Crozat. In 1717 Crozat surrendered his Charter, and a new one was issued to John Law's Company of the West, which provided for application of the same French laws. The Company of the West accomplished much for Louisiana. Bienville, a brother of D'Iberville, was sent out as a governor, and New Orleans was established by him in 1718. However, the company failed to realize profits, and eventually came to an end fatal to its creditors. It surrendered its Charter in 1731, and Louisiana became a crown colony, still governed by Edicts, Ordinances, and the Custom of Paris.

Louisiana was ceded to Spain in 1762 by the Treaty of Fontainebleau, but French laws continued to apply at least until November 25, 1769, when a newly appointed Spanish Governor, Don Alexander O'Reilly, issued an Ordinance designed to organize an efficient government and administration of justice in accordance with the Spanish laws.[6] In the preamble, Governor O'Reilly stated the reasons for his legislation [*sic.*]:

> . . . to establish . . . that form of political government and administration of justice prescribed by our wise laws, by which all the states of His Majesty in America have been maintained in the most perfect tranquility, content and subordination . . . And as the want of advocates in this country, and the little knowledge which his new subjects possess of the Spanish laws might render a strict observance of them difficult, and as every abuse is contrary to the intentions of His Majesty, we have thought it useful, and even necessary to form an abstract or regulation drawn from the said laws, which may serve for instruction and elementary formulary in the administration of justice and in the economical government of this city, until a more general knowledge of the Spanish language may enable every one, by the perusal of the aforesaid laws, to extend his information to every point thereof.[7]

The text of the Ordinance contains provisions of public law dealing with the *Cabildo* (City Council), the Ordinary *Alcaldes*, the *Alcalde* Mayor Provincial, the *Alguazil* Mayor, the Depositary General, the

Receiver of Fines, the *Mayordomo de Proprios*, the *Escribano* of the *Cabildo*, and the Jailer and the Prisons.

On the same day, November 25, 1769, Governor O'Reilly promulgated a second Ordinance containing:

> Instructions as to the manner of instituting suits, civil and criminal, and of pronouncing judgments in general, in conformity with the laws of the *Nueva Recopilación de Castilla*, and the *Recopilación de las Indias*, for the government of the judges and parties pleading, until a more general knowledge of the Spanish language, and more extensive information upon those laws may be acquired.[8]

The text of the Ordinance, frequently referred to as O'Reilly's Code, contains provisions of public and private law dealing with civil judgments in general, executory proceedings, judgments in criminal cases, appeals, punishments and testaments. The substance of these provisions was taken, as O'Reilly indicated, from the *Nueva Recopilación de Castilla* and the *Recopilación de las Indias*.[9]

Louisiana was retroceded to France on October 1, 1800, by the Treaty of San Ildefonso but France assumed sovereignty only on November 30, 1803, for a period of twenty days. During the brief period of French control, Laussat, as Colonial Prefect representing Napoleon, abolished the Spanish authorities and created a municipal government for Louisiana. He organized a militia composed of Americans and Creoles, and bearing grudge for his treatment by the Spaniards, made himself as obnoxious to them as he could. He did not, however, have the time to organize a judiciary; and his only change to the laws governing Louisiana was the abrogation of Spanish slave legislation and the re-introduction of the French *Code Noir*.[10] Thus, the bulk of the pre-existing laws remained in force until the United States took possession on December 20, 1803.

The 1803 Act of Congress which authorized the President to take possession of the territories ceded by France provided a method of interim government and the basis for the protection of the inhabitants. In accordance with this Act, President Jefferson appointed W. C. C. Claiborne to exercise all the powers and authorities heretofore exercised by the Colonial Governor and Intendant. The first official act of Claiborne was to affirm the application of the laws then in force.

Despite clear indications that French law was replaced in 1769 by the system of Spanish law, both public and private,[11] there has been much disagreement whether this actually happened.

The question of which were the laws in force in Louisiana at the time of the Purchase was first considered by the territorial Superior Court in 1805. In that year, John Prevost, still the court's only judge, decreed that Roman, Spanish, and French civil law would be enforced as the customary law of the territory in all cases.[12] The next year, the Legislative Council and the House of Representatives passed an act "declaring the laws which continue to be in force in the territory of Orleans, and authors which may be referred to as authorities within the same."[13] The Act declared in part [*sic.*]:

> . . . the laws which remain in force, and those which can be recurred to as authorities in the tribunals of this Territory, save the changes and modifications which may have already been made by the Legislatures of the said Territory, save also whatever might be contrary to the constitution of the United States, to the laws of the federal government which have been extended to the said Territory by Congress, and to the acts of the said Congress which direct the present government of the said Territory, and save therefore the modifications, which necessarily result from the introduction which the act of the 22nd March 1804, has made into the said Territory of the two most important principles of the judiciary system of the common law, to wit, the writ of habeas corpus, and the trial by jury, are the laws and authorities following, to wit: 1.° the Roman Civil code, as being the foundation of the Spanish law, by which this country was governed before its cession to France and to the United States, which is composed of the institutes, digest and code of the emperor Justinian, aided by the authority of the commentators of the civil law, and particularly of Domat in his treaty of the Civil laws; the whole so far as it has not been derogated from by the Spanish law;
>
> 2.° The Spanish law, consisting of the books of the *recopilatión de Castilla* and *autos acordados* being nine books in the whole; the seven parts or *partidas* of the king

> Don Alphonse the learned, and the eight books of the royal statute (*fuero real*) of Castilla; the *recopilatión de Indias*, save what is therein relative to the enfranchisement of slaves, the laws *de Toro*, and finally the ordinances and royal orders and decrees, which have been formally applied to the colony of Louisiana, but not otherwise; the whole aided by the authority of the reputable commentators admitted in the courts of Justice.

Governor Claiborne vetoed this act, pointing out that it was the prerogative of Congress to determine whether the civil law should or should not apply to the territory. Following Claiborne's veto, the legislature adjourned in protest, claiming that their best acts were rejected by the Governor. Within a few days, a manifesto signed by a number of representatives was published in New Orleans newspapers, which purported to be a resolution for the dissolution of the legislature on account of the Governor's veto.[14] Nevertheless, the legislature convened on June 7, 1806, and adopted the resolution for the preparation of a civil code for the territory. James Brown and Moreau Lislet were charged with this task, and were specifically directed to base codification on the civil law by which the territory was governed. Governor Claiborne acceded to this resolution.

Shortly, thereafter, in the spring of 1807, the question of which laws were in force at the time of the Purchase, was raised in the framework of a celebrated litigation involving Edward Livingston and President Jefferson. A detailed analysis of this litigation, known as the *Batture Question*, is to be found in Dr. Dargo's monograph and in a lengthy article published in 1841 by Gustavus Schmidt in the *Louisiana Law Journal*.[15] At this point, it is interesting to note the arguments of President Jefferson and Edward Livingston concerning the question of the law in force at the time of the Purchase.

President Jefferson argued that O'Reilly's Ordinances of 1769 did not abrogate the entirety of the French laws. O'Reilly introduced:

> only a specific and not a general change in the jurisprudence of the colony, as is evident from the inspection of his ordinances which only substitute a *cabildo* for the council, introduce Spanish offices and Spanish of-

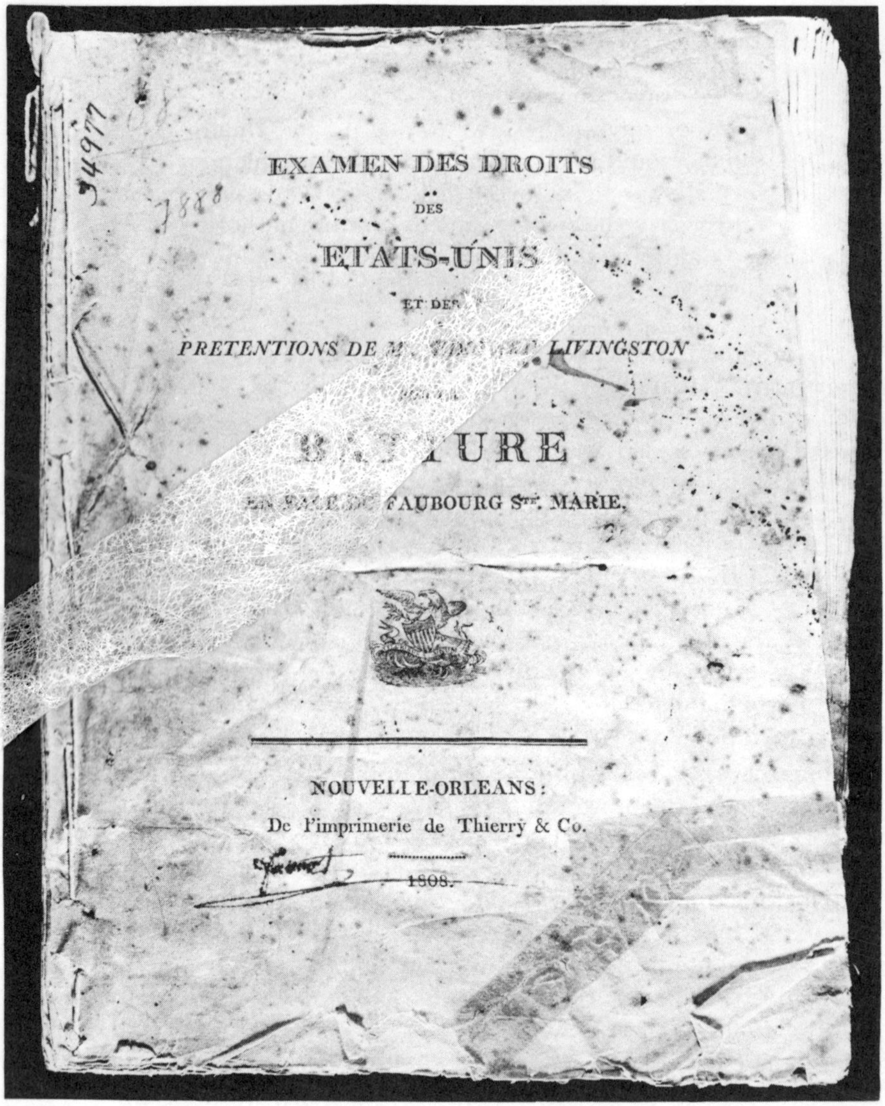

"Examination of the Rights of the United States and of the Claims of Mr. Edward Livingston to the Batture in Front of Faubourg Ste. Marie," 1808. Louisiana State Museum.

> ficers for analogous French functions and functionaries which had previously existed.[16]

President Jefferson admitted that O'Reilly also changed the modes of proceedings in civil and criminal cases, and that the Ordinances were obligatory, so far as they introduced specific changes; but he denied that they either abolished or intended to abolish the whole system of jurisprudence of France then in force; and he insisted that the introduction of specific changes in the law, proves that no general change was intended. He conceded that there were certain loose expressions in the ordinance, which would lead to conjecture, that more extensive changes were contemplated at some future period; but as it did not appear that they were ever made, there is no pretext for saying that the entire French law was abrogated.

Edward Livingston's position was that, in general, the cession of a territory does not involve a change in its laws. However, the cession of a territory changes the fundamental laws that affect the prerogatives of the sovereign. Further, Livingston's position was that O'Reilly changed not only the form of government but also the administration of justice, and with it all the laws of the province. And he pointed to the *Recopilación de las Leyes de las Indias*, applicable to all Spanish colonies, which declared that these laws governed not only the present colonies but also colonies acquired in the future.[17]

A generation later, Gustavus Schmidt appraised critically the arguments of both Jefferson and Livingston. He had this to say:

> If we examine the question, whether the laws of France or Spain were in force in Louisiana, and place the arguments of Jefferson and Livingston in juxtaposition, we shall find, that the former have at least as much in their favor as the latter. The position of Mr. L., that the subjects of one country, when transferred to another, stand in the same relation to the new sovereign as all his other subjects, is evidently erroneous. The reverse of this is usually the case, because the subjects, even of a conquered country, generally retain their laws, and the privileges they enjoyed under their former sovereign, while the new one acquires those he enjoyed; that is, the *status ante bellum* or *ante cessionem* remains unchanged

> as to the laws and prerogatives of the inhabitants of the new territory.
>
> The second position, that the laws of France were abrogated by the ordinances of O'Reilly, seems to us likewise untenable.[18]

Schmidt admitted that the secret treaty of cession did not contain a provision for the preservation of the laws of France, but nevertheless questioned O'Reilly's authority to change the laws of Louisiana. O'Reilly had declared in the Ordinance of November 25, 1769 that he had acted by virtue of a patent issued at Aranjuez on April 15, 1769, but no copy of that patent was ever procured, despite repeated efforts by the United States. Schmidt specifically disputed O'Reilly's authority to make a total change to the laws of Louisiana and argued that such authority was negativated by the ordinances themselves which refer to future sanctions of the measures by the King of Spain.

Further Schmidt referred to a number of other documents, which were not procured until 1833, and which:

> seem to support fully the position of Mr. Jefferson, that O'Reilly introduced only a partial change in the legislation of the colony, and left to the King of Spain to determine, after advising with the Council of the Indies, whether it would be advisable to subject Louisiana to the same laws as all other Spanish colonies in America. This advice appears to have been given, although we have no evidence that it was ever followed.[19]

Schmidt concluded that the third position of Mr. Livingston, that the laws of the Indies became the law of Louisiana, *proprio vigore*, cannot be true.

On October 12, 1841, Julien Seghers, "an able and intelligent jurist,"[20] wrote a letter to the Editor of the *Louisiana Law Journal*, in which he took issue with the statements of Gustavus Schmidt that the laws of France were not repealed by the Ordinances of O'Reilly. Seghers quoted statements by Derbigny and Judge Martin, and concluded:

> The Spanish laws were already in full operation in Louisiana. . . . The inhabitants were compelled, through

> necessity, to apply for legal advice to the Spanish lawyers, that had accompanied the expedition; and hence we at once see the reason, why the laws of Spain became, without opposition, the sole guide of the tribunals in their judgments. Besides, whoever would have been daring enough, in 1769, to inquire into the nature of O'Reilly's instructions, or to contest the expediency of repealing the French laws, might well have paid the forfeit with his life; he would have died without avengers; for men, that had been repudiated by their mother country, had no redress to expect under a foreign yoke.[21]

Gustavus Schmidt replied with a forceful leading article in which he refuted each of the arguments made by Seghers.[22] Schmidt's central thesis was that according to well-settled principles of public international law the cession of the territory to Spain did not abolish ipso facto the prior laws and that the new sovereign did not exercise its prerogative to replace the prior laws. Schmidt asserted that O'Reilly did not have authority to change the laws of Louisiana, did not intend to usurp such authority, and if O'Reilly had in fact exceeded his authority, his illegal acts were never ratified by the King of Spain. Schmidt concluded;

> If we examine the ordinances themselves, it will be apparent, that O'Reilly confined himself strictly within the limits he had assigned, and that all his regulations had reference to matters of administration, with the exception perhaps of testaments, in which he introduced some changes, which do not appear to be within the scope of his authority. . . . We consequently believe, that the opinion, that the French legislation was abolished in Louisiana has been adopted without sufficient examination, and without adequate authority; that it has, like many other doctrines, equally fallacious, circulated and gained credit more on account of the respect entertained for those, who had sanctioned the belief by their authority, than on account of its intrinsic merit; and that it is not yet too late to dispel the illusion, and to restore to facts and to reason their authority on this interesting subject.[23]

The question of the laws in force at the time of the Purchase lay subsequently in suspended animation for more than a century and a quarter, when it rose again in the Pascal v. Batiza debate.[24] In the meanwhile, Louisiana courts, practicing lawyers, and doctrinal writers had generally accepted the view that O'Reilly had in fact changed the laws of the colony, with the exception of the French *Code Noir*.[25] The arguments of President Jefferson and Gustavus Schmidt were all but forgotten. Following the Pascal v. Batiza debate, research undertaken by an eminent legal historian was shown that undoubtedly;

> the law of Castile and of the Indies, including the Private Law of Castile, was introduced into Louisiana soon after Spain formally took possession in August 1769. O'Reilly was authorized to introduce this system of law, subject to subsequent approval; he did in fact introduce Spanish-Castilian law, and received approval by royal *cédula*.[26]

Nevertheless, there are strong indications demonstrating an unusual attachment by the French population to their own laws and customs. Rather than resorting to the official Spanish judicial system, the French population frequently settled affairs among themselves extrajudicially on the basis of French laws, customs, and usages.[27]

II. The Sources of the Louisiana Civil Code of 1808

The second issue concerning the early sources of Louisiana law is whether the redactors of the Louisiana Civil Code codified French or Spanish laws. This issue was hotly debated in 1972 between Professor Pascal of the Louisiana State University law faculty and Professor Batiza of the Tulane law faculty.[28] Subsequently, others entered the fray and sided with one or the other of the protagonists.[29] For a proper understanding of the issue another brief historical excursus is required.

In 1806, James Brown and Moreau Lislet were commissioned by the legislature "to compile and prepare jointly a Civil Code" and to "make the civil law by which this territory is now governed the ground work of said code."[30] In accordance with the legislative mandate, the commissioners prepared a code and submitted it to the legislature. On March 31, 1808, the legislature adopted their work under the title of "A Digest of the Civil

Laws now in Force in the Territory of Orleans, with Alterations and Amendments Adopted to its Present Form of Government."[31] The Digest, known as the Louisiana Civil Code of 1808, gained Governor Claiborne's approval. It was published in both French and English, but the English version was merely a translation from the French original.

The 1808 Digest did not repeal all prior laws. The enabling statute provided that "whatever in the ancient laws of this territory, or in the territorial statute, is contrary to the dispositions contained in said digest, or irreconciliable with them, is hereby abrogated."[32] This provision was compatible with the notion of a digest or compilation rather than a true civil code. Civil codes are conceived as comprehensive enactments, designed to be complete within their area of application, and are intended to break with the past. It is neither proper nor necessary to go outside a civil code and to look at previous legislation for the purpose of ascertaining the law. The provision in the enabling statute has been criticized, therefore, as an inadvertance in draftmanship and as an entirely useless precaution.[33]

Indeed, if the 1808 Code was actually a digest of existing laws, the provision accomplished nothing that would not have been equally well accomplished by its omission. According to the principle of tacit abrogation, the latest expression of legislative will would have been given precedence over ancient laws. If the intention of the legislature was to retain some of the ancient laws in force, it would have been preferable legislative technique to re-affirm the application of these laws by specific designation in the enabling statute. Be this as it may, the Louisiana Supreme Court held in 1812 that the 1808 Code was "but a digest of the civil law, which regulated the country under the French and Spanish monarchs";[34] and, in 1817, the same court declared that the ancient laws "must be considered as untouched, wherever the alterations and amendments, introduced in the digest, do not reach them."[35]

The 1808 Digest is not a collection of Spanish legislative texts, translated into French and English. It is organized like a civil code, and its provisions were derived from a variety of legislative texts and doctrinal writings. For a long time, the assumption prevailed that the redactors of the 1808 Digest had copied, for the most part, provisions from the French Civil Code of 1804 or from the 1800 *Projet du Gouvernement*.

The assumption was verified only in 1971. In that year Professor Batiza published his monumental work, "The Louisiana Civil Code of 1808: Its Actual Sources and Present Relevance."[36] The author asserted that he was able to identify "the actual sources"[37] of 97% of the provisions of the 1808 Code; that 70% of the provisions of the Code were derived from the *Projet du Gouvernement* and the Code Napoleon, a total of 1,516 articles; that another 15% of the provisions of the Code were derived from a variety of works, including Spanish and Roman legislation and doctrinal works. Thus, 1,837 out of 2,160 articles (or about 85% of the whole) were derived from French "sources," while most of the remaining articles were derived from predominantly Spanish "sources."[38]

Professor Batiza did not assert that Louisiana law prior to 1808 was French. It is apparent that Professor Batiza used the word "sources" to mean the works, legislative and doctrinal texts, from which the provisions of the Code were derived. This use of the word *sources* is common among legal historians.

Having asserted that the sources of the 1808 Digest were French, Professor Batiza felt compelled to dispute the view that the sources of the 1808 Digest were those indicated in the de la Vergne volume, attributed to Moreau Lislet. These so-called sources were not actual sources but mere "concordances."[39] It would seem that few scholars would disagree with Professor Batiza's use of the word *sources*, and few Louisiana lawyers would take issue with the statement that the citations in the de la Vergne volume are references to texts that deal sometimes directly and most frequently tangentially with matters dealt with in the relevant provisions of the 1808 Digest. As a matter of fact, random research indicates that the "sources" in the de la Vergne volume are at times contrary to rules adopted in the 1808 Code.[40]

However, a prominent Louisiana legal scholar, Professor Pascal of the Louisiana State University law faculty, thought it was his academic duty to respond to Professor Batiza because the latter challenged the thesis that the Digest of 1808 "though written largely in words copied from, adapted from, or suggested by French language texts, were intended and does for the most part, reflect the substance of the Spanish law in force in Louisiana in 1808" and "questioned the source reference character of the Moreau notes in the de la Vergne volume."[41]

Professor Pascal began his discourse with the assertion that Spanish law was in force in Louisiana in 1806 when Moreau Lislet and James Brown were commissioned to prepare a civil code and were directed to make the civil law by which the territory of Orleans was then governed the ground work of the Code. According to Professor Pascal, the redactors of the 1808 Code acted as intelligent and practical men. Without in any way vio-

violating their mandate, they used readily available texts in the French language which expressed existing rules of Spanish law or which were modified to accomplish this end. When there was an obvious difference between Spanish and French law, the redactors were careful to adopt Spanish solutions, and in this way a great number of distinctively Spanish rules and institutions were codified in the 1808 Digest.

Professor Pascal also took issue with Professor Batiza's methodology, according to which an article "is to be classified as having its substantive source in French law to the degree its specific phraseology can be traced to borrowings from French legal writings, even though the substance of the rule expressed by the article conforms to Spanish-Roman law in force in 1808."[42] Finally, Professor Pascal re-asserted his view that the actual sources of the 1808 Digest are those cited in the de la Vergne volume, and concluded:

> Professor Batiza's work emerges finally as a work of concordances rather than an index of sources. It is not reliable as an index of sources of the substantive content of individual articles of the Digest of the 'source' cited may be different in substantive content from the relevant Digest provision.[43]

In a rejoinder, Professor Batiza restated his credo:

> An article is to be classified as having its "verbatim" or "almost verbatim" source in French law to the degree its specific phraseology can be traced to borrowings from French legal writings showing either "verbatim" or "almost verbatim" language. The fact that the substance of the rule expressed may conform to Spanish-Roman law in force in 1808 is entirely irrelevant.[44]

Further, Professor Batiza stated that "in adopting rules from various French and other sources, Moreau Lislet did not, and could not have intended to reflect the Spanish law in force in Louisiana."[45] In fact, Moreau Lislet "took considerable liberties with the instructions since the civil law of the territory that was to be codified was almost entirely Spanish, and the Code of 1808 shows an overwhelming French influence."[46] The redactors adopted the structure, or organization, of the French Civil Code and as the framework of the Louisiana Civil Code and "French codal and doctrinal texts pervade the Louisiana code, adopted no doubt on the theory that the Roman law tradition shared by the French and Spanish legal systems made them substantially similar."[47] When, however, French laws were in conflict with Spanish rules and institutions, as in the fields of illegitimacy, curatorship, succession law and community of gains, the redactors deviated from the French models because "to have ignored Spanish laws in those areas would have been in open disregard of the instructions received, but even here French texts are found throughout the code."[48]

Conclusion

The dust has now settled. On the basis of the works of all those who devoted time and energy to the resolution of the "mystery"[49] surrounding the early sources of Louisiana law, one may attempt to state conclusions. In so doing, one should be aware that such conclusions are a matter of opinion rather than objective truth because in the absence of authoritative contemporary documentation the determination of the question of the early sources of Louisiana law depends on reconstruction of the past. This is history, "not an objective reality, but rather an evocation of events vanished in time."[50]

1. At the time of the Purchase, the *official law* of Louisiana was Spanish. Governor O'Reilly had the authority to change the laws of the colony and did introduce Spanish law by his Ordinances of November 25, 1769.

However, the word *law* is polysemantic and its meaning in a particular context is frequently colored by philosophical orientation. In the case of eighteenth-century Louisiana, one may legitimately speak of *official law* and of *law in action*. While the official law of Louisiana was Spanish, its law in action had various components.

In late eighteenth-century "civil law" was considered to be the common law of Europe, having its roots in the "*ratio scripta*" of Roman law. This law was superseded, of course, by royal decrees and local customs, but even these were interpreted and applied in conformity with the general body of the civil law, as expounded in the works of the commentators. It was after the era of codification that civil law was "nationalized,"[51] that is, acquired a distinctive national flavor in the various countries of Europe. Prior to the era of codification the civil law prevailing in southern France, in Spain, in Italy, or in Germany, was thought to be essentially the same, in the absence of directly applicable royal decrees and local customs. Thus, the law of Louisiana at the time of the Purchase was thought to be the *civil law* as modified by directly applicable Spanish legislation and local customs.

Libraries were few and collections of Spanish laws were scarce.[52] Courts, lawyers, and administrative officials were relying on few general works, such as Febrero and the treatises of Domat and Pothier. Since the majority of the population spoke French, it was natural to use French materials in the belief that they were expositions of the prevailing civil law. Moreover, French customs antedating the transfer of the colony to Spain continued to be followed by the French population, and notaries, in outlying areas especially, incorporated in contracts and other juridical acts provisions of French law as governing law.[53] One should note in this context that most provisions of the civil law were, and still are, suppletive. Parties could, and still can, derogate from such provisions by express stipulation.

The tension between official law and folkways in eighteenth-century Louisiana is not without historical precedent. In the year 212 A.D., Emperor Antoninus Caracalla promulgated the *Constitutio Antoniniana* by which he conferred Roman citizenship on large segments of the population in the provinces. Consequently, Roman law would apply to the relations of all citizens, including the predominantly Greek population in the East. The following centuries witnessed a struggle between the official law of Rome and the Greek law that continued to be the governing folksway for the ordering of the life of the citizens.[54] The matter has been historically documented by the work of Mitteis.[55]

2. Turning to the sources of the Louisiana Civil Code of 1808, Professor Batiza has demonstrated that about 85% of the provisions of this code were derived from French "sources." Professor Pascal, however, has asserted that the "sources" of the same Code were predominantly Spanish. It is obvious that the protagonists of the 1972 tournament of scholars did not use the word sources in the same sense.

The term *sources of law* has a variety of meanings. For example, in the field of legal philosophy, the term refers to the very foundation of legal order; in the field of legal history, the term ordinarily refers to the documents which contain information about the past of a legal system; and for purposes of analysis of legal institutions, especially by civilian scholars, the terms refers to the processes from which legal rules derive their existence.[56]

A prominent member of the school of analytical jurisprudence admonishes that the term *sources of law* "is a frequent cause of error unless we scrutinize carefully the particular meaning given to it in any particular context."[57] He further points out that there is a distinction between formal sources of law and material sources of law. A formal source is "that from which is derived the matter, not the validity of the law. The formal source of law is the will of the State. . . . The material sources are very comprehensive, since they include anything that may be drawn into the process of creation."[58]

In the light of the foregoing, it is apparent that Professor Batiza means to say that 85% of the provisions of the Louisiana Civil Code of 1808 were derived from French legislation, preparatory works and doctrinal writers. These were the "actual sources" of the 1808 Code. Professor Batiza's research is convincing, despite an occasional omission or overstatement[59] and criticism of his methodology.[60] The use of the word "sources" to denote the works from which legislative provisions were taken is legitimate. It would take a stretch of imagination to assert that 85% of the provisions of the 1808 Code were taken from the works indicated in the de la Vergne volume.

By basing 85% of the provisions of the 1808 Code on French sources, as defined, the redactors did not consciously violate their mandate. It is true that Moreau Lislet took certain liberties with the instructions.[61] However, one should remember that the instructions were to make the civil law in force the *groundwork* of the codification and that the law in force included Spanish legislation, the general body of civilian jurisprudence, and local customs. The redactors, in keeping with the legislative mandate, codified what they thought to be the civil law in force in the territory, placing more emphasis on the words *civil law* rather than *in force.* In areas in which they were aware that official Spanish law was different from French models, they generally took care to adopt Spanish solutions. But they also felt free to innovate and to change the law in certain particulars. If the 1808 Code had not been intended to change the law in any respect, but to be merely declaratory of the law in force, the enabling statute would have so decreed; it would not have abrogated all contrary laws.[62]

There remains the question whether the provisions of the Louisiana Civil Code of 1808 were essentially French or essentially Spanish in origin. The answer to this question will await a study of the *substance* of the provisions of the 1808 Code in comparison with French and Spanish laws.[63] It may be that, as to most of the provisions of the 1808 Code, there was no material difference between French and Spanish law; or it may be that there was a pronounced difference.

Be this as it may, the Louisiana Civil Code of 1808 despite the origin of its provisions in Spanish, French, or other sources, was Louisiana law. The question of the origin of its provisions could have influenced the processes of interpretation and application in the light of the intent of the legislature. But the 1808 Code was short lived, and it was abrogated and replaced by the Louisiana Civil Code in 1825. The question of the actual sources of the 1825 Code may well form the basis of another tournament of scholars and of another critical appriasal. But this is another story.[64]

[1]See John H. Tucker, Jr., Foreword, in *Louisiana Civil Code* (1981 edition), vii-ix. See also, id., Effect on the Civil Law of Louisiana Brought About by the Change in Sovereignty 2-4 (Soc'y of Bartolus, Juridical Studies No. 1, 1975).

[2]Tucker, *Louisiana Civil Code*, vii-viii.

[3]See Yiannopoulos, *The Civil Codes of Louisiana, in Louisiana Civil Code* (1981 edition), xi-xxvi.

[4]See Dargo, *Jefferson's Louisiana: Politics and the Clash of Legal Traditions* (1975), 111-113.

[5]For bibliography, see Brown, "Law and Government in the 'Louisiana Purchase': 1803-1804," 2 *Wayne L. Rev.* 169 (1956); Brown, "Legal Systems in Conflict: Orleans Territory 1804-1812," 1 *Am. J. Legal Hist.* 35 (1957); Dart, "Courts and Law in Colonial Louisiana," 22 *Rep. La. B.A.* 17 (1921); Groner, "Louisiana Law: Its Development in the First Quarter-Century of American Rule," 8 *La. L. Rev.* 350 (1948); Hood, "A Crossroad in Louisiana History," 22 *La. L. Rev.* (1962), 709, 710-720; Schmidt, "Ordinances and Instructions of Don Alexander O'Reilly," 1 *La. L. J.* (1841), 1; Smith, "Edward Livingston and the Louisiana Codes," 2 *Colum. L. Rev.* (1902), 24; Stone, *The Reception of Law in Louisiana in Legal Thought in the United States of America* (Hazard and Wagner, eds., 1970); Dargo, *Jefferson's Louisiana* 3-50 (1975).

[6]See Schmidt, "Ordinances and Instructions of Don Alexander O'Reilly," 1 *La. L. J.* (1841), 1-60 (English translation by Schmidt). The Spanish original of the Ordinances is reprinted in B. Torres Ramirez, *Alexandro O'Reilly en las Indias* 187-225 (1969).

[7]Schmidt, "Ordinances and Instructions of Don Alexander O'Reilly," 1 *La. L. J.* (1841), 1-3.

[8]See Instructions of Nov. 25, 1769, Preamble, reprinted in English translation in Schmidt, "Ordinances and Instructions of Don Alexander O'Reilly," 1 *La. L. J.* (1841), 1, 27.

[9]The *Nueva Recopilación* of the Kingdom of Castile was enacted in 1567. The *Recopilación de Leyes de los Reinos de las Indias* is a selective and systematic rearrangement of major legal

texts up to 1680. See Baade, "The Formalities of Private Real Estate Transactions in Spanish North America," 38 *La. L. Rev.* (1978), 656, 667. If no later enactment furnished the rule of decision, reference was made to the laws of the *Siete Partidas*. This is a compilation of laws made in 1263 and formally enacted in 1348. See Moreau Lislet and Carleton, *The Laws of Las Siete Partidas, which are still in Force in the State of Louisiana* (1820), iii-xxv.

[10]See Baade, "The Law of Slavery in Spanish Luisiana," text at note 86, this Symposium. The *Code Noir* was a collection of rules regulating ownership, discipline, and control of slaves. See also note 23 *infra*.

[11]*Beard* v. *Poydras, 4 Mart.* (O.S.) 348 (La. 1816); Moreau Lislet and Carleton, *The Laws of Las Siete Partidas*, Translators' Preface (1820), iii, xviii. "O'Reilly issued a proclamation, changing the form of the government of Louisiana, abolishing the authority of the French laws, and substituting those of Spain in their stead. From the time of its promulgation until now, the French law ceased to have any authority in this country, and all controversies were tried and decided conformably to the Spanish laws . . ."

[12]The original decision has not been found. See Dargo, *Jefferson's Louisiana: Politics and the Clash of Legal Traditions* (1975), 132, note 16, citing Hatcher, *Edward Livingston: Jeffersonian Republican and Jacksonian Democrat* (1940), 118-119.

[13]The proposed legislation in manuscript is printed in the *Territorial Papers, Orleans Series*, National Archives. It has been reprinted in Brown, "Legal Systems in Conflict; Orleans Territory, 1804-1812," 1 *Am. J. Legal History* (1857), 35, 46-48; and Franklin, "The Place of Thomas Jefferson in the Expulsion of Spanish Medieval Law from Louisiana," 16 *Tul. L. Rev.* (1942), 319, 323-26.

[14]See *Le Telegraph*, New Orleans, Tuesday, June 3, 1806, reprinted in part in A. N. Yiannopoulos, *Louisiana Civil Law System* - Part I (1977), 191-193.

[15]See Dargo, *Jefferson's Louisiana: Politics and the Clash of Legal Traditions* (1975), 74-101; Schmidt, "The *Batture Question*," 1 *La. L. J.* (1841), 84-151.

[16]Schmidt, "The *Batture Question*," 1 *La. L. J.* (1841), 84, 93.

[17]Id., at 96-97.

[18]Id., at 98.

[19]Id., at 99.

[20]Schmidt. "Were the Laws of France, Which Governed Louisiana, Prior to the Cession of the Country to Spain Abolished by the Ordinances of O'Reilly?" Introductory Note, 1 *La. L. J.* (1842), 23-38.

[21]Id., at 26.

[22]Id., at 27-38.

[23]Id., at 37-38.

[24]See note 28 *infra*.

[25]See Wallach, *Research in Louisiana Law* (1958), 166; Hood, "A Crossroad in Louisiana History," 22 *La. L. Rev.* (1962), 709; Dargo, *Jefferson's Louisiana Politics and the Clash of Legal Traditions* (1975), 238, note 62. *But see* note 10 *supra*.

[26]Baade, "Marriage Contracts in French and Spanish Louisiana: A Study in 'Notarial' Jurisprudence," 53 *Tul. L. Rev.* (1978), 3, 74; see also Baade, "The Formalities of Private Real Estate Transactions in Spanish North America ," 38 *La. L. Rev.* (1978), 656, 682, citing recommendation for royal approval by the Council of the Indies on February 27, 1772, and formal approval by royal *Cédula* dated August 17, 1772.

[27]See Baade, "Marriage Contracts in French and Spanish Louisiana: A Study in 'Notarial' Jurisprudence," 53 *Tul. L. Rev.* 3, 87-88 (1978).

[28]See Batiza, "The Louisiana Civil Code of 1808: Its Actual Sources and Present Relevance," 46 *Tul. L. Rev.* (1971), 4; Pascal, "Sources of the Digest of 1808: A Reply to Professor Batiza," 46 *Tul. L. Rev.* (1972), 603; Batiza, "Sources of the Civil Code of 1808, Facts and Speculation: A Rejoinder," 46 *Tul. L. Rev.* (1972), 628.

[29]See Sweeney, "Tournament of Scholars over the Sources of the Louisiana Civil Code of 1808," 46 *Tul. L. Rev.* (1972), 595; Dargo, *Jefferson's Louisiana: Politics and the Clash of Legal Traditions* (1975), 163; Tucker, Effect on the Civil Law of Louisiana Brought About by the Change in Sovereignty (Soc'y of Bartolus, Juridical Studies, No. 1, 1975), 2-42.

[30]Res. of June 7, 1806, Territory of Orleans Acts 215 (1806).

[31]La. Acts 1808, No. XXIX, An Act providing for the promulgation of the Digest of Civil Laws now in force in the Territory of Orleans.

[32]La. Acts 1808, No. XXIX, sec. 2.

[33]See Yiannopoulos, *Louisiana Civil Law System* - Part I (2nd ed., 1977), 32.

[34]*Hayes* v. *Berwick, 2 Mart.* (O.S.) (La. 1812), 138, 140.

[35]*Cottin* v. *Cottin, 5 Mart.* (O.S.) (La. 1817), 93-94.

[36]46 *Tul. L. Rev.* (1971), 4-165.

[37]Id., at 10.

[38]Id., at 11-12.

[39]Id., at 9, note 34.

[40]See *e.g., Dickson* v. *Sandefur, 250 So. 2d* (La. 1971), 708, 717, note 5: "It is most obvious from a study of our Civil Code Article 518 that Moreau Lislet's references in the Digest to writers and laws opposite its predecessor (Art. 17, Book II, Title II, Chapter III, p. 107) – are not the source of that article but to the contrary state the opposing Roman legal principle. Not one of the cited authorities gives any basis or support for the Article 17 appearing opposite these references. They contradict Article 17. It appears that we should accept Moreau Lislet's notes for what he says they are: '*de notes qui referent aux Loix civiles et Espangnoles qui y ont raport.*' " *Holland* v. *Buckley, 305 So. 2d* (La. 1974), 113, 119: "In the particular instance here argued, the alleged sources cited bear little resemblance in text and substance to the Louisiana code article adopted, being only generally related in subject matter. In actual fact, the 1808 article is a verbatim enactment of the equivalent article of the Projet of the year VIII (1800) for the French Civil Code. We are unable to attach any relevance to the notes found in the de la Vergne volume, insofar as their interpretation of this article of the Louisiana code as to the issue before us."

[41]Pascal, "Sources of the Digest of 1808: A Reply to Professor Batiza," 46 *Tul. L. Rev.* (1972), 603-604 (emphasis deleated).

[42]Id., at 607-608.

[43]Id., at 623-624.

[44]Batiza, "Sources of the Civil Code of 1808, Facts and Speculation: A Rejoinder," 46 *Tul. L. Rev.* (1972), 628, 639.

[45]Id., at 645.

[46]Id., at 649.

[47]Batiza, *The Verbatim and Almost Verbatim Sources of the Louisiana Civil Codes of 1808, 1825, and 1870: The Original Texts* (1973), Preface to vol. 3.

[48]Ibid.

[49]Tate, "The Splendid Mystery of the Civil Code of Louisiana," 3 *La. Review* (1974), 1, 11, reprinted in 25 *L. B. J.* (1977),29. For a different explanation of the mystery, see Baade, "Marriage Contracts in French and Spanish Louisiana: A Study in 'Notarial' Jurisprudence,"

53 *Tul. L. Rev.* (1978), 3, 84; *cf.* Dargo, *Jefferson's Louisiana* (1975), 160, 164.

[50]Sweeney, "Foreword," 46 *Tul. L. Rev.* (1971), 2.

[51]See Yiannopoulos, "Louisiana Civil Law: A Lost Cause?" 54 *Tul. Rev.* (1980), 830, 832.

[52]See Franklin, "Libraries of Edward Livingston and of Moreau Lislet," 15 *Tul. L. Rev.* (1941), 401-402.

[53]See Baade, "Marriage Contracts in French and Spanish Louisiana: A Study in 'Notarial' Jurisprudence," 53 *Tul. L. Rev.* (1978), 3, 40.

[54]See Yiannopoulos, *Louisiana Civil Law System* (1977), Part I, p. 8.

[55]See Matteis, *Reichsrecht und Volksrecht in den Östlichen Provinzen des Römischen Kaiserreichs* (1891).

[56]See Planiol, *Traité élémentaire de droit civil* (trans. by the Louisiana State Law Institute, 1959), vol. 1, part 1, 10-11.

[57]Patton, *Jurisprudence* (1951), 140-141.

[58]Ibid.

[59]See Batiza, "Sources of the Civil Code of 1808, Facts and Speculation: A Rejoinder," 46 *Tul. L. Rev.* (1972), 628, 640.

[60]See Dargo, *Jefferson's Louisiana: Politics and the Clash of Legal Traditions* (1975), 163.

[61]See note 46 *supra*.

[62]See note 32 *supra*.

[63]See Batiza, "Sources of the Civil Code of 1808, Facts and Speculation: A Rejoinder," 46 *Tul. L. Rev.* (1972), 628, 651.

[64]See Yiannopoulos, *The Civil Codes of Louisiana, in Louisiana Civil Code* (1981 edition), xix-xxi; Batiza, "The Actual Sources of the Louisiana Projet of 1823: A General Analytical Survey," 47 *Tul. L. Rev.* (1972), 1.

AN OVERVIEW OF THE WORK OF THE TERRITORIAL COURT, 1804-1808, A MISSING CHAPTER IN THE DEVELOPMENT OF THE LOUISIANA CIVIL CODE

By
Richard H. Kilbourne, Jr.

Introduction

Almost a year elapsed following the cession of Louisiana to the United States before the territorial judiciary could begin functioning. Suits instigated in the Spanish tribunals and others presented to Governor Claiborne for decision were in abeyance, awaiting the constitution of the judiciary created by act of Congress in March, 1804. Perhaps the provision granting the new Superior Court of the Territory both original and appellate jurisdiction in civil matters was intended to expedite the flow of accumulated litigation, thus providing both immediate and permanent relief for the most pressing claims.[1] Not until November, 1804, did the Superior Court actually commence hearing cases, and another six months passed before the Legislative Council enacted legislation regulating the practice of the court.[2] The congressional statute creating the Superior Court provided for three judges "any one of whom could constitute a court."[3] The first apointee to the court was John B. Prevost, a native of New York and the stepson of Aaron Burr. Prevost alone presided during the first two years of the court's existence, and not until 1807 was there a full complement of three judges, with the additions of Joshua Lewis and George Mathews.

One of the first petitions to assail Prevost concerned the Superior Court's jurisdiction. The petitioner queried whether Judge Prevost sitting alone could take cognizance of an appeal from Governor Claiborne's tribunal.[4] In reality the plaintiff was saying that a final judgment had already been rendered in the Governor's court, a court which was now defunct. In the event Governor Claiborne's decision was subject to appeal, the plaintiff also petitioned for a jury trial.

Jury trials appear to have been used in a number of civil cases during the eight-year life of the Superior Court. In one particularly complicated case involving a dispute between the city of New Orleans and one Metzinger over title to lots located on or near the levee fronting the city, Metzinger agreed to submit questions of fact to a jury for decision; nevertheless, he refused the submission of "points of law, as they [were] . . . the most difficult of jurisprudence."[5] Set against the background of the batture controversy and the city's frequent attempts to evict trespassers from land in the vicinity of abandoned fortifications which had been denominated as commons, Metzinger's concern was justified.

A wide spectrum of factual and legal questions were litigated during the life of the Superior Court, and those questions likewise bore on important historical events in the life of the territory, such as the batture controversy between Edward Livingston and the city of New Orleans, the Baron de Bastrop land concession, Father Walsh's dispute with Father Antonio, liquidations of important merchant houses, and even a dispute over the contract for printing the 1808 Digest.[6]

The present work, however, will focus only upon those areas of substantive law that appear to have been most frequently litigated in the Superior Court in an effort to determine whether there were wide divergencies between the court's appreciation of civil law regimes in the early years of the territory and the formulation of such regimes in the 1808 Digest. The docket of the Superior Court runs about thirty-five hundred cases, and about forty percent of those pre-date the enactment of the 1808 Digest. Regretably, neither judgment books nor indexes appear to have survived,[7] thus the areas of substantive law treated have been drawn from a survey of petitions and answers filed in that court.

Insolvency

While insolvency proceedings bore most directly on questions of commercial law, their significance for Louisiana's civil law heritage and the work of the Superior Court should not be minimized. Roughly two-thirds of the litigation in the Superior Court concerned insolvency proceedings wherein debtors petitioned the court to stay proceedings and executions against them by their creditors so that none of the creditors might "have any advantage to the prejudice of the others."[8] Such petitions frequently contained elaborate summaries of a debtor's business activities, a schedule of his creditors, and instruments evidencing his debts.

Because New Orleans was an important commercial center for the United States even during the last years of Spanish rule, the cession of the territory in 1803 was not merely anticipatory of a vast augmentation of business in consequence of the opening of the west bank of the Mississippi

River for settlement. The importance of the river trade and the influence of the Anglo-American merchant community in New Orleans probably insured that Louisiana's commercial law would be assimilated to the law merchant of the United States* when the territory was ceded in 1803; nevertheless, the judiciary's authority for the subsequent transformation of commercial law is obscure.[9]

One important Spanish regulation did escape dismantlement, that being the institution governing insolvency proceedings. The continuance of Spanish insolvency regulations probably received some encouragement from the facts that the United States itself lacked a national bankruptcy law and that the laws of the various states on that subject were completely chaotic. In any event the Legislative Council enacted a statute in 1805 for the relief of insolvents which, in the words of Judge Joshua Lewis, was passed "in aid of the Spanish law upon the subject."[10] The statute itself clearly indicates a recognition of a background of Spanish commercial law and that the statute was a supplement in a general scheme of regulation not yet posited legislatively, because it provides that when any debtor who "shall, subsequent to the passing of this act, be sued or imprisoned for any debt, shall deliver in a schedule *as now required by law* . . . every suit against such debtor shall be stayed."[11]

One of the institutions of the Spanish regulation that remained in force was the *Espera*,* or delay, which a majority of creditors "in number and amount" could agree to give the debtor.[12] The *Espera* had the effect of forcing all the creditors to allow the debtor an additional period for discharging his obligations. The Superior Court recognized the validity of the *Espera* but there can be little doubt that all such debtor-relief measures could be opposed by the federal Constitution's prohibition against laws imparing the obligations of contract.[13] Furthermore, the discharge of the insolvent as provided for in the 1805 legislation was equally repugnant to the federal Constitution; nevertheless, Louisiana and all the states of the Union continued to adopt such relief measures throughout the nineteenth century.

An important subject for elucidation in this context are privileges and other security devices such as mortgages. It was quite usual to find a wife asserting her dotal rights* in insolvency proceedings, as an examination of the case of *Le Bourgeois* vs. *His syndics* will show. Le Bourgeois's wife had obtained a decree from the Superior Court ordering a sale of his estate

*See Glossary.

to satisfy her claims and demands, as well as those of other creditors. Before any sale could take place Le Bourgeois demanded that the syndics* of his creditors reconvey "his said effects or estate according to law."[14] He made a tender to the syndics of money and "offered good and sufficient security" for any remaining balance.[15] It is obvious that Le Bourgeois planned to use his wife's separate and dotal assets, her entitlement to which already had been confirmed by the Superior Court, as a set-off against creditors of inferior rank. The syndics refused the offer, and Le Bourgeois responded with a suit substantiating his claim with generous citations to Spanish authorities that supported his right to have his estate reconveyed to him.

Matrimonial Regimes

Most litigation in the Superior Court of the Territory involving marriage contracts arose in the context of insolvency proceedings usually with the wife's seeking to safeguard her dotal rights and paraphernal property* where syndics were liquidating the husband's estate to satisfy the claims of secured and general creditors. Where an express marriage contract in notarial form evidenced the wife's dotal rights, the Superior Court always recognized her priority vis-a-vis any of the husband's other creditors, because such an act usually created in her favor a mortgage over all the husband's estate.

Prior to the 1808 Digest the wife had a privilege "by the ancient laws of the country" for her dowry that primed even the husband's antenuptual secured creditors.[16] The Digest reduced substantially the wife's privilege and simply required the husband to give security upon receiving the dowry, unless he had been bound to do otherwise by an express marriage contract. But, when a husband sought to mortgage property, even his separate property, and the wife already had a mortgage over the whole of his estate to secure her dotal rights, the prospective mortgagee usually required the wife's consent so that his mortgage would outrank hers.[17] Furthermore, the purchaser of an immovable from the husband would require her assent to the sale so that the immovable would not be encumbered with the wife's mortgage. The wife's petition in the case of the *Wife of Pierre Lartique* vs. *the Syndics of Lartique*, wherein she was represented by Edward Livingston, asserts that the purchasers of a plantation from Pierre Lartique had "as a present and acknowledgment for... [her] consent to the sale [had] agreed to give to her the customary gift made on the occasion of the like nature and known in the province by the name of Epingles (pin money) as her money . . . for her separate use."[18]

It is significant that the examination of litigation affecting matrimonial regimes in the Territorial Court revealed only two cases where spouses attempted to dissolve the legally imposed regime, the community of acquets or gains.* The community of acquets or gains, of which the husband was deemed to be head and master, was part of the husband's patrimony.*[19] The community of gains took place whether there was an express marriage contract between the spouses or not, but it should be remembered that the husband could not gain access to the wife's antenuptual property or property which came to her separate estate during marriage, unless an express marriage contract between them placed these assets in a dowry. As early as 1805, a man and his wife attempted by notarial act to "dissolve the community existing between them . . . and divide between themselves all the effects belonging thereto, whether movable or immovable."[20] The spouses jointly petitioned the Territorial Court, alleging that the "aforesaid instrument of writing . . . [could] be put in force and execution, but when sanctified by the honorable court."[21] They prayed that the court would "order and decree that the said act be lawfully executed."[22] How Judge Prevost disposed of their petition is not known but, in a subsequent case, a partition of community property by notarial act was voided because the spouses had predicated the partition on a voluntary separation from bed and board, and the law required a judicial pronouncement. In *Catherine Morin* vs. *Bernard Genois* the plaintiff sought a confirmation of the separation from bed and board and "in consequence thereof a new partition of the goods of the community hitherto existing between them."[23] She claimed that by their partition her husband had received "three times as much property as she [had] received for her share, although the said property was common between them, and their rights to the same equal."[24] In his answer Bernard Genois admitted that "though he had signed [the voluntary act of separation] he never [had] considered himself as separated, in as much as the same . . . [was] null and void in law."[25] The case was decided after the 1808 Digest was in force, and the judgment was for the defendant-husband.

The substance of matrimonial regimes in the Territorial period, as revealed in the litigation examined thus far, appears consistent with what was true of contemporary Spanish law, that neither a separation of property to secure the wife her dotal rights nor a separation from bed and board would dissolve the community of acquets or gains between the spouses. This assumption is reinforced by the 1805 alimony statute which granted the county courts jurisdiction over applications "from wives against their husbands, for alimony, on the husband's deserting his wife for one year successively, and in cases of cruel, inhuman treatment."[26] An award of alimony carried with it criminal penalties if the husband failed to comply with the judgment and "released the . . . [wife] from the power of her husband," thus permitting her to live separate from him.[27] She might then "acquire, use, and dispose of any property uncontrolled by her husband, as if she were a single woman."[28] What is especially significant about the 1805 alimony statute is that an award of alimony was tantamount to a judgment of separation from bed and board. Additionally the judge might make provision "for the maintenance of the children of any parties . . . according to the age and sex of such children, and to the circumstances of their parents."[29]

The 1805 alimony act is a singular, if not unique, piece of legislation in the realm of familial relations, and perhaps an explanation of the need for such legislation will be found in the context of rude frontier conditions where husbands frequently deserted their wives, migrated to distant lands, and set up housekeeping anew. Another explanation is that the legislation provided the wife with more expeditious access to the husband's patrimony for her maintenance and that of any children. Such an interpretation reinforces what is implicit in the cases themselves: that a judgment of separation from bed and board did not dissolve the community between the spouses. Indeed, the wife's desertion of the husband resulted in her forfeiture of all her rights "to the property acquired in the community."[30]

From almost the beginning of the Territorial period there was litigation respecting the wife's binding herself personally for the husband's debts, whether antenuptual or community. The wife's suretyship* permitted the husband's creditors to reach her separate and dotal property; hence, the Spanish legal system, which was very protective of the wife's separate personality and property, contained a variety of positive safeguards affecting the wife's separate estate. A wife might, however, waive all of her protections and contract a suretyship in favor of her husband. In the case of *Bartelemi Beauregard* vs. *Piernas* the creditor-plaintiff noted in his petition that his debtor's wife had "executed as a security for her said husband, and hypothecated and pledged* in conjunction with the said Piernas, all her property present and to come, renouncing for herself the laws of the Emperor Justinian, and Senatus Consultus, the laws of *Toro*, the *Partidas Nuevas*, and the old constitutions and other authorities, and making at the same time, the oath prescribed by [the Spanish practice], and solemnly swearing that she was not influenced by [her husband] . . . nor by any other person."[31]

Not infrequently the wife would bind herself jointly with her husband to secure the repayment of a particular obligation, in which case she had to have her husband's authorization to bind herself jointly with him. The nature of her obligation in this instance differed considerably from a contract of suretyship for repayment of a husband's debts; here the wife required only the husband's authorization to become a joint obligor. Finally, as previously noted, creditors usually required the wife's permission or waiver of her priority ranking with regard to her dotal privilege when the husband sought to secure repayment of a loan with a mortgage on property. In one early case the wife complained that fear and threats of ill treatment from her husband had been the cause of her consent.[32] Presumably, if she was able to establish the truth of her accusation she retained her priority ranking vis-a-vis the husband's other secured creditors.

The community of acquest or gains between the spouses dissolved when the marriage terminated, that is, either when a spouse died or a special act of divorce* was obtained from the Territorial Legislature. In one suit, *Dupre* vs. *Dupre*, which was instituted in 1808, the plaintiff-wife, who had been married in 1804, petitioned the Territorial Court with the following rescitation of facts:

> [A]t the time of the said marriage no matrimonial contract, or marriage articles, were entered into between [the spouses] . . . and that her said husband secured to her no dower, nor any other gift out of his property; that a few months ago her husband died intestate, leaving an only child, issued from the aforesaid marriage, for his only heir; and that no property, or if any a very inconsiderable portion, having been acquired during the said marriage, your petitioner's child . . . inherits the whole... estate of her father; so that your petitioner will be reduced to poverty, if your honorable court does not take into consideration her distressed situation and allow her to that share, which the laws of her country grant in such cases to widows, to wit, one fourth part of the estate of

her deceased husband.[33]

Judge Lewis of the Territorial Court decreed that the plaintiff was to recover one-fourth of the estate of her deceased husband "to be by her enjoyed during her lifetime in a quality of usufruct."*[34] His authority was Title V, Chapter II, Section II, article 55 of the 1808 Digest, Moreau Lislet's source notes for which cite the *Partidas* and *Febrero*.*[35] No corresponding article is to be found in the Code Napoleon. Such confirmations of the continuing influence of Spanish legal institutions at the litigation level tend to confirm that many aspects of Spanish legal culture relative to matrimonial regimes remained quite viable after the cession of the Louisiana territory to the United States in 1803.

Successions

Forced heirship* being one of the most conspicuous features of Louisiana successions law, it is important to observe that the petitions filed in the Superior Court, which involve donations *inter vivos* and *mortis causa** confirm the provisions in the 1808 Digest that regulated the size of the disposable portion* where there were forced heirs, whether in the ascending or descending lines. In the words of one petitioner "by the laws of this land, the father, mother, or other ascendants, [could] . . . dispose, either *inter vivos* or *mortis causa*, to the prejudice of their children in favor of strangers, only of a fifth part of their property. That when they [had] . . . exceeded that portion fixed by law, their children and other legitimate descendants [could] . . . obtain a reduction of the liberalities of their parents, as being made to the prejudice of their lawful inheritance."[36] The disposable portion, where there were forced heirs in the ascending line, was a third of the decedant's estate.[37]

Relative to forced heirship and ascendants, one of the most important cases to emerge in the survey of the Superior Court Archives was *Darby* vs. *Darby*, wherein suit was instituted on behalf of the testator's* natural children,* all of whom were offsprings of his illicit union with a black concubine. The descendants claimed status as natural children duly recognized as such by their father's testament. The defendant was the testator's mother, who deemed the prosecution of their suit to be "contrary to all the laws and rules of the Territory, an action also contrary to the manners of the country . . . and very prejudicial to all the inhabitants" of the Territory.[38] She asserted her right to inherit as her son's forced heir in accordance with the laws governing the country and sought to invalidate his testament arguing that he had "no lawful progeny . . . [to] institute for his heirs," for the law stated positively that the natural children had to be born of a free mother "who might without lawful hinderance" marry their father.[39] Marriage between blacks and whites was strictly forbidden by "the laws of Louisiana, laws which existed ever since the establishment of the country" to forbid such marriages.[40] The disposition on which the plaintiffs set their claims therefore was void. That the father was barred from acknowledging his illegitimate children, when the only conceivable impediment was that his concubine was a woman of color, seems unlikely; certainly, subsequent decisions of Louisiana courts during the ante-bellum period confirmed a father's power to acknowledge such children, thus raising them to the status of natural children.[41] Children of color were, nevertheless, barred from proving filiation* where they claimed descent from a white father.[42]

It is significant that none of the provisions governing the rights of illegitimate children of color in the 1808 Digest are to be found in the Code Napoleon, and the Moreau Lislet source notes* indicate that they were drawn from Spanish sources.[43] The natural father could bestow one-third of his estate on his natural children, either by donation *inter vivos* or *mortis causa*, even when he left legitimate ascendants; so the plaintiffs in *Darby* probably prevailed. The 1825 Civil Code, however, limited the benefits that could be given to natural children when there were ascendants to one-fourth of the decedant's estate, thus reducing the disposable portion in the case of illegitimates.[44]

Illegitimates born of a miscegenous union appear to have been numerous in the Louisiana Territory, and decades later François Xavier Martin would observe that:

> A part of the population of this state has been placed by law under certain disabilities and incapacities, from which it is not the province of courts of justice to relieve them. Cases of bastardy, of very rare occurence in France, are, unfortunately, much more frequent among us. The decisions of no tribunal in France are binding upon us, and there are very important considerations which impose on our courts a stricter observance of the

> laws relative to illegitimate children, especially those of colour.[45]

What Martin was alluding to is likely attributable to the more expansive protections afforded the legitimate family in France, rather than a lesser incidence of bastardy in that country. In any event, the rights of illegitimates frequently were the subject of litigation in the Territorial period, particularly in the context of succession proceedings.

The 1808 Digest codified an elaborate succession provision from the Spanish legal system which prescribed that collaterals of the whole blood,* in intestate successions,* inherit to the exclusion of collaterals of the half blood where there were neither descendants nor ascendants. The redactors clearly codified one provision that was a precise feature of Louisiana succession law in the period between the cession of the Territory to the United States and the enactment of the Digest.[46] A more difficult question concerns the pre-1808 practice with regard to setting aside donations wherein a disposition was made through hatred, anger, suggestion, or captation. The Digest positively prohibited evidence of a donor's being subject to "undue influence" when making a disposition either *inter vivos* or *mortis causa*, in order to attack the donor's capacity.[47] It is, therefore, somewhat surprising to find a petition, drafted by Moreau Lislet and filed in 1809, wherein the plaintiff complained that both a testament and codicil were null and void, "having been made through captation and suggestion."[48]

It appears that by the end of the Spanish period, a custom had evolved respecting executors* and curators'* fees. In the case of *Denis de la Ronde executor by will of the late Philip Marigny* vs. *Bernard Marigny* the plaintiff-executor had obtained "the letters of administration* ordered by law, in consequence of which he put himself in the full and entire possession of all the properties movables and immovables."[49] De la Ronde had been "remitted the said properties to the heirs of [the testator] . . . by an act of remittance" passed before a notary.[50] It appears that de la Ronde claimed an executor's fee of five percent of the net estate of Philip Marigny, as well as a five percent fee from the estate of John Marigny, a deceased son. The defendant-heir, Bernard, resisted this imposition, no doubt because its cumulative effect was a double charge on the net estate of his father, Philip. Philip's son, John, had never reached majority, but had lived long enough to make a will naming de la Ronde his executor. Furthermore, de la Ronde, in his capacity as tutor* of John Marigny, claimed ten percent of the revenues of John's properties during the period of tutorship, which was customary and "agreeable to law and to the jurisprudence of the province."[51] Much of the revenue attributable to John's estate was in consequence of the liquidation of the estate of his father. De la Ronde noted that by John's testament he had been given "all power and faculty, that by him and without the interference of any part, he might form the inventory, estimation and sale of the estate, on terms or for ready cash, as he might think most fit."[52] Fortunately for the heirs de la Ronde agreed to "deliver to them the said estate as it existed . . . and [he] was thus abdicated of the right and faculty of selling."[53] The plaintiff's only alternative was to get a judgment based on the merits of his claim because his surrender of the property had reduced substantially his leverage with the heirs.

The 1808 Digest reduced the commission of the testamentary executor with seizin* to two and a half percent "whether he was charged to sell it or not."[54] Furthermore, the Digest made a clear distinction between testamentary executors according to whether or not they had a general seizin. Where the executor "had not a general seizin, his commission [could] . . . only be on the estimated value of the objects which he had in his possession, and on the sums put into his hands for the purpose of paying off the legacies."[55] It appears that the distinction was based primarily on Spanish sources, and no corresponding articles are indicated in the Code Napoleon.[56] Assuming John Marigny was above the age of sixteen when he made his testament, he had capacity to make donations *mortis causa*. Whether he could name de la Ronde executor is questionable, because such a disposition might well have been opposed by a prohibition similar to the one enacted in the Digest which prohibited dispositions by minors in favor of their tutors.[57] It is significant that Bernard Marigny was represented by Moreau Lislet; so, while it is impossible to determine whether such a prohibition existed prior to the enactment of the 1808 Digest, one of the redactors was certainly aware of problems that could arise with testamentary executors. De la Ronde was awarded nine thousand dollars by a special jury and assessed with the court costs. It is perhaps of some relevance that public perception of lawyers and judges in the context of succession proceedings associated them with corrupt practices, and this perception lasted well into the antebellum period.[58]

Supplementary Role of Legislation and the Sources of Law

It has been suggested that Governor Claiborne's veto of an enactment of the First Territorial Legislature declaring what civil laws were in force in the Louisiana Territory proceeded from political considerations, specifically Claiborne's desire to introduce the institutions of the common law into the Territory, rather than from an awkward interpretation of the congressional statutes extending the common law modes of procedure to Louisiana.[59] There seems to be some evidence, however, for finding a less hostile attitude on Claiborne's part toward the civil law and more concern for expositing the institutions of a system of law which was to him entirely foreign.

Louisiana legal culture was too provincial in the Territorial period to have received much influence from Jeremy Bentham's reform philosophy of legislative positivism,* and the supplementary role of legislation during the period of the Legislative Council, as reflected in the alimony and insolvency statutes, is perhaps most indicative of the mixed sources of law in Louisiana legal culture.[60] Cession alone might truncate institutions inherited from the colonial period to the extent that they were incompatible with the new regime's constitution, but it could not terminate altogether those institutions' subtle and various influences. Separation of powers among three branches of government was entirely new to the Louisiana environment, and this reality had a vital significance for the way in which the Legislative Council and its successor, the Territorial Legislature, enacted laws. A colonial heritage wherein the governor had combined all the functions of lawgiver, executive, and judge no doubt sharpened the nostalgia of those charged with positing laws for a country whose judicial administration and executive authority were now diversified in distinct channels. Those charged with explicating the subtleties of law probably saw their task hamstrung with foreign innovations such as the decentralization of authority in legislative, executive, and judicial branches of government.

Some inkling of the discomfiture of the Legislative Council may be seen in the Act for the Punishment of Crimes and Misdemeanors enacted in 1805 which specifically excluded slaves who were to be "punished according to the laws of Spain for regulating her colonies: Provided, however, that no cruel or unusual punishment (should) . . . be inflicted."[61] Section forty-eight ordered the governor to compile an exposition of all crimes and misdemeanors mentioned in the act which were not therein precisely defined, and additionally an explication of the "rules of evidence, the mode of trial, the forms of writs and indictments, and all other proceedings" as provided for in the thirty-third section.[62] Section thirty-three declared that all crimes and misdemeanors specified in the act were to be construed "according to and in conformity with the common law of England."[63] The Legislative Council's primary concern appears to have been with exposition of the laws in force, and in no way suggests a preoccupation with an exclusive authority to make laws.

Positing laws via the legislative branch certainly was one method for explicating laws already in force, thus settling for good ambiguities of interpretation that arose in the litigation context. The Legislative Council simultaneously with the supplementary compilation for the Crimes and Misdemeanors Act, which Governor Claiborne charged Lewis Kerr to prepare, authorized a Digest of Civil Laws.[64] Subsequently money was appropriated in a single resolution of the Council to pay the redactors for their work on the Civil and Criminal Codes.[65] An important theme in understanding the workings of the Territorial government at this crucial juncture in Louisiana's civil law heritage was the need to exposit laws and not just posit them.

Although the records of the Territorial Court are all too abbreviated, there are some indications that an exposition of the civil laws in force in the Louisiana Territory was indeed prepared and circulated in the court's deliberations. Sections from the *Curia Phillipica,** Feberero, and the *Partidas* were translated and cited as authority in debates centering on questions of law, and obviating for a moment the issue of which laws were in force after the cession; it is clear that apprizing Governor Claiborne, Judge Prevost and other officials of civil law institutions and their sources presented many practical problems. There is no evidence in the records of the Territorial Court to suggest that the application of traditional civilian regimes in the litigation context was interrupted at the cession or at a subsequent time.

When Claiborne vetoed the First Legislature's enactment identifying by reference only what civil laws were in force he may well have believed that such an enactment was unnecessary because their identities were known and the institutions of Spanish law had never ceased to have the force of law. Abrogation of existing legal institutions at the cession would have required the introduction of incompatible institutions and a blanket repeal, neither of which ever happened in the context of civil law regimes.[66] Claiborne's famous letter to Madison contains evidence of the Governor's surprise at the public consternation which his veto had aroused and his well supported belief that the "bill was useless."[67] It is, however, easy to confound the expositional problem with abrogation of existing laws by a new sovereign. In the case of commercial law, for example, it is obvious that most institutions of Spanish legal culture simply died from ignorance and obscurity, but the Louisiana judiciary never was able to establish that Spanish commercial law had either been abrogated at the cession or at a subsequent time.[68] Criminal laws were substantially altered by the acts of Congress and the Legislative Council's statute regulating crimes and misdemeanors. In the latter instance concern about exposition led the Council to authorize Governor Claiborne to prepare a compilation which would supplement the abbreviated text of the statute and thus inform a community largely ignorant of the common law institutions of criminal law. There is no evidence at present which suggests that Claiborne or the members of the Legislative Council philosophically grounded the Louisiana legal system in legislative positivism; hence, the expositional problem takes on additional importance in the criss-cross of tensions which converged to determine the destiny of the civil law in Louisiana. There was, in other words, no constitutional necessity for making law an expression of legislative will, except that the new sovereigns were not likely to tolerate ambiguities or obscurities in the ancient laws which governed the province.

That the Legislative Council authorized the drafting of a Digest of the civil laws in 1805 at the behest of Claiborne and Prevost, primarily as an exposition of the laws in force, is a certainty; that it was actually drafted finds a supporting complement in the criminal law compilation prepared by Lewis Kerr. In his introduction Kerr states;

> Congress, therefore, have wisely fixed a period when the laws of the Territory of Orleans are to be administered in the same manner as the laws are generally administered throughout the United States. By the ordinance of Congress of the 13th Of July, 1787, for the government of the territory North West of the Ohio, which by the late act of Congress, (8th Con. 2nd sess. chap. 82) is extended, with a few alterations, to this territory, it is declared that the judges "shall have common

law jurisdiction." And afterwards, by the second article of compact, in the same ordinance it is declared, that "the inhabitants of the said territory shall always be entitled to the benefit of the writ of habeas corpus, and of the trial by jury; of a proportionate representation of the people in the legislature, and of judicial proceedings according to the course of the common law." By these clauses, the substance of our preexisting law appears to be untouched; the form of administering them alone is changed; and the first legislature of the territory, sensible of the advantages of that change, at least in criminal proceedings, and desirous of preparing the way for the future operation of the ordinance (have adopted that statute for the punishment of crimes and misdemeanors). . . .

The introduction of English law in this territory is said to have given some offense. . . . Exception also may have been taken against it as being foreign law. But the truth is, that the common law as recognized in the United States, is no more the law of England than the civil law can now be deemed the law of Rome.

However as this new mode of practice is as yet but little known in Louisiana, and this has been one of the reasons urged against its introduction, there is a clause of the same statute of crimes and punishments intended to remove that objection.[69]

The palliative Kerr was referring to was, of course, the exposition he had been charged to prepare.

Conclusion

During the eight years the Superior Court of the Territory was in existence, the names of no more than a dozen attorneys appear on the petitions and answers filed with the clerk of court. Nevertheless, the bar of the Territorial Court was a distinguished one, and the frequency with which

Etienne Mazureau, an early Louisiana attorney. Louisiana State Museum.

certain names appear is hardly a disappointment when they are Livingston, Moreau Lislet, Derbigny, Brown, Workman, Ellery, Alexander, Mazureau, and Kerr. Their cumulative effort contributed to a solidification of the civil law in Louisiana, and their contribution seems especially significant in the years between 1804 and 1808. The indigenous legal institutions suited to the habits and manners of the people, and grounded in local customs or usages, needed to be articulated for the benefit of a bench composed almost exclusively of judges drawn from common law jurisdictions.

The Superior Court was a forum wherein the particulars of Louisiana's civil law heritage could find concrete expression through everyday application. Something more than the vague allusions to the "ancient laws of the province" or the "customs and usages of the Spanish government" was needed to insure the continuance of civilian regimes in Louisiana, particularly when the governing authorities were ignorant of those legal institutions. It is significant that the redactors of the 1808 Digest, Moreau Lislet and Brown, were prominent in litigation bearing on both the appropriateness and application of civil law institutions in settling disputes between claimants.

Finally, the pre-1808 Superior Court's importance to the survival of the Louisiana civil law heritge might be juxtaposed with the dramatic decline of litigation in that court bearing on questions of civil law after the enactment of the Digest. That juxtaposition seems to suggest a resolution of many ambiguities that arose in the litigation context. This impression is strengthened by a cursory examination of the first volume of *Martin's Reports** that presumes to digest the most important decisions of the Superior Court for the period 1809-1812. Probably the enactment of the Digest satisfactorily settled the most important questions of civil law at least for the duration of the Territorial period. The Superior Court as a forum wherein the particulars of the civil law regimes could be expounded presents an invaluable contribution to the survival of institutions which otherwise could not have gained exposure. In most instances the work of the redactors of the 1808 Digest faithfully represents civil law institutions as assimiliated from the petitions and answers submitted to the court prior to 1808.

[1]An act erecting Louisiana's two territories, and providing for the temporary government thereof, 1804 Acts of the Territory of Orleans, lst Sess. 284.

[2]G. Dargo, *Jefferson's Louisiana: Politics and the Clash of Legal Traditions* 113 (1975) [hereinafter cited as Dargo]; An Act Regulating the practice of the Superior Court in civil cases, 1804 Acts of the Territory of Orleans, lst Sess. 210-61.

[3]An act erecting Louisiana into two territories, and providing for the temporary government thereof, 1804 Acts of the Territory of Orleans, lst Sess. 284.

[4]*Heirs of Percalis de la Barre* v. *Pierre de la Ronde*, Docket No. 38 (Records of the Superior Court of the Territory of Orleans, New Orleans Public Library).

[5]*Corporation* v. *Metzinger*, Docket No. 2832 (Records of the Superior Court of the Territory of Orleans, New Orleans Public Library).

[6]*Renard* v. *Bradford* & *Amderson*, Docket No. 2482 (Records of the Superior Court of the Territory of Orleans, New Orleans Public Library).

[7]Because of the absence of docket and judgment books, as well as indexes, and the lack of a reporter system, three months were required for this writer to examine the available records on a case by case basis.

[8]*Bouligny* v. *His Creditors*, Docket No. 1658 (Records of the Superior Court of the Territory of Orleans, New Orleans Public Library).

[9]R. Kilbourne, *Louisiana Commercial Law: The Antebellum Period* (1980), pt. two [hereinafter cited as Kilbourne].

[10]*Kenner* & *Henderson* v. *Hunt* & *Smith*, Docket No. 1303 (Records of the Superior Court of the Territory of Orleans, New Orleans Public Library).

[11]An act for the Relief of Insolvent Debtors, 1805 Acts of the Territory of Orleans, 2d Sess. 60-66.

[12]*Bouligny* v. *His Creditors*, Docket No. 1658 (Records of the Superior Court of the Territory of Orleans, New Orleans Public Library).

[13]Kilbourne, *supra* n. 9, at pt. one.

[14]*Le Bourgeois* v. *His Syndics*, Docket No. 736 (Records of the Superior Court of the Territory of Orleans, New Orleans Public Library).

[15]Id.

[16]*Loucy Tounoir* v. *Thomas Bailey*, Docket No. 825 (Records of the Superior Court of the Territory of Orleans, New Orleans Public Library).

[17]*Wife of Pierre Lartique* v. *Syndics of Lartique*, Docket No. 942 (Records of the Superior Court of the Territory of Orleans, New Orleans Public Library).

[18]Id.

[19]See generally *La. Digest of 1808*, ch. II, sec. IV, arts. 63 *et seq.*

[20]Petition of Cornellius Deploy & Marguerite Des Bordes, Docket No. 30 (Records of the Superior Court of the Territory of Orleans, New Orleans Public Library).

[21]Id.

[22]Id.

[23]*Morin* v. *Genois*, Docket No. 1812 (Records of the Superior Court of the Territory of Orleans, New Orleans Public Library).

[24]Id.

[25]Id.

[26]An act Concerning Alimony and for other purposes, 1805 Acts of the Territory of Orleans, 2d Sess. 54-59.

[27]Id.

[28]Id.

[29]Id.

[30]*William Despau* v. *Sophie Carriere, his wife*, Docket No. 561 (Records of the Superior Court of the Territory of Orleans, New Orleans Public Library).

[31]*Bartelemi Beauregard* v. *Piernas*, Docket No. 85 (Records of the Superior Court of the Territory of Orleans, New Orleans Public Library).

[32]*Lartique* v. *Lartique*, Docket No. 942 (Records of the Superior Court of the Territory of Orleans, New Orleans Public Library).

[33]*Dupre* v. *Dupre*, Docket No. 1936 (Records of the Superior Court of the Territory of Orleans, New Orleans Public Library).

[34]Id.

[35]*A Reprint of Moreau Lislet's Copy of A Digest of the Civil Laws now in force in the Territory of Orleans (1808): The de la Vergne Volume*, bk. 3, tit. V, ch. II, sec. II, art. 55 (2d ed., 1971) [hereinafter cited as *de la Vergne Volume*].

[36]*Heirs of Ximenes* v. *Mary Joseph Carol*, Docket No. 951 (Records of the Superior Court of the Territory of Orleans, New Orleans Public Library).

[37]*Widow Oliveau* v. *Louis Chevers*, Docket No. 997 (Records of the Superior Court of the Territory of Orleans, New Orleans Public Library).

[38]*Darby* v. *Darby*, Docket No. 532 (Records of the Superior Court of the Territory of Orleans, New Orleans Public Library).

[39]Id.

[40]Id.

[41]*Jung et al.* v. *Doriocourt et al.*, 4 La. 180 (1832).

[42]*La. Civ. Code* arts. 221, 226 (1825).

[43]*de la Vergne Volume, supra* n. 35, at bk. 1, tit. VII, ch. III, arts. 1-8.

[44]*La. Civ. Code* art. 1473 (1825); *Compton and others* v. *Prescott and another, Executors, and others*, 12 Rob. 70 (1845).

[45]*Jung et al.* v. *Doricourt et al.*, 4 La. 180 (1832).

[46]*La. Digest of 1808*, ch. II, sec. IV, art. 29; *de la Croix* v. *Le Breton Dourgenois*, Docket No. 641 (Records of the Superior Court of the Territory of Orleans, New Orleans Public Library).

[47]*La. Digest of 1808*, tit. II, ch. II, art. 18.

[48]*de la Bouraliere* v. *John Poyfare*, Docket No. 2213 (Records of the Superior Court of the Territory of Orleans, New Orleans Public Library).

[49]*Denis de la Ronde* v. *Bernard Marigny*, Docket No. 1248 (Records of the Superior Court of the Territory of Orleans, New Orleans Public Library).

[50]Id.

[51]Id.

[52]Id.

[53]Id.

[54]*La. Digest of 1808*, tit. II, ch. VI, sec. VI, art. 179.

[55]Id.

[56]*de la Vergne Volume, supra*, n. 35, at bk. III, tit. II, ch. VI, sec. VI, art. 179.

[57]*La. Digest of 1808*, tit. II, ch. II, art. 8.

[58]Kilbourne, *supra* n. 9, at pt. three.

[59]Dargo, *supra*, n. 2, at 129-30.

[60]An Act for the Relief of Insolvent Debtors, 1805 Acts of the Territory of Orleans, 2d Sess. 60-66.

[61]An Act For The Punishment of Crimes and Misdemeanors, 1805 Acts of the Territory of Orleans, lst Sess. 416.

[62]Id.

[63]Id.

[64]Dargo, *supra* n. 2, at 129-30.

[65]Resolution of Legislative Council, 1805 Acts of the Territory of Orleans, lst Sess. 458.

[66]P. Duponceau, *A Dissertation on the Nature and Extent of the Jurisdiction of the Courts of the United States* 68-76 (1824).

[67]III D. Rowland, *Official Letter Books of W. C. C. Claiborne* 309 (1972).

[68]Kilbourne, *supra* n. 9, at pt. two.

[69]L. Kerr, *Exposition of the Criminal Laws of the Territory of The Territory of Orleans* 2-6 (1806).

GLOSSARY

community of acquets or gains — The legally imposed matrimonial regime in Louisiana which the spouses could vary in an antenuptual agreement. Formerly the husband was the administrator of the community and could alienate assets acquired during the marriage which were deemed to be community property.

Curia Philipica — A comilation of ancient Spanish laws collected in the seventeenth century.

disposable portion — That portion of one's estate which one may dispose of to the prejudice of forced heirs.

donations ***inter vivos*** **and** ***mortis causa*** — A donation *inter vivos* is an act by which the donor divests himself, at present and irrevocably, of the thing given, in favor of the donee who accepts it. CC. 1468. A donation *mortis causa* is a revocable donation made in prospect of death which act is to take effect when the donor dies.

dotal rights — Pertaining to dowry. Any of several privileges arising by operation of law encumbering the husband's property for the protection of the wife's dowry.

Espera — A delay accorded to a debtor by law, when consented to by a majority of creditors in number and amount, which stayed all proceedings pending against the debtor's property. The Louisiana Civil Code provision on Respite is comparable to the *Espera*.

filiation — Paternity.

forced heirship — A limitation on one's capacity to alienate property, whether by donation or testamentary disposition, where there are children in the descending line, or parents in the ascending line. Forced heirship in the ascending line was eliminated in the 1981 legislative session.

hypothecated and pledged — Language customarily recited in a mortgage agreement hypothecation being synonymous with mortgage. Likewise the mortgage is a species of pledge; hence the language reflects a Roman law conception which did not distinguish between the mortgage and the pledge. Generally the mortgage encumbers immovable property and the pledge effects the same result with movable property.

law merchant of the United States — A system of law regulating commercial relations in the United States during the nineteenth century, derived almost exclusively from the customs and usages of merchants, either judicially recognized or legislatively posited. That system was deemed to be uniform throughout the United States, but was subject to many local variations.

legislative positivism — A philosophy of law which acknowledges legislative sanction as the premiere authority for all law.

letters of administration — Letters granted to a person by a probate court evidencing such person's authority to act as an administrtor for the succession of the decedent.

Martin's Reports—A compilation of decisions rendered by the Territorial Court and the Louisiana Supreme Court for the years 1809-1830 compiled by François X. Martin.

Moreau Lislet source notes—An interleaved edition of the 1808 Digest with annotations to various French and Spanish sources which correspond to the code articles. The annotations are attributed to Louis Moreau Lislet, one of the redactors of the Digest.

Natural children—Acknowledged illegitimate children.

paraphernal property—Extradotal property, that is the wife's property which forms no part of her dowry.

patrimony—An inherited estate.

Partidas **and** *Febrero*—The *Partidas* is a compilation of ancient Castilian laws gathered in the thirteenth century at the behest of Alphonso X. Febrero—A book for judges, lawyers, and notaries, comprehensive of the civil, criminal and administrative codes, as much as in the theory as in the practice, in accordance with current legislation. This compilation was prepared in the eighteenth century.

seizin—The immediate passing of an inheritance to the legal heir upon the death of his ancestor by operation of law. The heir is seized before he has taken any step to put himself in possession, or has expressed any will to accept it. This concept was more or less eliminated by the Code of Civil Procedure in 1961.

Special act of divorce—A special act passed by the legislature divorcing a named husband and wife, predicated on a legislative investigation of the grounds for requesting the legislative enactment. This was the only route for obtaining a divorce during the territorial period.

suretyship—A security device, whereby one person, the surety, contracts to guarantee the obligation of another, the principal.

syndic—A trustee appointed to represent the creditors of the estate of an insolvent.

testator—A deceased person who died leaving a valid will.

tutor—A guardian who has authority over a minor. There are four kinds of tutorship in Louisiana—by nature, by will, by the effect of law, and by the appointment of a judge.

usufruct—The right of enjoying a thing, the property of which is vested in another, "and to draw from the same all the profit, utility and advantages which it may produce, provided it be without altering the substance of the thing." La. CC. 533.

STEAMBOATS, TOWBOATS, AND LEGAL HISTORIOGRAPHY: THE LAW IN LOUISIANA AND THE NEW NATION

By
George Dargo

To begin, here is a short description of the Mississippi as it appeared to the River's most astute observer, surely the most famous and probably the most talkative river pilot who ever lived:

> The majestic bluffs that overlook the river, along through this region, charm one with the grace and variety of their forms, and the soft beauty of their adornment . . . And then you have the shining river, winding here and there and yonder, its sweep interrupted at intervals by clusters of wooded islands threaded by silver channels; and you have glimpses of distant villages, asleep upon capes; and of stealthy rafts slipping along in the shade of the forest walls; and of white steamers vanishing around remote points. And it is all as tranquil and reposeful as dreamland, and has nothing this-worldly about it—nothing to hang a fret or a worry upon.[1]

The writer was, of course, Mark Twain. The approach of a Mississippi steamer and the commotion and excitement which it caused in every river town is what first drew boys like the young Samuel Clemens to a life aboard the steamers.[2]

And here is Mark Twain describing one of the great pastimes of river pilots, steamboat racing:

> I think that much the most enjoyable of all races is a steamboat race . . . Two red-hot steamboats raging along, neck-and-neck, straining every nerve,—that is to say, every rivet in the boilers,—quaking and shaking and groaning from stem to stern, spouting white steam from the pipes, pouring black smoke from the chimneys, raining down sparks, parting the river into long breaks of

> hissing foam—that is sport that makes a body's very liver curl with enjoyment.[3]

A somewhat more obscure source, an account which appeared in a newspaper called the *Louisiana Chronicle*, described in some detail what sometimes happened during such a steamboat race—a boiler explosion which struck a steamboat called the *Clipper* in the year 1843:

> All the boilers bursting simultaneously—machinery, vast fragments of the boilers, huge beams of timber, furniture and human beings in every degree of mutilation, were alike shot up perpendicularly many hundred fathoms in the air. On reaching the greatest height, the various bodies diverged like the jets of a fountain, in all directions—falling to the earth, and upon roofs of houses, in some instances as much as two hundred and fifty yards from the scene of destruction. The hapless victims were scalded, crushed, torn, mangled and scattered in every possible direction—many into the river, some in the streets, some on the other side of the Bayou, nearly three hundred yards—some torn asunder by coming in contact with pickets and posts, and others shot like cannon balls through the solid walls of houses at a great distance from the boat . . . [The] 2nd engineer [was] thrown against the fence—one arm torn off and fragments of his carcass scattered over the trees. The watchman . . . was thrown alive, one hundred yards through the solid wall of Baker's Hotel, into a bed. He retained his senses perfectly for some time after, but the poor fellow expired during the evening. The cabin boy was thrown about two hundred yards through the roof of a shed, and was picked up in a mangled condition.[4]

In recalling the romantic days of the Mississippi steamboat (as well as one of its less romantic moments) we are reminded of the great dependence of the western settlements upon inland water transportation in the early and middle decades of the nineteenth century. This was particularly true in Louisiana whose trade and commerce were so completely tied to the Mississippi Basin's vast network of rivers, bayous, and canals.

Prior to the War of 1812, goods and people often came to New Orleans by flatboat, a journey that was long, arduous, and full of hazard. Average time from Pennsylvania in 1810, for example, was about six weeks in fair weather. But the return journey could take as much as four months, sometimes even longer. In fact, the common practice was simply to break up the flatboat, sell the wood, and return to the point of origin on horseback. Interestingly enough, while the steamboat would eventually displace the flatboat, the two forms of river transportation grew side by side for several decades. The steamboat solved the problem of the return voyage for flatboatmen, so that until the mid-1840's the annual number of flatboats arriving in New Orleans actually increased—from about 600 in 1814 to over 2500 in 1846.[5]

Clearly, however, this was to be the Age of Steam. In the West it began in the winter of 1811 when a ship appropriately called *The New Orleans*, owned by the Fulton-Livingston group of New York, steamed from Pittsburgh to New Orleans. Thereafter steamboats became "the most important factor in the great industrial [and commercial] development of [the] region. . . ."[6] Indeed, no other section of the country was so dependent upon steam for transport as was the Mississippi Basin. In no other part of the world were so many steamboats built or operated. And New Orleans led the way in this expansion. In the year 1820, for example, there were 198 reported arrivals of steam-powered vessels in this city. Not until the mid-1820's did any other western inland port even approach that figure.[7]

But along with the increase in the number of steamboats in use was the growth in the number of steamboat accidents. The hazards of steamboating were unique, dramatic, and even awesome as the explosion aboard the *Clipper* in 1843 so graphically demonstrated. Steamboat accidents represented the first major example of industrial accidents which affected the general public. While steam-powered machines were already injuring, maiming, and killing early industrial workers, particularly in textile factories, steamboat accidents put the public in direct contact with the dangers of the new energy technology.

Given the riskiness of life in general in that era of economic scarcity, frontier violence, and primitive public health it is a little surprising how agitated the public became over steamboat accidents and their resulting casualties. Perhaps the explanation lies in their communal impact which neither railroad accidents nor factory accidents ever duplicated. Railroad mishaps often occurred somewhere along the right-of-way, and their effects were confined to the passengers, the crew, or the hapless farmers

H. Lewis pinx. Lith. Inst. Arnz & C° Düsseldorf.

CONVENT DU SACRAMENT.

The sinking of the steamboat *Brilliant*. "Convent du Sacrament" from *Das Illustrit Mississippi Thal*. *ca*. 1849. Louisiana State Museum.

whose flax near the tracks caught fire. Similarly, factory accidents usually happened behind closed doors and were restricted in their social impact to workers and their families. But steamboat explosions occurred most often on the approach to or the departure from the river port. As in the case of the *Clipper*, these events were witnessed by entire communities. Their dramatic character can best be compared to airline disasters in our own century and the obsessive concern we have about them even though we all know that statistically we run a much greater risk when we take a cab to the airport than in the flight itself.

Exploding boilers on steamboats were clearly the most startling and novel kind of accident. One half of the number of lives lost on steamboats before the Civil War were caused by these explosions. But fires were equally spectacular and, in terms of property loss if not mortality, equally devastating. Unlike boiler explosions, however, fires had a certain comforting familiarity about them. But while the threat of fire on sailing vessels or flatboats was always present, fires aboard steamboats occurred with greater frequency because of the proximity of combustible cargoes to flying sparks, smoldering embers, and blazing furnaces. As one writer has put it:

> [The] floors and partitions [of these boats, their] light framing and siding, soft and resinous woods, the whole dried out by the sun and wind and impregnated with oil and turpentine from paint, made the superstructure . . . little more than an orderly pile of kindling wood.[8]

With cargoes of cotton, hay, straw, oil, spirits, and even gunpowder, and with dry wood for fuel, it is truly amazing that any steamboats completed the voyage of any inland river. Lifeboats and life preservers were unknown. Tiller ropes made of hemp burned along with everything else on board so that there was no way to steer a blazing boat back to shore. With nothing but wooden buckets for fire control, it is no wonder that fires aboard steamboats often caused tremendous loss of life and property.

Snags, collisions, and storms were the other main causes of accidents to steamboats on western waters. Snags were the biggest single cause of accidents, but they were also the least costly. Snags were usually caused by logs or other debris which breached the hull with tremendous force. Collisions occurred because navigational space was limited, rules of the road were rudimentary at best and ships were not yet required to have running lights at night. The sharp bends in the river and the flat bottoms of the boats afforded limited maneuverability. Founderings caused by sudden storms or by running aground on hidden shoals were another familiar source of mishap.

Of these five major causes of steamboat accident—boiler explosions, fires, collisions, snags, and founderings—the last two were thought to be beyond human control, pure accident which even the most careful seamanship could not avoid. Fire and collision, on the other hand, were attributable to human error which created at least a presumption of negligence. But boiler explosions fell somewhere in between. Their cause or causes were not yet fully understood in the early years of steam navigation. One body of opinion held that boiler explosions were "unavoidable accident," a "peril of the sea" (or the river). Thus in a marine insurance case decided as late as 1845, the Supreme Court of Missouri concluded "that whatever natural philosophers may think of this . . . the elements which combine to create the power of steam, are . . . entirely within the reach of accident. . . ."[9] On the other hand, just a few years before, the Supreme Court of Ohio, in a similar case, held that "a steam engine, properly constructed, is entirely within man's control . . . The laws of steam are as well understood as the laws which regulate any other power. . . . Of all the great moving powers, [steam] is the most completely manageable. . . . [A]n explosion . . . presupposes negligence."[10]

The Louisiana courts adopted the second theory. In an explosion case decided in 1859 the Louisiana Supreme Court rejected the argument that "an explosive something, probably electricity, is generated in the steam boiler, which no care can prevent." Instead it held that despite the

> unsatisfactory state of science on the subject of the explosion of steam boilers . . . we think it might be safely assumed, that where steam boilers and engines are properly constructed, of good materials and proper strength, and are managed with that prudent and reasonable care which the powerful agent employed requires, they will not explode. . . . The long period of prosperity and freedom from explosions which followed the passage of the Act of Congress of 1852, and the comparative security of steamboats constructed and managed under the regulations of the French Government . . . give great weight to this inference.[11]

The movement for statutory regulation of steamboating to which this Louisiana case referred, began with the first catastrophes of the 1820's. At first the states most immediately affected tried their hand at regulatory schemes. Legislative investigations of accidents, licensing requirements for engineers, and the imposition of penalties and fines for violations evidenced an emerging governmental interest in the subject. None of the legislation proposed was designed to protect steamboat crews, however—only the life and property of the public at large, which is not surprising since it was public outrage over steamboat accidents that triggered these regulatory efforts. But state regulation had little effect since the steamboat traffic was interstate. There was little that local authorities could do to regulate out-of-state companies.

Thus what little legislation there was in the 1830's caused no change in the general trend of accident statistics. The decline in the average age of steamboats destroyed on western rivers continued: from 1811 to 1819 it was 4.2 years, from 1820 to 1829 it was 4.0 years, and from 1830 to 1839 it was 2.65 years.[12] Not until Congress stepped into the regulatory field, first in 1838 and then again in 1852, was there significant change. But until the 1850's steamboats continued to blow up, burn, collide and founder with alarming regularity. As Charles Dickens, one of many European travellers to America in these years, once put it, "Western steamboats usually blow up, one or two a week, during the season."[13] Or as our old friend Mark Twain later reported: "between St. Louis and Cairo . . . steamboat wrecks average one to the mile—two hundred wrecks, altogether."[14]

But while statutory solutions were slow in coming the courts were called upon to deal with the steady flow of litigation which the high rate of accidents produced. The question presented in many of these cases turned on the standard of liability to be applied to the steamboat as a carrier of goods or of passengers. In Louisiana the Digest of 1808, known also as the Civil Code of 1808, established a statutory scheme which often but not always was the starting point of analysis. Article 63 of the Digest provided that

> Carriers and watermen may be liable for the loss or damage of the things entrusted to their care unless they can prove that such loss or damage has been occasioned by accidental or uncontrollable events.[15]

The source for Article 63, as confirmed by the de la Vergne edition of the Digest, was Article 1784 of the Civil Code of Napoleon.[16] The chief difference in the Louisiana version of the provision is that the mandatory language of the Napoleonic formulation ("they *are* liable for the loss or damage") was changed to the permissive language of Article 63 of the Digest ("carriers and watermen *may be* liable"). Interestingly enough, the Revised Civil Code of 1870, which is the present version of the statute, returned to the mandatory language of the French Code possibly because the leading cases decided in the aftermath of the adoption of the 1808 Digest pointed in that dirction, as we shall see.

The Digest seemed to offer an open invitation to judicial construction which the Louisiana courts did not hesitate to accept. In *Hunt* v. *Morris*, the first important case to construe Article 63, goods placed on board a steamboat in New Orleans for delivery at Natchez were destroyed by fire when, in preparation for the voyage, the vessel went on a short nighttime excursion to secure wood for fuel.[17] The Louisiana Supreme Court applied an ordinary care standard to the defendant's conduct. The Court held that a carrier was not an insurer as at common law but a bailee for hire answerable only for ordinary neglect which it defined as "the omission of that care, which every man of common prudence . . . takes of his own concerns."[18] But the Court also held that loss by fire created a presumption of negligence which put a burden of proof of non-negligence on the defendant. Since masters of steamboats were "in the constant habit of running them by night" the master of this one did not deviate from what later courts would call the "standard of care" of his profession. The Court also noted that the risk of fire was less by night than by day "because its commencement in any part of the boat would be more readily discovered in the dark."[19] In effect, the defendant in this case met the burden of proof of accident by showing that he had acted with due diligence.

More important than *Hunt* v. *Morris* in terms of the influence of Louisiana law upon other American jurisdictions, however, was another steamboat case decided about ten years later. In *Smith* v. *Pierce* the captain of a vessel under tow by a steamboat was ordered to come around to starboard.[20] As was the practice, the two boats were lashed together. The towed vessel went aground and was damaged. There was a dispute as to the number of degrees to starboard the steamboat captain had ordered and whether or not the shouted orders were obeyed at all. The defendant steamboat owners alleged negligence on the part of the captain and crew of the towed vessel as a defense. The Louisiana Supreme Court upheld a judgment for the plaintiff and applied to steam towboats the same standard of liability as any other common carrier. Judge George Mathews, one of Louisiana's distinguished early jurists who had also written the opinion in *Hunt* v. *Morris*, reasoned that towboats were common carriers since their "trade is to carry goods for hire."[21] Mathews allowed no "distinction . . . between the towers [*sic.*] of vessels by means of steamboats and ordinary carriers" even though the master of the steam towboat had no direct control over the rudder of the towed vessel because "the vessels which are towed are almost entirely passive."[22] The master of the steamboat was bound to carry the vessel in tow safely to its destination even if this required placing his own men on board the vessel. Only uncontrollable events would relieve the steamboat master of liability.

The defendants in *Smith* v. *Pierce* attempted to put steamboats within one of the exceptions to strict common carrier liability developed by Chief Justice John Marshall in a Kentucky case where four black slaves drowned while being transported from shore to a steamboat in the steamboat's tender.[23] Marshall said that slaves were not goods but passengers. He reasoned that since slaves were, as he put it, "intelligent beings," the master of the vessel did not have the same control over them as he would over inanimate objects. Marshall applied the lower standard of liability applicable to passengers. But in *Smith* v. *Pierce*, Judge Mathews rejected this reasoning. Instead, the court, following *Hunt* v. *Morris*, said that the accident created a presumption of negligence rebuttable by evidence of ordinary care. Since the defendant had failed to meet that burden, judgment for the plaintiff was upheld.

The rule that steam towboats (or tugboats) would be held to the same standard of liability as ordinary steam carriers in Louisiana was not followed in most other American jurisdictions.[24] But *Smith* v. *Pierce* was cited as authority in order to establish the proposition that steamboats would be held to the strict common law standard of common carrier liability in the ordinary carriage of goods. A leading New York case, *Alexander* v. *Greene*, cited Judge Mathews' opinion in *Smith* v. *Pierce* at some length. In particular the New York Court of Errors noted the importance of Louisiana decisional law in this area:

> Situated as the people of that state are, upon one of the greatest inland thoroughfares of the new world, their example should have great weight in deciding this cause.[25]

While this New York case was a steam towboat case similar on its facts to *Smith* v. *Pierce*, its holding was later used as authority to extend common carrier liability to steamboat carriers rather than to tugboats in that jurisdiction.[26]

Thus, in a curious and roundabout way, Louisiana's application of common carrier liability to steam towboats helped to establish the foundations for the extension of common carrier liability to ordinary steamboat carriers in common law jurisdictions even though Louisiana itself was a state which placed the lighter standard of the civil law upon regular steam carriers of goods.

This narrow area of the law's development illustrates the importance of Louisiana law to the law of the nation in its formative period. In these early steamboat cases the courts were pressed into developing a searching analysis of the meaning of negligence. In the early nineteenth century negligence had not yet become a separate cause of action. But these early industrial accident cases do suggest that negligence law really got going with the dramatic increase in accidents generated by the steam engine. Louisiana steamboat cases are especially apposite precisely because Louisiana applied a standard of ordinary care rather than strict common carrier liability to steamboats and towboats. The fault principle and industrialization grew side by side in the nineteenth century. However, historians have traced the origins of negligence law to cases drawn from such pre-industrial contexts as jailhouse escapes and stagecoach collisions.[27] It would seem, therefore, that this explanation requires significant modification and amplification.

But even larger themes deserve further comment. For too long Louisiana law and its history have been viewed as an oddity by American common lawyers. Since American legal education remains focused upon the common law tradition and since the average law student in the typical American law school can easily escape such esoteric subjects as comparative law and comparative legal systems, it is not surprising that the best professorial advice a law student may get is, "When litigating in Louisiana refer to local counsel."

This excursion into early steamboat law suggests that such insularity is not only unfortunate but misplaced. Early nineteenth century Louisiana jurists faced the same kinds of commercial and technological realities which confronted their counterparts in common law jurisdictions. The reasoning in *Alexander* v. *Greene* by the New York Court of Errors was not all that different from what must have been in the mind of Judge

George Mathews in deciding *Smith* v. *Pierce*. The New York Court of Errors was faced with the obvious commercial fact that in New York, as in Louisiana, "The towing of boats by steam power has become a matter of great and increasing importance to the interests of the whole community." The application of strict standards of liability to this new form of transportation would induce shippers to use it. Clearly, the same impulses worked upon the Louisiana Supreme Court in *Smith* v. *Pierce*. The case was decided as it would have been in any common law state at that period of our history—on the basis of its facts and through the application of natural reason and legal logic. Public policy considerations, while unstated, lurked just beneath the surface, and the Civil Code was not even cited.

The law of common carrier liability as applied to the new technological phenomenon of the steamboat was in an unsettled state in the early decades of the Steamboat Era.[28] But while Louisiana law was different from the common law in the standard which it applied to steamboat carriers, the result in practice was not all that different. By shifting the burden of proof of non-negligence (or due care) onto defendants, the Louisiana rule approached the more exacting tests of common carrier liability in the common law. Moreover, with respect to tugboats, the standard of liability proved to be even higher in Louisiana than it was in common law jurisdictions. There the prevailing rule was that tugboats were not common carriers at all but bailees for hire bound only by an ordinary care standard with proof of negligence on the plaintiff, not the defendant. Thus, Louisiana law seems to have been more natural, less counter-intuitive, and more consistent.

On an even deeper level, however, these doctrinal developments suggest that the law was shaped by historical forces which transcended the differences in the given rules of law which separated the civil law and the common law worlds. Historians need to resist the narrow provincialism which still afflicts much historical writing about law and to look more searchingly into the underlying historical processes and social realities which did as much to shape the law in modern times as the ancient systems of law which are part of the American and the Louisiana legal heritage. Legal historians need to be as sensitive to the history which lies beneath the surface of legal doctrine as were the judges whose decisions still supply the chief historical source for most of the legal history that is written today. Above all, historians of the legal system of Louisiana have to be particularly alert to the fact that courts of law in the civil law world as well as in the common law community were faced with novel problems in the nineteenth century, problems caused by a rapidly changing economic, technological, and social environment. More often than most legal historians have liked to think, those problems were approached in much the same fashion in both the common law and the civil law worlds.

This point is best reinforced with comments drawn from the writings of two of the most eminent scholars which the civil law and the common law have produced in America, Gustavus Schmidt of Louisiana and Oliver Wendell Holmes, Jr., of Massachusetts. First Schmidt:

> Customs, when not contrary to good morals, or opposed . . .to positive legislation, have, . . . in all civilized countries, acquired the dignity of laws; but customs vary from age to age, and what may be regarded as reasonable and just at one period, often becomes obsolete at another; this proves the necessity of studyng with care the spirit of every epoch, at which a custom has been formed and has received judicial sanction, in order to appreciate its force and effect.[29]

And finally Holmes:

> The life of the law has not been logic: it has been experience. The felt necessities of the time, the prevalent moral and political theories, intuitions of public policy, avowed or unconscious, even the prejudices which judges share with their fellow-men, have had a good deal more to do than the syllogism in determining the rules by which men should be governed. The law embodies the story of a nation's development through many centuries, and it cannot be dealt with as if it contained only the axioms and corollaries of a book of mathematics.[30]

Even Mark Twain never did any better than that!

[1]*Life on the Mississippi* (New York, 1944), p. 338.

[2]Ibid., p. 29.

[3]Ibid., pp. 268-269.

[4]L. C. Hunter, *Steamboats on Western Rivers: An Economic and Technological History* (Harvard, 1949), p. 288.

[5]G. R. Taylor, *The Transportation Revolution: 1815-1866* (New York, 1951), p. 65.

[6]Ibid., p. 63.

[7]Hunter, *Steamboats on Western Rivers*, p. 644 (Appendix, Table 2).

[8]Ibid., p. 278.

[9]*Citizens Insurance Co.* v. *Glasgow, et al.*, 9 Mo. 243, 246 (1845).

[10]*Adm'rs. of Perrin* v. *Protection Insurance Co.*, 11 Ohio 148, 152-154 (1842).

[11]*Poree* v. *Cannon, et al.*, 14 La. Ann. 506-507 (1859).

[12]Hunter, *Steamboats on Western Rivers*, p. 654 (Appendix, Table 13).

[13]Charles Dickens, *Pictures From Italy and American Notes for General Circulation* (New York, 1892), p. 366.

[14]*Life on the Mississippi*, p. 153.

[15]La. Civ. Code, Bk. 3, Tit. 8, Art. 63, p. 384 (1804).

[16]See. R. Batiza, "The Louisiana Civil Code of 1808: Its Actual Sources and Present Relevance," 46 *Tul. L. Rev.* 4 (1971).

[17]6 Mart. (O. S.) 676 (1819).

[18]Id., at 680.

[19]Id., at 684. *Hunt* v. *Morris* remained good law until the early twentieth century. In *Lehman, Stern & Co.* v. *Morgan's La. & Tex. Rail & Steamship Co.*, 38 So. 873 (La. 1905), the Louisiana Supreme Court placed a greater burden on the defendant at least in fire cases. Defendants now had to show, in addition to proof of care, evidence as to causation. See C. Girard Davidson, "Liability of Carrier for Destruction of Goods Through Fire Originating on Premises of Shipper," 6 *Tul. L. Rev.* 111 (1931). While *Hunt* v. *Morris* had established the ordinary care standard it was not as favorable to defendants as it might appear since it did create the rebuttable presumption of negligence which placed the burden of proving non-negligence on the defendant. See 6 Mart. (O. S.) at 682.

[20]1 La. 349 (1830).

[21]Id., at 355.

[22]Id., at 356.

[23]*Boyce* v. *Anderson*, 27 U. S. (1 Pet.) 150 (1829).

[24]See Joseph K. Angell, *A Treatise on the Law of Carriers* (5th ed. 1877) § 86, 668. The two great nineteenth century authorities on American common law, Chancellor James Kent of New York and Justice Joseph Story, differed on this issue. Kent included tugboats in his list of carriers held to the higher common law standard of strict liability whereas for Story tugboats represented an exception to that rule. Compare 2 J. Kent, *Commentaries on American Law* 599 (3rd ed.) with J. Story, *Commentaries on the Law of Bailments* § 496 (4th ed. 1846). See also *Bussey & Co.* v. *Miss Valley Transp. Co.*, 24 La. Ann. 165-167 (1872); 80 C. J. S. Shipping § 101; 86 C. J. S. Towage § 13; 63 D. J. Towage at p. 19 (n. 19).

[25]*Alexander* v. *Greene*, 7 Hill 533, 550 (1844).

[26]See *e.g.*, *Dorr* v. *New Jersey Steam Navig. Co.*, 11 N. Y. 475 (1854). Likewise for Massachusetts see *Sproul* v. *Hemmingway*, 31 Mass. (14 Pick.) 1 (1833) and *Vermont & Mass. Railroad Co.* v. *Fitchburg Railroad Co.*, 96 Mass. (14 Allen) 462, 470 (1867).

[27]Morton J. Horwitz, *The Transformation of American Law, 1780-1860* (Harvard, 1977), pp. 85-89.

[28]See *Gordon* v. *Little*, 8 Serg. & Rawl. (Pa.) 533 (1822); *Harrington et al.* v. *McShane*, 2 Watts (Pa.) 443 (1934); *supra*, note 26.

[29]"History of the Jurisprudence of Louisiana," 1 *La. L. Journ.* 1, 3-4 (1841).

[30]*The Common Law* 1 (1881).

NEW LIGHT ON THE SLAUGHTERHOUSE MONOPOLY ACT OF 1869

By
Ronald M. Labbé

The *Slaughter House Cases* are one of Louisiana's most important contributions to the development of American constitutional law. In the narrowest sense of readily applicable legal precedent the United States Supreme Court's 1873 decision seems routine: it merely affirmed the power of a state to legislate for the health, safety and well being of the public, in this instance by regulating slaughtering in a populous metropolitan area. But the dispute presented the Court with its first opportunity to interpret the Fourteenth Amendment and it was here that the doctrine of substantive due process of law, the eventual nationalization of the bill of rights and a greatly expanded role for the judiciary in the protection of fundamental rights all got their start. Indeed, Professor Charles Fairman has commented that the case contains the key to an understanding of "a good third" of American constitutional law.[1]

Scholarly attention regarding the *Slaughter House Cases* customarily focuses on the issues of enduring importance as they were developed in the Supreme Court and as they evolved in subsequent decisions. Since the case arose out of the quagmire of the Reconstruction Era certain assumptions have often been made regarding the facts which, while not wholly inaccurate, deprive the collision of interests of some of its force. This paper is an effort to examine the roots of the case as a means of developing a more accurate and richer idea of the circumstances out of which this great controversy arose.

The *Slaughter House Cases* stemmed from an act of the Louisiana legislature of 1869 which sought, according to its title, "to promote the health of the City of New Orleans" by centralizing slaughtering. The measure would force the removal of numerous small slaughter houses scattered throughout the densely populated area and required slaughtering to be conducted in a single slaughterhouse where high sanitary standards and an effective system of animal inspection could be maintained. The details of its provisions strongly suggest, however, that the backers of the measure had something besides public health in mind.

The act spared no redundancy in its twelve sections and risked a good deal of confusion to secure its sponsors in its benefits. It incorporated seventeen persons into the Crescent City Live Stock Landing and Slaughter House Company and granted the company "the sole and exclusive privilege" for twenty-five years of conducting the business of landing, keeping or slaughtering animals for food in the Parishes of Orleans, Jefferson and St. Bernard. The company was required to erect, by June 1, 1869, "a grand slaughterhouse of sufficient capacity to accommodate all butchers" together with stock yards for all animals received at the port. Thereafter no stock was to be landed, yarded or slaughtered for the New Orleans market except at the company's facilities. The benefits to the Company were by a detailed schedule of fees which it was authorized to charge for the use of its facilities and by provisions allowing it to retain portions of each slaughtered animal presumably for their value when processed into fertilizer. An inspector of beef was to be appointed by the governor whose certificate was required, at set fees, before any animal could be slaughtered. Violations of the act were punishable by fines of as much as $250 for each infraction. These penalties were collectable by ordinary suit filed by the company and were to be divided equally between it and the Auditor of Public Accounts.[2]

Critics tended to exaggerate the value of the act but no one denied that the slaughterhouse franchise had substantial financial potential. New Orleans was keenly aware of the importance of an increased trade with Texas as a means of recapturing the prominent position as a trading center that it had occupied at an earlier time. The city was linked to Texas by water and hopes were high that a rail connection would be completed soon. At the close of the Civil War there were more than two million head of cattle in Texas and they could be purchased for almost any price. The Mississippi River furnished an avenue to the beef-starved markets of the North. Experiments with refrigerated shipping were already under way. As early as 1866 the ease of manufacturing ice had caused the New Orleans *Daily Picayune* to urge the formation of a company to slaughter beef on the Texas coast and then to transport it under refrigeration to New Orleans and other markets beyond.[3]

It was just the sort of act that many New Orleans Democrats had come to expect from a legislature made up of an unprecedented proportion of Republicans and blacks. With the exception of the *Times* whose publisher was believed to be financially interested in the new slaughterhouse, all of the New Orleans newspapers, including the *Republican* and the city's black journal, the *Tribune*, were critical of the slaughterhouse act. To the *Daily Picayune*, the measure's chief antagonist among the city's newspapers, the slaughterhouse bill was a sign that the "real people" of the state had been deprived of power and "a set of new men, greedy for the rapid acquisition of wealth, and utterly unscrupulous as to the means of getting it, have come among us, and joining with the lately emancipated slaves and the meanest portion of the resident population, have concocted plans for public plunder."[4] Acts creating public positions for the inspection of hay, flour and other cargoes arriving in the port or those granting long term franchises to conduct a state lottery or operate navigational canals for a profit were bitterly criticized but the slaughterhouse act was considered uniquely odious because it created a monopoly over a staple item of food and in effect placed a population of nearly 300,000 "under embargo to a few right men."[5] It was said that the act set a precedent for a monopoly over bread and could only cause higher meat prices as the stockholders raked in profits estimated at over fourteen million dollars over the life of the franchise.[6]

Attempts to defend the act on grounds of health were dismissed by the *Daily Picayune* as "sophomoric scribbling." The company was composed, it said, of "nearly all unknown men" with no experience in the livestock industry. They were interested in "keeping off sickness" only to the extent that it resulted in "the transfer of money from the pockets of our people, into their capacious iron safes, located in colder climes." Only a few days after the slaughterhouse bill passed the Senate the *Daily Picayune* charged that no "sensible men" could deny that bribery was being practiced for "the creation of monopolies designed to enrich a few." Later it was rumored that the act had cost the incorporators a million dollars. Even Governor Warmoth was believed to be implicated. When he failed to veto the bill after its legislative opponents had allegedly refrained from amendments in order to present it to him "with its most repulsive features untouched" the conclusion seemed inescapable that "the Governor holds stock to a very large amount."[7]

Years later, a principal opponent of the monopoly argued that the "main cause" of the resistance among the butchers and stockmen was the prospect of having to relocate their operations.[8] The company had chosen to establish the new slaughterhouse at Slaughter House Point on the west bank of the river, opposite from the city, where the New Orleans slaughterhouses had been confined during the city's colonial period. This location could be defended both on sanitary grounds and by the presence of a railhead belonging to the New Orleans, Opelousas and Great Western Railroad, a line which ran westward for eighty miles and which was regarded as a segment in a line that would eventually connect New Orleans and the beef-rich Texas plains. But the site meant that the butchers would have to commute across the river and pay fees to transport their meat to market.

As June first drew near the company did everything it could to stem the tide of opposition, but to no avail. It publicly disavowed any interest in interfering with the smooth operation of business. It even entered into a contract with one of the largest firms of stockdealers in which it agreed to transfer 1,500 shares of preferred stock in return for their agreement to relocate and withdraw their opposition.[9] None of this was sufficient to avert a judicial collision and before long the New Orleans skies were black with criss-crossing injunctions issuing from a confusing tangle of over three hundred suits. Six of these were eventually appealed to the state supreme court and consolidated for decision as the *Slaughter House Cases*. Together they illustrate the character of the parties, the range of immediate issues and the course of the litigation.

The first suit was filed on May twenty-sixth in the Sixth District Court by the Butchers Benevolent Association to enjoin the Crescent City Company from asserting any of its rights under the act.[10] No stranger to threats from monopolies, the Association was an organization of the city's French and German butchers which had been formed in 1866 to combat the informal monopolies of the large stock dealers by pooling small capital and making stock available at the lowest possible prices. Simultaneously, in the Fifth District Court, the Crescent City Company hastily obtained an injunction of its own to prevent the Butchers Benevolent Association from interfering with its exclusive statutory privileges.[11] A few days later the butchers' injunction was vacated because the Company had posted the necessary injunction bond before the butchers had posted theirs.[12] A short time later the Company proved that it meant business by having the President of the Butchers Association and two of his fellow officers jailed and fined for violating its injunction.

On the advice of their leaders the butchers responded by resigning from the Association in droves.[13] Then, using a printed form of petition and solemnly disavowing membership in the Butchers Association, they filed at least one hundred seventy new suits to enjoin the Company in the Seventh District Court.[14] The leading case in this new barrage was filed by Inbau, Aycock and Company, a large firm of stockdealers at Jefferson City. It became the third *Slaughter House Case* on Appeal.[15]

The Company answered this volley with two dozen new actions against individual butchers, stockmen and steamship operators to force compliance with the act. One of these actions, filed against the Steamboat *B. L. Hodge No. 2* and its owners to collect wharfage fees for cattle landed at a place other than the Company's wharf, would be the fourth of the *Slaughter House Cases* on appeal.[16] In the most controversial of these new actions, George W. Carter, the newly appointed inspector of beef under the act, obtained individual writs of injunction against one hundred seventy-eight elusive butchers.[17]

From the beginning of the litigation the butchers and stock dealers had been under enormous pressure to relocate their businesses. In mid-July they mounted their ultimate effort to invalidate the act. A group of thirteen stock dealers and prominent butchers incorporated the Live Stock Dealers and Butchers Association of New Orleans for the purpose of purchasing property just below the city from Charles Cavaroc, a wealthy merchant, and erecting a huge, consolidated slaughterhouse of their own. By voluntarily relocating the slaughterhouses, the Live Stock Dealers hoped to make it impossible to rationalize the act as a necessary health measure.[18]

This new development called for a special response. It came a week later when Simeon Belden, the state Attorney General, entered the fray in an action that would become the sixth of the *Slaughter House Cases* on appeal. Insisting that the act was a bona fide health measure and that the state had an interest in seeing it successfully implemented, he obtained an injunction from the Fifth District Court to prevent the Live Stock Dealers or Cavaroc from consummating their plans. A few days later Cavaroc obtained an injunction of his own against the Attorney General from the Third District Court. Thus shielded, construction of the new slaughterhouse and wharves proceeded unhindered.[19]

The butchers were represented in all of these actions by three firms of attorneys, but most notably by John A. Campbell, a former associate justice of the United States Supreme Court from Alabama who had resigned from the Court at the outbreak of the Civil War and eventually established a law practice in the Crescent City. A lawyer since the age of eighteen, his professional reputation was summarized in the adage, "Leave it to God and Mr. Campbell."[20] Campbell and his associates attacked the slaughterhouse act on numerous federal and state grounds in the lower courts. But their principal attack as formulated by the former Mr. Justice Campbell was based on the theory that constitutional government meant limited government and that no constitutional government worthy of the name ought to permit the kind of legislative action involved here. The newly adopted Fourteenth Amendment with its sweeping restrictions on the exercise of state power in terms of "privileges and immunities" of citizenship, "due process of law" and "equal protection of the laws" made a convenient vehicle for this argument and gave special force to Campbell's arguments concerning monopoly and bribery.[21]

It is one of the great ironies of our constitutional history that an amendment intended primarily to secure the rights of newly freed slaves should first be used to secure the property rights of New Orleans butchers, but it is not surprising that Campbell saw this possibility. There is less cynicism in his argument than there is a realistic admission of defeat. To him the Civil War had been an explosion that had revolutionized the federal system. He interpreted the amendment perhaps somewhat bitterly, but precisely as its radical sponsors in Congress intended—as a means of placing all civil rights, as opposed to private rights obtained by contract, under the protection of Congress and national courts.

Campbell's principal opportunity to articulate his argument came early in the lower court proceedings on the trial of an exception filed by the Company to prevent him from introducing evidence to prove his allegations concerning bribery. His argument spanned nearly two days and took the *Daily Picayune* almost ten columns of its finest print to report. He argued that very man has a natural light of "property in his person and a right to employ that in every lawful trade."[22] He made no effort to deny the regulatory power of the state. But he scorned the contention that this act could be justified as a health measure. "What do they say on their part?" he asked concerning the motivations of the incorporators.

> That this monopoly is just? That this monopoly is right? . . . No, sir. They say that the great object of this bill was to secure the health of the city; that the great purpose of this bill was to convey pure air and pure water, nutritive food, wholesome food, to the members of this community.[23]

Campbell dismissed this contention as pretense. Quite to the contrary, he contended that the act was a private financial scheme of unprecedented audacity, a "grinding and odious monopoly," obtained by fraud from the legislature all too willing to be corrupted.[24]

As he concluded he made it quite clear that he was arguing for a greatly expanded role for the courts, for "all the judiciaries of the country," in the defense of fundamental rights against unreasonable legislative intrusions. The legislative and executive branches had defaulted in their obligation to respect fundamental rights. "Woe!, woe!, woe! to this country if these tribunals falter in the performance of their duty."[25]

It is possible to accept Campbell's view of the act, if not the constitutional conclusion that he reached, and still recognize that the roots of the slaughterhouse act extend beyond the financial ambitions of its sponsors. The controversy is rooted deeper than that in long-standing efforts to rid New Orleans of the terrible pestilence, particularly in the form of yellow fever and cholera, that seemed perennially to plague the city during the first half of the nineteenth century.

The *Slaughter House Cases* arose at a time when New Orleans was riding the crest of a wave of sanitary reform that swept the nation following the Civil War. The dark ages of the American public health movement had come to a close and by 1869 an era of "State Medicine" had been ushered in which was characterized by an increasing awareness of the role of the community in safeguarding public health.[26] The bacteriological age was still a few years off and at first the new movement had little that was new to say about the cause and prevention of disease. But even medical misconception abetted the concern for cleanliness. From the beginning of the century the miasma theory, which held that disease was caused by breathing the gaseous emanations from decaying animal and vegetable matter had focused attention on the relationship between good health and environmental cleanliness. As early as 1859, papers delivered at the Third National Quarantine Convention had stressed the importance of keeping offal out of the municipal water supply and warmly advocated the French and English system of centralized public abattoirs.[27] By 1869 centralization of slaughtering had already been accomplished or was well under way in New York, San Francisco, Boston and Philadelphia. In New York one instance of reform occurred when a group of railroad stockholders from New York and Chicago obtained a charter from New Jersey to operate a mammoth slaughterhouse at Harsimus Cove near a western railroad terminus located across New York Bay from the city.[28] This arrangement bears such striking resemblances to the system later adopted in New Orleans as to justify speculation that it served as a model for the organization of the Crescent City Company.

Leading figures in the Crescent City's active medical community played a major role in the new national movement and frequently served as spokesmen for reforms that had their roots elsewhere. Their concern was understandable. New Orleans had a reputation as "one of the most unhealthy cities in the United States." Its death rate was compared unfavorably to London and Paris, the condition of its streets to Cairo and Constantinople.[29]

In spite of repeated urgings from the medical community, the city proved highly resistive to meaningful reform. Two obstacles, one ideological and one political, had to be overcome. New Orleans shared in the nation's deeply rooted tradition of minimal government which emphasized personal freedom and frowned on the use of governmental power for regulatory purposes. Then, too, New Orleans was keenly aware that it was competing for commercial trade with other cities and was extremely reluctant to admit that there was anything unhealthy about it.[30] Even the Board of Health was accused of being too quick to allow the "commercialism and prosprity of the city" to discourage the enactment or vigorous enforcement of appropriate legislation.[31] Moreover, the price of reform would be paid mainly by the local butchers and stock dealers and they could mount formidable political resistance.

However deeply rooted, ideological resistance to sanitary reform in New Orleans, as elsewhere in the country, was eventually overcome by the devastating effects of major epidemics, particularly of cholera and yellow fever, that repeatedly plagued the city. In New Orleans the turning point came with the yellow fever epidemic of 1853 which killed a tenth of the population in a single summer.[32] By the time it subsided, a regulatory impulse had been set in motion that can fairly be traced directly to the slaughterhouse act. As Dr. Edward Barton, a long-time advocate of reform, concluded in a seminal sanitary report on the tragedy, "the 'let-alone' system has been tried long enough."[33] The political path to reform was a long one, however,

The slaughterhouses had been a source of complaint in New Orleans since the beginning of the century. Originally concentrated across the river, they had eventually been moved into the city for the sake of convenience and they steadily migrated upstream with the expanding population. Following the 1853 epidemic, Barton's sanitary report had singled them out as a nuisance and urged their removal.[34] Slaughterhouses operating within the city had to be licensed by the city council, but its permission was seldom withheld.[35] By 1869 the Board of Health reported that there were forty located in the Fourth District alone.[36] An even larger number were scattered throughout adjacent Jefferson City, an incorporated suburb, where the city's main stockyards were located. Even the sympathetic *Daily Picayune* had reminded the butchers at the height of the slaughterhouse controversy that "public opinion is on their side only so far as it relates to the monopoly."[37] It repeatedly urged relocation of the slaughterhouses.

The most serious threat to the city's health posed by these establishments was believed to be the contamination of the water supply. The slaughterhouses were located upstream from the city's waterworks. When offal was disposed of at all, it was deposited into the river at nuisance wharves located only about a mile upstream from the intake pipe of the city's waterworks. The situation was described by a New Orleans Health Officer in 1867:

> The amount of filth thrown into the river above the source from which the city is supplied with water, and coming from the slaughterhouses is incredible. Barrels filled with entrails, liver, blood, urine, dung, and other refuse, portions in an advanced stage of decomposition, are constantly being thrown into the river but a short distance from the banks, poisoning the air with offensive smells and necessarily contaminating the water near the banks for miles.[38]

The waterworks fended off carcases of dead animals thrown from the cattleboats with a cage of pilings it had constructed around the mouth of the intake pipe but it had little defense against entrails and bits of decaying matter which occasionally clogged the pumping system.[39]

The cause of permanent reform was aided immeasurably by the sanitary campaign undertaken by the federal troops who occupied the Crescent City between 1862 and 1866. The campaign was launched by General Benjamin Butler out of fear for the health of his troops shortly after taking possession of the city in May, 1862. Because of Butler's own theories concerning yellow fever, particular attention was paid to the removal of decaying animal matter. The absence of serious epidemics for the four years of federal occupation provided a powerful illustration of the potential benefits of an effective use of governmental power in maintaining a clean city.[40]

By the time the military returned the city to civilian control on March 19, 1866, a popular movement toward reform was clearly evident. Only four days earlier in a long proclamation, the mayor urged strict adherence to the sanitary rules, including the ordinances regarding the conditions of the slaughterhouses.[41] In May the superintendent of the waterworks presented a petition signed by five hundred citizens to the city council requesting that slaughterhouses be forbidden above the waterworks. Soon the city countil was battling over a health ordinance said by the *Times* to embrace "the prominent features of ordinances in force in New York, Philadelphia and Baltimore."[42] Perhaps to forestall stricter measures the butchers themselves began to take the initiative in suggesting regulatory measures.[43] No important new ordinance resulted from all this and sanitary conditions soon deteriorated. When yellow fever returned to the Crescent City in the summer of 1867 the arguments of those urging reform seemed to have been confirmed in the costliest of ways. But the clamor for reform in 1866 achieved one crucial result: it shifted the demand for relief from the city to the state government.

If the epidemics had made sanitation an imperative function of local communities, it did not follow in Louisiana or elsewhere that this was considered a legitimate concern for the state government.[44] In Louisiana attention shifted to the state partly because the slaughterhouse problem strattled jurisdictional lines and was beyond the reach of either New Orleans or Jefferson City, and partly because it repeatedly proved politically impossible to achieve reform at the local level. The butchers and stock dealers were strongest in Jefferson City and even in the summer of 1866 when the reform movement was at its height the most that could be expected there was an ordinance forbidding cattle to run at large in the streets or requiring nuisances to be removed within a day after notification.[45] The butchers were less strong in New Orleans proper, but they had sufficient representation on the city council to mitigate effective reform. Owing mainly to the efforts of the representative from the Fourth District, where many of the slaughterhouses were located, the council responded to the petition lodged by the superintendent of the waterworks in May, 1866 with two weakly written provisions which left the slaughterhouses in place and, at most, prohibited offal from being thrown into the river above the waterworks. At this the superintendent took his problem to the grand jury which, by special report of August 21, 1866, urged passage of a state act forbidding slaughterhouses above the city within a specific number of miles.[46]

Thus, in 1867 a thoroughly Democratic legislature gave serious consideration to a bill to require all slaughterhouses in New Orleans and Jefferson City to relocate below the city in St. Bernard Parish. Though even the Board of Health had reservations—perhaps, politically inspired—concerning the necessity of forcing the butchers to relocate, the bill was a sign of the momentum of the removal movement. Moreover, a record of medical testimony and documents assembled in connection with the bill by a select committee of the House of Representatives provided a scathing and authoritative indictment of the slaughterhouses as a menace to public health. Opponents were relegated to specious denials that a problem existed or to pleas based on the cost and inconvenience to the butchers in having to move. The very weaknesses of their arguments suggested that reform was not far off.[47]

In the end the 1867 effort proved unsuccessful. Opponents succeeded in persuading the legislature to accept a substitute requiring New Orleans and Jefferson City to pass ordinances forbidding waste from the slaughterhouses to be thrown into the river any place above Slaughter House Point and declaring null and void any ordinance that either municipality might pass before enacting the one mandated by the statute.[48] New Orleans responded by instructing the city surveyor to prepare specifications for the nuisance boats needed to carry the offal away but passed no new ordinance. Jefferson City enacted a new ordinance but attached no penalties to its violation.[49] Although the 1867 act only required the relocation of the slaughterhouses and not their consolidation, it was praised by its sponsors as a desirable step toward greater public control and condemned by its opponents as "the beginning wedge in a vast monopoly."[50] These points of view suggest the extent to which centralization had come to be recognized as a necessary aspect of slaughterhouse reform. In fact by 1867 the centralized slaughterhouse had become widely regarded in the local live stock industry as a fit subject for a profitable franchise.

The organizers of the Crescent City Company were not the first to attempt to capitalize on the city's need for slaughterhouse reform. As early as April, 1862, Jefferson City had adopted an ordinance giving to the local firm of Hepp, Rochereau and Pochelu the "exclusive privilege of slaughtering" there for twenty-five years in a general slaughterhouse which they ageed to construct.[51] The ordinance was never implemented, perhaps because federal troops took control of New Orleans the next month. As soon as the federal troops withdrew in 1866, however, butchers began to compete with offers of $40,000 and $50,000 for a city franchise to operate a centralized slaughterhouse in the sparsely settled Third

District. These plans were scuttled in the city council by a decision to take bids for a fifteen-year franchise to operate slaughterhouses in both the Third and Fourth Districts. It was a self-defeating ploy that predictably was never implemented.[52] In early 1868, a newly formed company of local stockmen and others acquired the Hepp and Rochereau franchise for Jefferson City and made an unsuccessful attempt, with the enthusiastic support of the *Daily Picayune*, to convince the local butchers and stockmen to provide the capital needed to launch the venture.[53]

The entrepreneurs who finally won the competition for an exclusive slaughterhouse franchise were a motley group but no more mottled than the general population of New Orleans at the time. Most were not natives of New Orleans, but some were, like Joachim Viosca, the progenitor of a line of distinguished New Orleans lawyers. Most of the non-natives considered themselves residents of Louisiana and some had settled in the state permanently before the war and had amassed sizeable property holdings. They included former officers of both the Union and Confederate Armies. Few, if any, of them had previously had anything to do with the live stock market, but they included brokers, shippers, mercantilist and others in a position to appreciate the potential value of the Texas cattle trade. Some were indeed men of scant capital who were attracted to the venture by a sense of opportunism. Robert Bloomer, the chief lobbyist for the bill, for example,had been involved in a cotton brokerage firm in Shreveport. No stranger to bankruptcy, he was later implicated in a bribery scandal concerning the state's purchase of property for Audubon Park. George W. Carter, the first inspector of beef and fellow traveller of the original incorporators, was a native of Virginia and formerly a popular Methodist minister. He had served as a colonel in a Texas regiment and at the time of the slaughterhouse act he was making his way through several minor offices with Governor Warmoth's help, "trying to bear defeat manfully."[54] His reputation as an opportunist and his complete lack of qualifications as an inspector made him an ideal representative of the monopoly in the eyes of the opposition. Franklin Pratt, the chief organizer of the company and its first president, was a genuine speculator who seemed constantly on the move between New Orleans, New York, and his home in Massachusetts. Some of the organizers, however, were simply businessmen with capital to invest who regarded the slaughterhouse as a promising venture. Some later acquired important positions in the financial community and one later served as president of the city's prestigeous Pickwick Club. Only six of the seventeen original incorporators were acquainted with one another. Three of these were partners in a New Orleans mercantile firm. The others were recruited to help capitalize the enterprise by promises of stock and were, according to one of them, "pretty much strangers to one another — a promiscuous party of men each looking out for his own interest."[55] They were also a devious lot, given to frequent "side agreements" among themselves. And the slaughterhouse was not their only venture into the domain of semi-public enterprise. The organizers were represented among the directors of two companies franchised to operate navigable canals and they had connections with another famous monopoly, the Louisiana lottery.

Whether John Campbell could have proven bribery to the extent necessary to invalidate the act will never be known. It is clear, however, that the organizers of the Crescent City Company made no effort to mix ethical reform with sanitary reform. Evidence adduced later in connection with several suits among the incorporators provides an intriguing glimpse into the manner of conducting business in those days.

The organizers held regular meetings during the legislative session to hear reports on their mutual effort to get the bill through. Some later admitted to incurring expenses for "treating, wine, sandwiches"[56] but their efforts went far beyond that. Their method of persuasion had to be powerful enough to overcome stiff opposition by the butchers and to preempt the franchise from their competitors. Promissory notes in varying amounts were issued by some of the organizers, usually without consideration. These found their way into the hands of legislators who used them as a kind of warrant to collect what they could of their face value either from the makers or from other investors who had been recruited with stock pledges. In addition, large amounts of stock were pledged to members of the legislature on condition that the bill passed. The measure was enacted without much serious debate and with a good deal of humor in both houses by margins of four to one. Radicals voted for it heavily, while the conservative vote was split. Non-voting was very high, especially among the conservatives.[57]

Immediately after the act passed, the incorporators, by formal resolution, allocated half of the stock, or ten thousand shares with a par value of one hundred dollars each, to themselves declaring it to be preferred and fully paid up. Six-tenths of this allocation, however, was given to the six principal organizers "in consideration," according to the resolution, "of all disbursements made and liabilities incurred in perfecting the organization of the Crescent City Live Stock Landing and Slaughter House Company."[58] This extra portion was to be used to make good on the stock pledges made in the legislature and to financial backers to secure passage of the act. The six had promised more stock than they could deliver, however, and a spate of confusing litigation resulted in the course of which a lower court judge branded the venture "a wholesale bribery concern."[59]

The same resolution allowed the incorporators to subscribe to the remaining half of the stock by paying only ten percent of the par value. It is very unlikely that the Company was launched with capital amounting to more than a fraction of the total suggested by the par value of the stock. In any event, large numbers of shares ended up in the hands of members of the legislature and others, like Michael Hahn, the publisher of the *Republican* who served as a representative for several of the legislators. There is no evidence that any of the stock found its way to Governor Warmoth, but it was not for lack of effort on the part of the organizers. To assure the governor's assent to the act, the incorporators transferred two thousand shares to three of his lieutenants "as a matter of policy." One of the organizers later admitted that when it was discovered that the governor has signed the act without acquiring any of this stock they realized that they "had been great asses to make the donation."[60]

In the end John Campbell was never accorded an opportunity to prove his allegations of bribery. Even before the courts could dispose of the various preliminary defenses filed by both sides, it became obvious that the dispute could never be settled in the lower courts. As soon as the state supreme court's term began in early November steps were taken to have a sample of six principal suits decided summarily by the district courts so that they could be appealed for final resolution by the state's highest court. Meanwhile proceedings in all other cases would be held in abeyance. Results in the lower courts were predictable. The slaughterhouse act was upheld and permanent injunctions were issued against the butchers in the Company's three suits decided by the Fifth District Court. The act was declared invalid and the company was permanently enjoined in the actions filed by the butchers and decided by the Sixth and Seventh District Courts. On appeal the state supreme court brushed aside as strange indeed Campbell's argument that it could apply provisions of the Fourteenth Amendment to declare the act invalid as an unconscionable violation of property rights. Verbal assurances by counsel for the company that the act was a bona fide sanitary reform were accepted as adequated and, as the United States Supreme Court would later do in its turn, the state court upheld it as a valid exercise of the state's police power.[61]

Apart from being deprived of an opportunity to prove his allegations concerning bribery, Campbell's failure to suceed at either the state or federal level may be attributed to his inability to overcome a very practical view of the slaughterhouse act as simply an effective means of addressing a persistent public problem in a manner consistent with the mid-nineteenth century emphasis on minimal government. The contemporary understanding of the act may have been captured best in the way it was described by a district court judge in a peripheral action in 1871. "For years," he said,

> the butchers of New Orleans had defied public opinion and the express provisions of laws and ordinances in relation to the locality of the slaughter houses . . .
>
> The legislature therefore did a wise and practical thing; the corporate defendant was created. . . . Such a corporation with such large interests involved became powerful and was strong enough to throttle the butchers. The Company did what the officials of the law had failed to do; they forced all butchering and stock landing below the city and instituted a thorough system of inspection in obedience to other provisions of the law aforesaid.[62]

This is a view of the act which accepts the profit motive as a legitimate incentive to reform precisely because it is likely to be effective. In this view the widely perceived linkage between the slaughterhouses and ill-health had provided the energy to reform, the development of the centalized abattoir elsewhere provided the form, and the public franchise to a private company, a readily available means of implementation. The accomplishment of public tasks by this means was consistent with the early nineteenth century ideological penchant for minimal government and was frequently used in New Orleans and elsewhere for a variety of purposes including early sanitary reform.[63] If the organizers of the Crescent City Company obtained their franchise by means that left a good deal to be desired, it was certainly true, as the *Republican* argued in 1873, that "rings, bargains for patronage, dealings in depreciated public paper and wasteful contracts are no modern invention in New Orleans."[64]

Mere regulation of the slaughterhouses had proven ineffectual time and again. Because of the uniquely noxious nature of slaughterhouses, even removal from inhabited areas, *vel non*, was not enough. What was needed was a return to the ancient system of consolidated slaughtering which had been firmly established in both New Orleans and New York, and almost certainly elsewhere, in the eighteenth century, of which the abattoir system of the nineteenth century was only a modern expression.

The problem for the Crescent City Company's organizers was that they had obtained their franchise at a time when the public was beginning to have serious second thoughts about the subsidies and franchises they had lavished on corporations in the past as a means of stimulating growth.[65] The slaughterhouse act was an ideal object for the ire of those who felt adversely affected because it differed from other more positive franchises like those to operate a railroad, or to furnish water to the community or to carry away its sewage. It was a strong regulatory measure and the precursor of much that the post-Civil War period held in store. The heat generated by the controversy did not result merely from a clash between honest and dishonest methods of government, but from a collision between methods of minimal government with post-war demands for forthright regulatory measures. It is in terms of this equation that the case remains continually and perhaps especially relevant today.

[1]Charles Fairman, ed., *American Constitutional Decisions* (New York: Holt and Company, 1948), p. 286. Two earlier treatments of the *Cases* deserve special mention: Fairman, *Reconstruction and Reunion, 1864-88* (New York: Macmillan Co., 1971), pp. 1301-1388; Mitchell Franklin, "The Foundations and Meaning of the Slaughter House Cases, Part I," *Tulane Law Review* 18 (October, 1943), pp. 1-88, Part II, Ibid. (December, 1943), pp. 218-288.

[2]Act No. 118 of March 8, 1869, (1869) *La. Acts*, p. 170.

[3]*Daily Picayune*, December 2, 1866, p. 2. The economic potential of the monopoly act is discussed in Franklin, "The Foundations and Meaning of the Slaughterhouse Cases," I, pp. 1-6; on the Texas cattle trade see Byron Price, "The New Orleans Market for Texas Beef, 1821-1867," paper presented at the Western History Association Meeting, San Diego, October 19, 1979; on New Orleans and the railroads see James P. Baughman, *Charles Morgan and the Development of Southern Transportation* (Nashville: Vanderbilt University Press, 1968); Merl E. Reed, *New Orleans and the Railroads* (Baton Rouge: Louisiana State University Press, 1966).

[4]*Daily Picayune*, June 7, 1869, p. 4.

[5]*Daily Picayune*, June 22, 1869, p. 1. On the other acts mentioned see ibid., February 18, 1869, p. 1; February 28, 1869, p. 2; February 23, 1869, p. 1, February 3, 1869, p. 3.

[6]*Daily Picayune*, June 20, 1869, p. 2; June 3, 1869, p. 1.

[7]*Daily Picayune*, June 22, 1869, p. 1; March 9, 1869, p. 1; June 30, 1869, p. 2; June 21, 1869, p. 4; March 14, 1869, p. 4; February 12, 1869, p. 1; June 19, 1869, p. 1.

[8]Testimony of William Fagan, *Record, Bertin et al.* v. *Crescent City Live Stock Landing and Slaughter House Company*, Docket No. 3917, Louisiana Supreme Court Archives, p. 147.

[9]Contract, Crescent City Live Stock Landing and Slaughter House Company to McQuaid, Mehle and Co., May 26, 1869, Selim Magner Archives, 28:1315, Orleans Parish Notarial Archives.

[10]*Butchers Benevolent Association of New Orleans* v. *Crescent City Live Stock Landing and Slaughter House Company*, No. 466, Sixth District Court, Orleans Parish, Louisiana; for the *Record* see Docket No. 2505, Louisiana Supreme Court Archives. On the organization of the Butchers Benevolent Association, see New Orleans *Times*, October 26, 1866, p. 13; *Tages Deutches Zeitung*, November 3, 1866, p. 8; *Daily Picayune*, October 26, 1889, p. 4.

[11]*Crescent City Live Stock Landing and Slaughter House Co.* v. *The Butchers Benevolent Association of New Orleans*, No. 585, Fifth District Court, Orleans Parish, Louisiana; for the *Record* see Docket No. 2509, Louisiana Supreme Court Archives.

[12]Another injunction taken by an independent firm of stock dealers was also vacated, viz: *Inbau, Aycock and Co.*, v. *Crescent City Live Stock Landing and Slaughter House Co.*, No 471, Sixth District Court, Orleans Parish, Louisiana, filed May 28, 1869, New Orleans City Archives.

[13]*Daily Picayune*, June 9, 1869, p. 8; June 18, 1869, p. 7; June 19, 1869, p. 1.

[14]Variously titled, the suits bear numbers 1544, 1548-1660, 1667, 1786-1826, 1838-1848, 1857 of the Seventh District Court, Orleans Parish, Louisiana, filed June 21-29, 1869, New Orleans City Archives.

[15]*Inbau, Aycock and Co.* v. *Crescent City Live Stock Landing and Slaughter House Co.*, No. 1537, Seventh District Court, Orleans Parish, Louisiana; for the *Record*, see Docket No. 2504, Louisiana Supreme Court Archives.

[16]*Crescent City Live Stock Landing and Slaughter House Co.* v. *Steamboat B. L. Hodge, No. 2 and Owners*, No. 720, Fifth District Court, Orleans Parish, Louisiana; for the *Record* see Docket No. 2507, Louisiana Supreme Court Archives.

[17]On Carter and his enforcement actions, see *Daily Picayune*, July 10, 1869, p. 2; July 15, 1869, p. 3; July 30, 1869, p. 4; August 19, 1869, p. 8; December 17, 1869, p. 2; April 10, 1870, p. 8.

[18]*Live Stock Dealers and Butchers Association of New Orleans* v. *Crescent City Live Stock Landing and Slaughter House Co.*, No. 1883, Seventh District Court, Orleans Parish, Louisiana; for the *Record*, see Docket No. 2506, Louisiana Supreme Court Archives. The motives in forming the Live Stock Dealers Association are discussed in *Daily Picayune*, March 14, 1869, p. 4; March 18, 1869, p. 1; June 11, 1869, p. 1; June 20, 1869, p. 2; July 11, 1869, p. 2.

[19]*State ex rel Belden* v. *Fagan*, No. 809, Fifth District Court, Orleans Parish, Louisiana; for the *Record*, see Docket No. 2508, Louisiana Supreme Court Archives. On Cavaroc's action see *Daily Picayune*, August 5, 1869, p. 1; September 16, 1869, p. 8.

[20]Walton H. Hamilton, "The Path of Due Process of Law," *Ethics*, 48 (April, 1938), p. 273.

[21]U. S. Const., Amend. 14.

[22]All references are to Campbell's argument as reported in the *Daily Picayune*, June 27, 1869, pp. 10-11.

[23]Ibid.

[24]Ibid.

[25]Ibid.

[26]Wilson G. Smillie and Edwin D. Kilbourne, *Preventive Medicine and Public Health*, 3rd

ed. (New York: Macmillan, 1965), p. 8; Wilson G. Smillie, *Public Health: Its Promise for the Future* (New York: Macmillan, 1955), pp. 3-6.

[27]John H. Griscom, "Report Upon Sewerage, Water Supply and Offal, " in *Proceedings and Debates of the Third National Quarantine and Sanitary Convention* (New York: Board of Education, 1859), p. 434; John Bell, "Report on the Importance and Economy of Sanitary Measures to Cities," ibid., p. 441.

[28]The New York reform movement is documented in a large file of newspaper clippings, "New York City Slaughter House," in Thomas F. Devoe Collection, New York Historical Society; see in particular *New York Evening Post*, June 16, 1866; for an early review of the abattoir movement in the United States, see Henry G. Crowell, "Sanitary Regulations Relating to Abattoirs," *Public Health Papers and Reports*, 3 (1877), pp. 16-23; regarding reform in the other states, see *Ex Parte Shrader*, 33 Cal. 279 (1867); Act of June 16, 1879, ch. 365 (1870), Mass. Acts and Resolves, p. 283; *Report of the Sanitary Committee of the Board of Health Upon the Subject of Slaughterhouses* (Philadelphia: King and Baird Printers, 1854).

[29]Stanford E. Chaillé, *Life and Death in New Orleans From 1787 to 1869* (New Orleans: Bronze Pen Printers, 1869), p. 9. On the condition of the streets, see Louisiana Board of Health, *Report of the Board of Health* (1858); on the role of the Louisiana medical community in fostering reform, see, among his other works, John Duffy, ed., *The Rudolph Matas History of Medicine in Louisiana* (Baton Rouge: Louisiana State University Press, 1962), vol. 2, pp. 160-197.

[30]John Duffy, *Sword of Pestilence* (Baton Rouge: Louisiana State University Press, 1966), p. 168.

[31]Editorial, *New Orleans Medical News and Hospital Gazette* (1859-60), p. 925.

[32]Duffy, *Sword of Pestilence*, p. 167.

[33]Edward M. Barton, "Report Upon the Sanitary Condition of New Orleans," in New Orleans Sanitary Commission, *Report on the Epidemic Yellow Fever of 1853* (New Orleans: City Council), p. 218; on the reforming effects of epidemics, see Wilson G. Smillie, "The Period of Great Epidemics in the United States (1800-1875)," in *The History of American Epidemiology*, ed. Franklin H. Top (St. Louis: Mosby Co., 1952), p. 52.

[34]New Orleans Sanitary Commission, *Report on the Epidemic Yellow Fever of 1853*, p. 453.

[35]New Orleans, Ordinance No. 2084 (O. S.), 1855.

[36]Louisiana Board of Health, *Report of the Board of Health* (1869), p. 30.

[37]*Daily Picayune*, June 20, 1869, p. 2.

[38]Testimony of Dr. E. S. Lewis in Louisiana House of Representatives, Special Committee on the Removal of the Slaughter Houses, *Minute Book* (1867), pp. 13-14, Louisiana State University Department of Archives and Manuscripts.

[39]Testimony of Mr. Blaid, ibid., pp. 8-10.

[40]Benjamin F. Butler, "Some Experiences with Yellow Fever and Its Prevention," *North American Review* 147 (1888), pp. 525-541; Elisha Harris, "Hygienic Experiences in New Orleans During the War," *Bulletin of the New York Academy of Medicine* No. 30 (Sept., 1865), pp. 463-479; George A. Avery, *A Lecture on the Progressive Spirit of the Medical Profession Delivered Before the New Orleans Academy of Sciences, April 10, 1871* (New Orleans: Hopkins Printers, 1871); Duffy, *History of Medicine* II, pp. 320-32.

[41]*Daily Picayune*, March 14, 1866, p. 4.

[42]*New Orleans Times*, July 22, 1866, p. 2.

[43]*New Orleans Crescent*, August 22, 1866, p. 1.

[44]Smillie, *Public Health*, pp. 4-7, 77, 311.

[45]Minutes of August 6, 1866, in Jefferson City, La., Minutes of the Board of Aldermen 2 (1861-68), p. 437, New Orleans City Archives; Minutes of August 20, 1866, ibid., p. 467.

[46]New Orleans, Ordinance No. 235 (N. S.), approved August 2, 1866, Secs. 25, 26. "Special Report of the Grand Jury of the Parish of Orleans, August 21, 1866, in Special Committee on Removal of the Slaughter Houses, *Minute Book*, p. 44; *Daily Picayune*, August 22, 1866, p. 2.

[47]See *e. g.*, Testimony of Mr. Kaiser, Special Committee on the Removal of the Slaughter Houses, *Minute Book*, p. 39.

[48]Act No. 111 of March 23, 1867 (1867), *La. Acts*, p. 207.

[49]New Orleans, Ordinance No. 605 (N. S.), approved June 3, 1867. Minutes of June 3, 1867, in Jefferson City, Minutes of the Board of Aldermen 2 (1861-68), p. 586.

[50]*New Orleans Daily Crescent*, February 16, 1867, p. 1; *Daily Picayune*, March 22, 1867, p. 2.

[51]Jefferson City, Ordinance No. 406, approved April 7, 1862.

[52]New Orleans, Ordinances Nos. 232 and 233 (N. S.), approved July 31, 1866; Testimony of Mr. Kaiser, Special Committee on the Removal of the Slaughter Houses, *Minute Book*, pp. 39-41; *New Orleans Times*, July 19, 1866, p. 15; July 21, 1866, p. 18.

[53]*Daily Picayune*, March 15, 1868, pp. 3-4.

[54]Ibid., December 17, 1869, p. 2.

[55]Testimony of Dr. E. B. Benton, *Record, Durbridge* v. *Crescent City Live Stock Landing and Slaughter House Co.*, Docket No. 3959, Louisiana Supreme Court Archives, p. 273.

[56]*Record, Durbridge* v. *Crescent City Company*, p. 44.

[57]Howard J. Jones, "The Members of the Louisiana Legislature of 1868" (Ph. D. dissertation, Washington State University, 1974), pp. 157-161, 172-180.

[58]*Record, Louisiana ex rel. Durbridge* v. *Pratt*, Docket No. 2832, Louisiana Supreme Court Archives, p. 104.

[59]Judge William H. Cooley, *Record, Durbridge* v. *Crescent City Company*, p. 409.

[60]Testimony of E. B. Benton, *Record, Durbridge* v. *Crescent City Company*, p. 270.

[61]*Louisiana ex rel. Belden* v. *Fagan*, 22 La. Ann. 545 (1870).

[62]Reasons for Judgment filed by Henry C. Dibble in *Pratt* v. *Crescent City Live Stock Landing and Slaughter House Company*, No. 528, Eighth District Court, Parish of Orleans, Louisiana, included in *Record, Bertin* v. *Crescent City Live Stock Landing and Slaughter House Company*, Docket No. 3917, Louisiana Supreme Court Archives, pp. 230-231.

[63]Smillie, *Public Health*, p. 171.

[64]*New Orleans Republican*, April 1, 1873, p. 4.

[65]Charles W. McCurdy, "Justice Field and the Jurisprudence of Government-Business Relations," *Journal of American History* 61 (1975), p. 970.

REFLECTIONS ON THE PLESSY V. FERGUSON DECISION OF 1896

By

Otto H. Olsen

The *Plessy* v. *Ferguson* decision of 1896, stands roughly half way between two closely related United States Supreme Court verdicts that span a century. At the end of that span stands the unanimous *Brown* decision of 1954, signifying that legally imposed segregation no longer has a legitimate place in our law. Fifty-eight years earlier, the nation's highest court concluded precisely the opposite, when in denying the complaint of Homer Adolph Plessy, a member of Louisiana's black community, it sanctioned the doctrine of "separate but equal" and thus invited the age of Jim Crow. Thirty-nine years before that, the *Dred Scott* decision of 1857 offered an even greater concession to racism in declaring that a Negro was not and could not be a citizen and denying Congress the right to restrict the spread of slavery.[1]

The usually recognized connection between these three famous cases is the race question. Less noted is the fact that each also marked a significant expansion of the role of the judiciary in attempting to determine major questions of national policy at moments of social crisis. The one instance in which this attempted mediation by the judiciary failed, culminated in a Civil War. It is difficult to avoid detecting in all of this a commentary on the ineffectiveness of the democratic political process itself in dealing with the problem of race relations in the history of the United States. It is also hard to resist the invitation to speculate once again on the proper function of the judiciary in a society ostensibly dedicated to popular rule as well as to human rights.

The first of these decisions, that of Dred Scott, has received more than its share of notoriety, recently being pronounced by one scholar "the most maleficient judgment in the Supreme Court's history."[2] There is much to suggest, however, that we might better accord that dubious honor to the decision in the *Plessy* v. *Ferguson* case. Certainly the *Dred Scott* opinion was an odious one, and as Don Fehrenbacher persuasively argues, it appears deficient in "law, logic, history, and factual accuracy,"[3] but it was also a case of far more bark than bite. *Dred Scott* provoked a mighty clamor, but it was not a decisive step on the road to war, and as law its immediate impact was essentially inconsequential. In an impressive commentary on the limitations of judicial power, that attempt to determine the course of national development was overwhelmed by more powerful social forces.

The *Plessy* opinion, in contrast, not only also appears odious in principle and weak in law, logic, and history, but it was of decisive importance in encouraging and institutionalizing racism in the United States. The judgment in that case legalized a soon pervasive system of imposed segregation that endured for over fifty years and the effects of which continue to plague us today. That system of Jim Crow provided a means for intensifying racism throughout the South in particular, while its legal endorsement bolstered racist belief and behavior everywhere in the United States. If *Dred Scott* was an effort that failed, *Plessy* was one that unfortunately succeeded.

Even accepting the legitimacy of such an assessment, some analysts have cautioned against casting the blame for this upon the court. The majority opinion in the *Brown* case of 1954, for example, was reluctant to condemn the performance of 1896, concluding simply that the process of social evolution had destroyed the legitimacy of the views expressed in *Plessy*. Somewhat parallel is the view that the *Plessy* verdict was an appropriate response to the racist demands of that time, although it is not clear how one should relate such considerations to the letter or the majesty of the law.[4] It is also not clear whether any such racist pressures should properly be attributed to the populace or the leadership of that day. One might assume that the court of the 1890's had learned not to resist the kind of public pressure that the *Dred Scott* decision foolishly defied. But was the essence of the transition really that simple? For one thing the specific issue as well as the direction of flow had changed. In each instance the court did bow to racist demands proceeding directly from the South, although one ruling failed while the other did not. This would suggest that what had changed was the relative attitude of the North, but the North certainly was not clamoring for Jim Crow in the 1890's. Nor is it clear that the population of the South was. Numerous studies have concluded that prior to this time southern race relations were flexible and diverse and that Jim Crow was primarily a heritage from the North.[5] The South was apparently changing too. As a way out of such confusion, this essay will propose that the demand for Jim Crow and the acceptance of that policy by the Supreme Court was less a reflection of racism per se than it was of an attempted solution to the general social crisis of the 1890's. As such, legally imposed segregation is perceived as primarily a product of an elitist rationale rather than of popular demand. Most of what follows will, therefore, slight the admittedly persisting influence of racist beliefs while focusing attention elsewhere.

Whatever its limitations, the Civil War destroyed slavery, and in the years that followed the concept of equal rights without respect to color or race was repeatedly confirmed in the Freedmen's Bureau bill of 1866, the Reconstructions acts, the Fourteenth and Fifteenth Amendments to the federal construction, and the Civil Rights acts of 1866, 1870, 1871, and 1875. Of course racism and a pattern of racial separation persisted, but it was in good part true that during the Reconstruction era Congress "sought to wipe out every racial distinction that had any form of legal support, whether that support came from legislation, regulation, custom, or judicial decision, and whether the racial discrimination was the result of government action or inaction."[6]

We all know, however, that failure and betrayal followed, in good part because racism was a national as well as a southern ill. It also was apparent, however, that in the retreat from Radical Reconstruction, racism had become so entwined with demagoguery, economic exploitation, home rule, political power, and reform, as to make it impossible to attribute developments on the racial front to the racist factor alone.[7] This was true in both North and South. One should not therefore minimize the public and legal commitments to racial justice that already had been achieved. The clearest measures of public will that were made during those years did endorse equal rights, and that endorsement had been inscribed in the national constitution and was impressive enough to obtain the professed endorsement of the South and the national Democratic party by 1872.[8] Thereafter there was a significant distinction between an outright opposition to Negro rights, continuing manifestations of selective types of prejudice, and a limited willingness on the part of whites to remain involved in the related struggle. Nevertheless, the southern Reconstruction governments were overthrown, and as blacks and whites maneuvered toward a new relationship, the Civil War crusade lost its force, older federalist principles reasserted themselves, and northerners turned their attention toward problems and opportunities at home. The outcome was the appropriately labeled reunion and reaction of 1877.

In succeeding years racism in the nation undoubtedly intensified. The 1880's witnessed an alarming increase in lynchings, the passage of segregation statutes by several southern states, and the endorsement of separate but equal transportation facilities by the Interstate Commerce Commission. Although some counter tendencies could be found in the adoption of equal rights laws by at least eighteen northern states during these same years, the flagging effort at the national level was clearly revealed when efforts to extend federal aid to education and to pass a federal voting act suffered a decisive defeat in the Republican dominated Congress of 1890. That same year blacks reacted to the trend by holding a variety of national conventions protesting racial prejudice and founding the Afro-American League and the American Citizens' Equal Rights Association. Indicative of a serious division among blacks, the latter biracial organization was prompted by opposition to the all black composition and separatist orientation of the Afro-American League. These conflicting strategies were in turn decisively affected by the Lake Mohonk Conference on the Negro Question held in upstate New York during the summer of 1890. This convention of prominent and influential white liberals, to which no Negroes had been invited, confirmed the abandonment of the struggle for racial equality by the nation's political and economic elite as they endorsed a paternalistic and separatist approach to the race question that would soon be epitomized by the leadership of Booker T. Washington.[9]

There still remained, however, the question of the precise meaning of existing federal law respecting racial equality. This was a matter of particular import to the South since the pertinent law had been inspired by the plight of the freed slaves and the bulk of the black population still resided in the South. As one might have expected, the courts reflected and contributed to the general retreat from the equalitarian principles of Reconstruction. In a vigorous reassertation of states rights principles, together with a declining empathy for, even some apparent annoyance with, the Negroes' quest for justice, a series of controversial decisions by the United States Supreme Court during the 1870's and 1880's seriously weakened the promise of federal protection for black. In essence the court curtailed the power of the federal government and restored responsibility for the protection of civil rights to the states. This created a situation in which the federal government could not, while too often the state governments of the South would not, act to provide equal justice for blacks.[10] There is little to indicate that the court was deliberately abandoning the blacks, however, and there is much to suggest that its course reflected the political rather than the racial ideology of that day. To put it simply, the black population was the victim of both a general hostility to any expansion of the power of the central government and a traditional faith in manhood suffrage, states rights, legal equality, and the competitive process. Those principles had served white democracy well, and it was assumed they would so serve the blacks. While this assumption undoubtedly misread reality, it did not constitute an endorsement of legal or practical inequality for blacks.

This was most clearly indicated in the *Strauder* v. *West Virginia* decision of 1880, which in overturning a state law barring blacks from jury service, affirmed the proposition that "the law in the States shall be the same for the black as for the white; that all persons, whether colored or white, shall stand equal before the laws of the States and, in regard to the colored race . . . that no discrimination shall be made against them by law because of their color." The court further held that blacks were entitled to "the right of exemption from unfriendly legislation against them distinctively as colored—exemption from legal discriminations, implying inferiority in civil society, lessening the security of their enjoyment of rights others enjoy, and discriminations which are steps toward reducing them to the condition of a subject race."[11] It was precisely this protection which was sought by Homer Plessy when he brought before the court his complaint against the Louisiana segregation law of 1890.

While the legal developments discussed above may properly be viewed as part of a resolution of the conflict over Reconstruction policy, the rise of the *Plessy* case represented something new. In the interim southern race relations had remained characterized by a significant degree of flexibility and interracial contact. Nowhere was this more true than in Louisiana, where blacks continued to vote, hold office, serve on juries, participate in the labor movement, and otherwise exert their rights. Integration in public affairs was not uncommon and on railroads seems to have been the rule rather than the exception. "Perhaps the most striking aspect of race relations in Louisiana from 1877 to 1898," concluded a recent study, "was the absence of a system."[12] What was being demanded by 1890 was an end to such flexibility and the establishment of an imposed system of Jim Crow. What is not clear is just what this demand represented.

Interpretations of racial prejudice too often have viewed that prejudice as a product of the emotional ignorance of the poor, while neglecting the role of white elites. Ever since the colonial era the racist segregation of blacks as slaves in some sense served all whites. So long as blacks, the lowest class, were excluded from the body politic, the threat associated with the spread of democracy was lessened for the white elite. This facilitated the admission of more whites to political participation, and gained broader white support for the existing class order by impressing all whites with the advantages of their color.[13] While this herrenvolk system drew all whites into the pattern of white supremacy, slavery made the distinction of race especially valuable to the slaveholding elite. Thus, when the sectional dispute over slavery erupted, not only did racism become the major justification for that institution, but the racist rationale was primarily developed by the slave-owning upper classes of the South. During Reconstruction, racism again served as a political weapon to disrupt a biracial Republicanism that threatened the wealth, power, and pride, including racial pride, of the traditional ruling class. After all of this, it is somewhat remarkable that southern race relations continued to remain as flexible as they did.

Despite its explicit racism, the post-Reconstruction program of white supremacy did not specifically oppose blacks voting, and black political participation continued until the turn of the century. This would become especially significant in the context of a growing radical response to the depressed economic conditions of the New South. In Louisiana, where blacks constituted a slight majority of the voting population, Republicans retained their organization and lucrative federal patronage, blacks held a variety of federal posts, and Republicans continued to win some legislative and congressional seats.[14] Perhaps more significant was the fact that as a variety of factions challeged the Democratic machine during these years, bids for the black vote came from all sides, with blacks catering to one side or the other in pursuit of their own needs or in response to fusion agreements made by the Republican party. As a consequence, memories of Reconstruction were repeatedly revived, and in the context of persisting racist demagoguery, whenever black voters favored one faction they stimulated racism within the other. Once damned for not dividing their vote, they were now doubly damned because they did, and the insidious influence of racism steadily mounted. This trend was intensified by depressed economic conditions. The ousting of the carpetbaggers had failed to solve the economic problems of the South, and the power of the so-called Redeemers was repeatedly threatened by a variety of reform movements that sought black and Republican support. At the same time, hard times and widespread unemployment stimulated a racial competition and conflict among workers that invited exploitation. Politicians repeatedly utilized racism to win votes, and employers were quick to take advantage of racial divisions in rural and urban labor conflicts.

In noticeable contrast was the extent to which equalitarian reform movements throughout the South once again made an explicit biracial appeal. This was true of the readjustor movements, the farmers' alliances, the Populists, the Knights of Labor, and even the American Federation of Labor, each of which achieved significant biracial support. In Louisiana political reformers repeatedly sought black and Republican support, though not always successfully, and during the 1880's the Knights of Labor established over forty locals in the state. In the midst of that decade, one observor believed that the establishment of a New Orleans confederation of workers did more "to break the color line in New Orleans than any thing" since emancipation. In 1887 a biracial labor strike swept the sugar fields of Louisiana that was denounced as a black insurrection and brutally suppressed, while in 1892 thousands of workers of both races paralyzed New Orleans with a four-day general strike. "With one fell swoop," exclaimed the astonished Samuel Gompers, "the economic barrier of color was broken down."[15] Unfortunately he was too sanguine. The New Orleans general strike was crushed by a proclamation of martial law, and throughout the South the tide already had been turned by a campaign of racist demagoguery directed against radical, democratic reform.

It is of crucial significance that it was the defeat of the southern Populist reform movement that led directly to the age of disfranchisement and Jim Crow. While it is true that racism infected all political groupings and made the Negro a general scapegoat for southern ills, a careful study of southern politics by J. Morgan Kousser firmly concludes that it was not hayseed Populists and the lower classes but southerners of intelligence, wealth, and patrician background that led the movement for racial disfranchisement in the South. Primarily at stake were matters of economics and political power rather than race, although the lines of divisions were seldom as consistent as this might suggest. In New Orleans, for example, a reform movement was led by the business community in opposition to a political machine with strong working class support, while the role of Republicans and blacks was ambiguous and divided. But this species of reform appears more akin to Progressivism than Populism, and a variety of recent studies suggest that southern Progressivism marked the defeat of equalitarian principles on both racial and political grounds. Racism, then, may have facilitated certain kinds of reform, but it also appears to have usually redounded to the benefit of established economic power groups and it certainly undermined real political democracy in the South. The demand for Jim Crow and the initiation of the *Plessy* case arose in the midst of that trend.[16]

Early in 1890 the federal Supreme Court indicated its amenability to segregation when it ruled that a Mississippi railroad segregation law did not constitute interference with interstate commerce. As Justice John Marshall Harlan pointed out in dissent, this decision conflicted with the court's ruling twelve years earlier that a Louisiana law prohibiting segregation did constitute such interference.[17] Two months later, a statute inspired by the court's ruling and modeled after the one in Mississippi was introduced into Louisiana legislature. In response a memorial protesting such discriminatory legislation was presented to the legislature by seventeen members of the American Citizens' Equal Rights Association of Louisiana, all of whom were apparently members of the black community. This eloquent memorial pointed out that similar measures recently had been rejected by South Carolina and Texas, and it condemned such caste legislation as "unconstitutional, un-American, unjust, dangerous," and in violation of "the high moral precept that men should not do unto others what they do not wish should be done unto them."[18] Many of the signers were veterans of the Reconstruction battle, the most prominent being Pinckney B. S. Pinchback, who had been a member of the constitutional convention of 1868, a state senator, and lieutenant governor of the state, and Paul Trevigne, a noted teacher and linguist who during and after the Civil War had been editor of the two most noted Negro newspapers in the nation, the New Orleans *L'Union* and *Tribune*. Three of the signers were to be leading spirits in the new fight against Jim Crow – Laurant Auguste, Rodolphe L. Desdunes, and Louis A. Martinet. Laurant Auguste, the least known of the three, had been a Republican leader during Reconstruction. The much younger Rodolphe Desdunes, who was of Haitian and Cuban ancestry, was an active Republican who had served as a clerk of Customs in the years preceding the Democratic administration of Grover Cleveland. He would later achieve recognition as a poet and the author of a history of the colored Creole community of New Orleans.[19] The third member of this group, Louis Martinet, was probably the leading spirit in the new struggle against Jim Crow. The son of a Creole father and a slave mother, Martinet was an attorney and notary who had held various minor Republican appointments during the 1870's and 1880's. He then became an advocate of cooperation with the Democratic party as a means of racial progress but was soon alienated by the unyielding racism of that party. Returning to the Republican fold, Martinet founded and edited, sometimes with the assistance of Paul Trevigne, the New Orleans *Crusader*. This militant, equalitarian newspaper carried on the struggle for equal rights from 1889 to 1897 when it finally collapsed.[20]

All three of the above men were members of that light colored, French speaking community in New Orleans known as Creoles of color. In the main these Creoles were descendants of ante-bellum *gens de couleur libres*—free people of color—who, aided by certain flexibilities and freedoms in the French and Spanish legal tradition of Louisiana, had achieved unusual progress and distinction in the slave South. Though still subject to racial discrimination, they enjoyed a degree of freedom and rights that was seldom experienced by free blacks elsewhere in the South. Accordingly they prospered, especially in New Orleans, where they developed a firm base of economic security and skill as well as an elite professional class characterized by substantial wealth, education, and cultural achievements. Free blacks had fought at the Battle of New Orleans in 1815, and in 1861 they organized two regiments of soldiers that offered their services to the Confederacy. Denied that privilege, they eventually served instead as a segregated unit in the Union army. Following the occupation of New Orleans by federal troops, the colored Creole community provided a uniquely talented portion of the state's black leadership and played a significant role in promoting equalitarian goals during and after Reconstruction.

It was little wonder that this portion of the state's black community was among the first and ablest in resisting the new tide of racism in the South. Nor is it surprising that the issue that aroused these men in 1890 was that of segregated public transportation. That, after all, was precisely where the racist attack was being made. Unlike the issue of separate schools, which many blacks favored, much as they favored separate churches, segregation in public transportation offered no advantage to blacks and remained an unsettled issue. Furthermore, public transportation had been the focus of repeated contests for decades, at both the state and local level and in both North and South. A variety of related cases already had reached the courts, and New Orleans itself had been the scene of a successful campaign against segregated street cars during and immediately after the Civil War.[21]

Opposition to the Louisiana Jim Crow law of 1890 also came from the eighteen black members of the state legislature and from railroad representatives who opposed the bother and costs of a system of enforced segregation. Black legislators were encouraged by the promise of votes against the segregation law in return for their support of an effort to override the governor's veto of a new lottery bill, and Desdunes and Martinet later charged that only ineptness in handling the matter permitted passage of the racist bill at all. The truth of the matter seems to have been that Negro legislators were impossibly handicapped as they stood caught, in usual fashion, between two opposing factions of whites. Obviously they alienated the liberal anti-lottery force, and they were betrayed by some of the racist pro-lottery men they had supported. In any event, the segregation measure was passed in July, 1890, and despite the impassioned protest of Martinet and his cohorts, Governor Francis T. Nicholls signed it into law. Throughout the controversy the supporters of Jim Crow had insisted that there was "an almost unanimous demand on the part of the white people of the State for the enactment of such a law," but there was little else to indicate that this was true.[22]

Martinet responded to the segregation law in the columns of the *Crusader* by calling for a boycott and a legal challenge. "We'll make a test case," he promised, "and bring it before the Federal court on the grounds of invasion of the right [of] a person to travel through the State unmolested."[23] His proposed resistance faltered until September 1, 1891, when at the urging of a former Reconstruction leader, the aged Alexander Aristide Mary, eighteen men of color, all but three of whom had French names, established a Citizens' Committee to Test the Constitutionality of the Separate Car Law.[24] Money was collected and a white man from Mayville, New York, Albion W. Tourgee, was brought into the case. This former carpetbagger and long time crusader for Negro rights was appointed "leading counsel in the case, from beginning to end, with power to choose associates." Of French Huguenot descent and a native of Ohio, Tourgee had served as an officer in the Union army and settled in Greensboro, North Carolina in 1865, where he became an active Republican and served with distinction as a Superior Court judge. He achieved his greatest fame and fortune after leaving the South by writing two powerful and popular novels about his Reconstruction experiences, *A Fool's Errand by One of the Fools* (1879) and *Bricks Without Straw* (1880). The success of these works launched Tourgee upon a literary career, a great deal of which remained primarily concerned with the race question in the United States. By means of additional novels and other books, a variety of significant articles, and a widely circulating editorial column in the Chicago *Inter Ocean*, Tourgee became probably the most publicized and persistent opponent of white racism and defender of Negro equality in the nation. At the 1890 Mohonk Conference on the Negro his had been the one voice of vigorous dissent to the new paternal trend, and as Tourgee joined the legal battle against Jim Crow he fully recognized the need to arouse the conscience of the country in behalf of that cause. Ever confident of the latent strength of the northern white commitment to equal justice, he intensified his anti-racist crusade and launched a new biracial organization, the National Citizens' Equal Rights League.[25]

During the final months of 1891, the Citizens' Committee, in cooperation with certain railroad officials, completed arrangements for a test case. A noted white criminal lawyer from New Orleans, James C. Walker, was retained to handle local legal procedures. Walker had served the Confederacy as a private from 1862 to 1865 and had been paroled at Greensboro, North Carolina, shortly before Tourgee's arrival there; during Reconstruction he allied himself with Louisiana's Republicans.[26] In preparing the test case Tourgee advised that a "nearly white" person be utilized to challenge the law, an approach which, according to Martinet, provoked accusations from some darker members of the Negro community that "the people who support our movement were nearly white, or wanted to pass for white." Actually the motivation for having a nearly white person challenge the law was a tactical one designed to expose the absurdity of Jim Crow, encourage sympathy from whites, and contribute to specific legal arguments. Undoubtedly urban Creoles of color, accustomed for generations to intermingling with whites, most immediately felt the new segregationist demands, while the majority of blacks in the state, especially those in rural areas, were less affected and less concerned. But the principle at issue would, in one way or another, ultimately affect everyone, and at no time was there any indication that the campaign against Jim Crow was perceived as anything less than an absolute opposition to the principle of enforced racial segregation. This is true even though one of the legal arguments that would be utilized in behalf of Homer Plessy, who was seven-eights white, was that segregation deprived him of variety of personal benefits associated with a white status.[27]

On February 24, 1892, Daniel F. Desdunes, the almost white, twenty-one year old son of Rodolph, purchased a ticket on the Louisville and Nashville Railroad for a destination outside the state and "took a seat in the white passenger coach which at the time was crowded with ladies and gentlemen." Upon his refusal to move, he was arrested and indicted for violating the Jim Crow law. "The great interracial conflict, the question whether a dark cuticle shall provide against its possessor's riding in the same railway coach with Caucasians, is at last before the courts," declared the New Orleans *Times-Democrat* on the following day. The Desdunes case came to an abrupt end, however, because of a related decision delivered by the state Supreme Court late in May. This case involved the Pullman Car Company, which had allowed a Negro passenger to travel into the state in an unsegregated car, the court holding that by reason of the commerce clause of the federal constitution, the Jim Crow law could not be applied to interstate travelers. Deplored by the white press, this decision was greeted with grossly exaggerated hopes by Martinet's *Crusader*: "Reactionists may foam at the mouth, and Bourbon organs may squirm, but Jim Crow is as dead as a door nail."[28]

Martinet was confident that Jim Crow travel would prove impractical in the face of a vigorous assertion by blacks of the right granted in this decision together with the difficulty of distinguishing between inter and intrastate passengers. Of course, this would not prove to be the case, and so long as the Jim Crow principle itself remained intact it also threatened a variety of other activities in addition to travel. Tourgee and Walker wanted a decision on the principle of segregation itself and immediately arranged another case that did not involve interstate travel.

Two weeks after the Desdunes case was dropped, Homer Adolph Plessy purchased a ticket in New Orleans, boarded the East Louisiana Railroad bound for Covington, Louisiana, and took a seat in a white coach. Stating he was colored when questioned by the conductor, Plessy refused to move to a Jim Crow car and was arrested by detective Christopher C. Cain. Waiving examination before a Recorder, he subsequently appeared before the Criminal Court of the Parish of New Orleans, where his attorneys raised fourteen specific objections against the segregation statute. The essential argument was that the law established "an insidious distinction and discrimination between Citizens of the United States based on race" and was therefore in violation of the Thirteenth and Fourteenth Amendments. The presiding judge, John H. Ferguson, while complimenting Plessy's counsel for their "great research, learning and ability," denied their contentions and upheld the segregation law in a decision jubilantly hailed by the New Orleans *Times-Democrat* which hoped that the judge's words would "have some effect on the silly negroes who are trying to fight this law. The sooner they drop their so-called 'crusade' against 'the Jim Crow car,' and stop wasting their money in combatting so well-established a principle—the right to separate the races in cars and elsewhere—the better for them." This newspaper also urged the immediate extension of the principle of Jim Crow, beginning with the prohibition of "intermarriage between the races."[29]

The controversy was not yet over, of course, since Judge Ferguson's ruling was appealed to the state Supreme Court thereby initiating the case of *Plessy* v. *Ferguson*. On December 19, 1892, that court, too, denied the arguments against Jim Crow in an opinion delivered by Associate Justice Charles E. Fenner and referring especially to two decisions by state supreme courts in the North. One was the noted Roberts decision of 1849 upholding school segregation in Boston against an abolitionist inspired legal attack led by Charles A. Sumner. The other was a postwar Pennsylvania decision which defended privately enforced segregation of the races on a railroad by concluding that "to assert separateness is not to declare inferiority in either. It is simply to say that following the order of Divine Providence, human authority ought not to compel these widely separate races to intermix." Of course it was human policy and not Divine Providence that was keeping the races apart on this railroad, and the Pennsylvania legislature prohibited this version of Divine Providence a short time before the court's pronouncement.[30]

After failing to obtain a rehearing at the state level, Tourgee and Walker carried their case on a writ of error to the United States Supreme Court. Hindsight should not be allowed to persuade us that the issue in this case was a lost cause. As the question of race had been disputed since the Civil War, certain compromises had emerged reflecting the fact that different specific issues invoked differing degrees of sensitivity, among both blacks and whites. Whites responded far more vehemently to integrated schools, for example, than they did to the presence of blacks in public places, and they expressed far more opposition to private than they did to public contact. One result was an attempt to distinguish civil and political equality from an ill-defined, but sensitive, area of social equality. During the early 1870's, such distinctions were at the heart of an intense national debate over the proposed federal Civil Rights Act of 1875. Provisions in that act prohibiting segregated schools and cemeteries were accordingly dropped, but the bill itself was passed. That bill firmly asserted the right of all persons to equal rights in all public travel, public accommodations, and public places of amusement, as well as to jury duty, without discrimination based upon color or race. Supporters of the law considered it not only a just but a practical measure in the context of the 1870's. The rights included were perceived not only as basic, but as involving matters of such limited sensitivity as to be amenable to law. Although this act was pronounced unconstitutional by the *Civil Rights* decision of 1883, it was only the right of Congress to enforce those rights by legislation that was voided. The concept of civil rights contained in the act of 1875 was still widely endorsed, and many still looked to the Supreme Court to protect those rights against direct infringement by the states.[31]

To the complete satisfaction of Plessy's attorneys, who continued to hope for a favorable revival of public concern in the North, his case was not heard by the federal high court for over three years. Meanwhile there were some encouraging signs. The initial response to Tourgee's National Citizens' Rights Association was inspiring, and there were continuing calls for equal justice from ministers and church organizations, from radical Republicans and former abolitionists, from college students and black leaders, and from ordinary citizens in every corner of the land. In 1892 blacks won suits against public segregation in New York and Michigan, and between 1891 and 1895 at least eleven northern states strengthened their civil rights law. During this time the Methodist Episcopal Church denounced Jim Crow and called for a national campaign against racial injustice, and an impressive boycott was instituted against the Chicago Exposition of 1893 because it had slighted blacks. In 1894 Tourgee testified in behalf of an antilynching measure in Ohio which subsequently became law.[32] Such encouragements, however, did not match in significance the intensified racist demagoguery that swept the South during these same years. Also discouraging was the markedly conservative composition of the United States Supreme Court.

Tourgee, who was convinced of both the necessity for constant resistance to racial oppression and the unconstitutionality of Jim Crow, was frightened by the Supreme Court's attitude and the public's limited concern with the race question. In 1891 he suggested delaying or even abandoning the *Plessy* case until a more favorable atmosphere or a more favorable court prevailed. "It is of the utmost consequence," he warned his colleagues, "that we should not have a decision against us," for the court "has *never reversed itself* on a *constitutional* question." Continued postponement apparently encountered resistance from the Attorney General of Louisiana, however, and the case was allowed to proceed.[33]

Arguments in behalf of Plessy were commenced by Tourgee before the Supreme Court on April 13, 1896. Walker supplied a separate brief, while a third brief in behalf of the plaintiff was delivered by Samuel F. Phillips for himself and F. D. McKenney. Phillips was of a well known North

Carolina family and had been a prominent Reconstruction Republican in that state. It was a bad sign, perhaps, that Phillips was the United States Solicitor General who had been defeated in the Civil Rights Cases thirteen years earlier. Also inauspicious was the dominant white setting of this effort in behalf of black rights. All of the attorneys involved were white, and they faced an all white bench. Other than the issue at stake, the only and most totally unnoticed black presence consisted of the silent movements of a Negro messenger staff and the murmurings and occasional clatter of dishes traceable to a Negro kitchen staff preparing the justices' lunch in the partially separated kitchen adjoining the court. Recollections by the son of one of the justices suggest that in appearance at least, Chief Justice Melville W. Fuller, seated at the center of the judigical bar, epitomized the color consciousness of the white world:

> In keeping was his pre-Raphaelite appearance: the fascinating pallor, the delicately chiselled features, the clear blue eyes, the ethereal snowy locks falling almost to his shoulders, the long white mustache. Fuller sat in a court beneath the American emblem, a fierce eagle holding in his gilded talons a bar supporting a bright red curtain that served beautifully to set off the whiteness of the Chief Justice. In fact, wrote reporter Arthur Brisbane, "Whistler's 'White Girl,' now hanging in the Metropolitan Museum of Art, is not as white a study in white as is Chief Justice Fuller."[34]

Ostensibly, however, everyone involved in the *Plessy* case agreed that blacks were entitled to equality before the law. What the issue boiled down to was the validity of the plaintiff's contention that legally imposed segregation on the railroads was an act of harmful discrimination. Declaring that it was not, the majority opinion, prepared by Justice Henry Billings Brown, rejected the "assumption that the enforced separation of the two races stamps the colored race with a badge of inferiority. If this be so, it is not by reason of anything found in the act, but solely because the colored race chooses to put that construction upon it." Experience would soon expose the absuridity of that assertion. Additionally exasperating was the court's insistence that unsegregated facilities would be attempting the impossible task of establishing social mores by forcing social integration. With a logic that must elude everyone, the *Plessy* opinion thus determined that the *absence* of legal restraint in public places was imposing social mores, whereas *enforced* segregation law was not. What was involved here was not social integration at all, but public rights, and the only force that was being applied was that of Jim Crow. Individuals were not to be allowed to function freely in society but were to be forced to separate according to race. While by no means equally oppressive, this was an interference with the freedom of whites as well as blacks, and once sanctioned by federal law it was carried to absurd extremes, precisely for the purpose of imposing social mores. The *Plessy* decision thus surrendered a promising opportunity to allow the principle of equal rights to operate gradually over time. In addition, the meaninglessness of the principle of separate but equal in the context of the issues involved in *Plessy*, helped discredit a concept that might have been of more positive significance in other realms, most obviously in education. And so the court helped create the problems that now plague us all.[35]

The weaknesses in the *Plessy* opinion were clearly exposed by Plessy's attorneys and in Justice Harlan's lone dissent. "The arbitrary separation of citizens, on the basis of race, while they are on a public highway," Harlan noted, "is a badge of servitude wholly inconsistent with the civil freedom and the equality before the law established by the Constitution." He also correctly predicted that the "thin disguise" of equal accommodations would fool neither blacks nor whites, and he warned that since "the destinies of the two races" were "indissolubly linked together . . . the interests of both require that the common government of all shall not permit the seeds of race hate to be planted under the sanction of law."

Justice Harlan's observations appear so obvious today, that one wonders what it was that drove his colleagues to a contrary conclusion. One recent response to this question has been that the court merely endorsed existing case law precedent by accepting Jim Crow as a proper exercise of the police power of the state.[36] Several objections can be registered to this line of argument. First, admitting that such precedent was convenient, even influential, it certainly was not binding. Second, the most important of those precedents dealt with school segregation, and we already have indicated that there was a perceived distinction of crucial significance between schooling and public accommodations. Third, while these legal precedents had sometimes dealt directly with the equal rights argument, the issue had yet to be decided by the federal court in the context of an explicit constitutional prohibition against discriminatory state legislation. Even more important is the fact that there was case law precedent on both sides of this question. Segregation practices had been nullified in both state and federal courts, and especially in those northern states whose constitutions contained strong equalitarian clauses.[37] Although Plessy's attorneys may have erred in not marshalling a thorough case law tradition in behalf of their client and in not stressing the similarity between the federal constitution and those state constitutions with rather than without equalitarian clauses, the Supreme Court was undoubtedly aware of these facts. Justice Brown admitted in his decision that segregation had not been "uniformly" upheld by the lower courts, but he conveniently refrained from citing decisions conflicting with his own conclusions on the matter.

What was at issue in the *Plessy* case was a matter of judgment, not case law precedent. The nation's highest court was being forced, for the first time, to make an explicit judgment as to the reasonableness and equity of legally imposed segregation in public transportation. While Plessy's attorneys did not present an effective case law precedent in his behalf, they certainly did focus effectively on the question at issue—whether or not such enforced segregation was an invidious discrimination against blacks:

> The exemption of nurses shows that the real evil lies not in the color of the skin but in the relation the colored person sustains to the white. If he is a dependent it may be endured; if he is not, his presence is insufferable. Instead of being intended to promote the general comfort and moral well-being, this act is plainly and evidently intended to promote the happiness of one class by asserting its supremacy and the inferiority of another class. Justice is pictured blind and her daughter, the Law, ought at least to be color-blind.
>
> * * *
>
> It is an act of race discrimination pure and simple. The experience of the civilized world proves that it is not a matter of public health or morals, but simply a matter intended to re-introduce the caste-ideal on which slavery rested. . . . The object of such a law is simply to debase and distinguish against the inferior race. Its purpose has been properly interpreted by the general designations of 'Jim Crow Car' law. Its object is to separate Negroes from

> whites in public conveyances for the gratification and recognition of the sentiment of white superiority and white supremacy of right and power.[38]

Although the court denied the compelling logic of the argument for Plessy, and although it did have selective case law to fall back upon, it is difficult to believe that the Supreme Court was merely accepting precedent. This would assume an incredible lack of awareness and is not consistent with the arguments of substance presented in both the majority and the minority opinion. In the South there was even some surprise at the verdict, the Richmond *Dispatch* confessing that "this decision was hardly expected"; and in the North expressions of protest were not uncommon.[39] All of which suggests that the *Plessy* verdict cannot be satisfactorily explained without again returning to the general social context.

By the 1890's it had become the habit of the federal Supreme Court to interpret the law to the advantage of propertied interests. Dedicated to Social Darwinism and economic progress, that court repeatedly nullified the popular will and frustrated reform in its determination to protect the rights and possessions of an economic elite. In pursuit of this end, the same court that minimized the promise of the Fourteenth Amendment to blacks, stretched its meaning in behalf of private property and business enterprise. It did so not only in the name of liberty and inalienable rights, but in what it believed to be the interests of social progress and order. In the midst of the extraordinary turbulence associated with the depression of the 1890's, a rash of major labor strikes, and the rise of the Populists, this defense of property was particularly on guard against a "thrust from below, an upsurge of *the democracy* resentful at the growth of concentrated wealth and determined to use its majority power to effect redistribution." Stephen J. Field, who was probably more responsible than any other justice for shaping the conservative philosophy of the court, was obsessed with the need to protect "the strong, who were bringing about superior achievements in the business and industrial world, against the restraining activities of the public."[40]

Ironically, when Homer Plessy sought his rights before a court that was so solicitous of minority rights, he invoked little sympathy. A court renowned for its firm resistance to government interference with rights of property holders, saw no need to protect blacks against Jim Crow. The catch was, of course, that Plessy represented a minority at the bottom rather than at the top of the social order, and in the context of the tumultous 1890's, established authority perceived people at the bottom as dangerous. It has been noted earlier that throughout the history of the United States the division between black and white served the interests of social order. Certainly the conservative mind of the South, and probably elsewhere as well, appreciated that fact and feared blacks as the lowest and potentially most dangerous members of society. In the 1890's the demand for racial equality could not be divorced from a cry for equalitarian democracy which conservatives viewed as the major threat of their day. As members of the lowest class, blacks were susceptible to egalitarian pleas. Furthermore, when interracial pleas were made, however weak, they usually came from radicals who advocated interracial unity as a means of defeating the power of concentrated wealth. These considerations might be expected to incline a conservative minded court to cooperate with southern leaders in establishing a new pattern of white over black as a means of preserving social order. Such a course conveniently accorded with the federal system, the northern heritage of Jim Crow, and a newly respected quasi-scientific racism that permeated the educated thought of that day.

C. Vann Woodward has noted that Francis T. Nicholls, Chief Justice of the Louisiana Supreme Court at the time it denied Plessy's complaint, had won a reputation for racial fairness as the state's first Redeemer governor thirteen years earlier. He was again the governor in 1890 who refused to veto the Jim Crow law, and as Chief Justice he concurred in upholding that law. By the 1890's, concludes Woodward, "the wave of Populist rebellion among the white farmers was reaching its crest in the South, and Judge Nicholls's change of course typified the concessions to racism that conservatives of his class made in their efforts to forestall or divert the rebellion."[41] Begging the question of whether conservatives were making concessions to or exploiting racism, let us at least note that Judge Nicholls's course was not as far removed from Southern paternalism as Woodward implies. Paternalism had always had two sides. On the one hand it was anxious to reward submissive behavior, but on the other it was prepared to crush threatening demands; and by the 1890's southern white leaders were no longer so sharply restrained by the threat of northern intervention as they had been twenty years earlier.

Enforced segregation met contrasting conservative needs. It minimized the threat of social disorder and biracial radicalism, and it promised some degree of justice and progress to blacks. Undoubtedly the conservative mind desired to avoid extremism and conflict, but in that age it frequently did so in a manner that violated equalitarian and democratic belief. The promise of benevolent and paternal conduct was a part of the rationale for that process, and at least three of the justices joining in the *Plessy* verdict, Brown, George Shiras, and Chief Justice Melville W. Fuller, displayed a paternal interest in the welfare of the Negro. The entire court, of course, enjoyed the services of a retinue of black messengers and servants.[42] The relevance of such considerations was highlighted at just this time by Booker T. Washington's endorsement of both the white establishment and the principle of an accommodating separatism. Washington was undoubtedly correct in his conclusion that blacks were more interested in survival, jobs, and cultural independence than they were in integration. The fact was that blacks had been driven toward separatism as a means of making progress and achieving freedom at the same time that white racists were demanding enforced and perpetual segregation as a means of keeping blacks down. Unfortunately the manner in which Washington presented black aspirations offered a convenient mandate for Jim Crow, which was something altogether different from what blacks themselves sought.

All of this is meant to emphasize that the *Plessy* decision was not forced upon the Supreme Court by popular demand, nor should one expect such to be the case for a court already so noted for frustrating the common will. One suspects instead that the aristocratic predilections of the justices inclined them toward racial as well as class distinctions, and that they moved toward segregation as a policy that fulfilled the needs or calmed the fears of a conservative elite. In his dissent in both the Civil Rights and the *Plessy* cases, Justice Harlan implied as much in insisting that the course of the court was directly defying what the popular will assumed it had achieved in adding the Thirteenth and Fourteenth Amendments to the federal Constitution.

This is not to say that the court of 1896 was defying a strong demand for racial equality. To the contrary, the lack of effective pressure in that realm undoubtedly contributed to the triumph of Jim Crow, something that Tourgee recognized and feared. The tie between the radical reform movement and the blacks, for example, was incredibly weak. During the crucial presidential election of 1896, while the Populists and Democrats joined in condemning the conservative role of the Supreme Court in economic matters, they registered no opposition to the *Plessy* decision. And although the Populists did condemn what they called "the wholesale system of disfranchisement adopted in some states," they avoided identifying that issue directly with the race question.[43] By this time the Knights of Labor, which was unusually outspoken in its biracial appeal, had been crushed by the reaction to the Haymarket riot; the A. F. of L. was moving rapidly toward its Jim Crow stance; and southern Populism was being undercut by racist demagoguery. Furthermore, all of the leading actors directly supporting Plessy were products of Reconstruction Republicanism who, like almost all of the Negro press, opposed the Populist crusade. Obviously biracial forces were weak and divided, and the virus of white racism infected equalitarian reformers or frightened them from an effective appeal to the most oppressed group in the nation. Booker T. Washington helped finalize that fact. In one way or another, race prejudice served as the Achilles heel of American reform.

Admittedly much of this interpretation is conjecture based upon circumstantial evidence, but circumstantial evidence does not always make a bad case. With a little more time, a stronger one could be made. Justice Stephen J. Field and Chief Justice Fuller closely fit the suggested conservative mold, while Justice Harlan fits that of the opposition. Other justices are more troublesome. Henry Billings Brown, who wrote the *Plessy* decision, was one of the dissenters in the income tax case, but he was also more clearly a racist and later confessed that perhaps he had made some mistakes in his *Plessy* opinion.[44] What is needed is a book-length study which effectively ties the thoughts of the participants themselves to the social context of that time.

And so Jim Crow was sanctified by national law, and before long it would spread to lengths easily as ridiculous as those mentioned derisively by Tourgee's brief in the *Plessy* case. Discouraged by the *Plessy* decision, the lack of white concern, and the growing power of Booker T. Washington's approach to race relations, the equalitarian crusade all but ceased. James C. Walker died in New Orleans only two years later, and his role was so far forgotten or suppressed that obituaries in the city's two leading newspapers agreed in lauding his long service in the Confederate army, his emminence as a criminal lawyer, and his recent successful fight before the United States Supreme Court in upholding the principle of Jim Crow! By 1905, the year of Tourgee's death, however, a new tide was rising. In November of that year, the newly formed black Niagara Movement sponsored nationwide memorial services in honor of "Three Friends of Freedom"—Frederick Douglass, William Lloyd Garrison, and Albion W. Tourgee. Within a few years the Niagara Movement was succeeded by the biracial National Association for the Advancement of Colored People which initiated a persisting legal struggle culminating in the victory of 1954. Louis Martinet, who had completed his medical studies during the 1890's remained in New Orleans pursuing a multiple career as notary, attorney, and physician until his death in 1917.[45]

[1]*Dred Scott* v. *Sanford*, 19 Howard 393 (1857); *Plessy* v. *Ferguson*, 163 U. S. 537 (1896); *Brown* v. *Board of Education of Topeka*, 347 U. S. 483 (1954). Since *Brown* dealt with education, the Plessy ruling on transportation was not directly overturned until *Gayle* v. *Browder*, 352 U. S. 903 (1956). Apparently Plessy's given name was Homère, but he himself used Homer throughout the judicial records. Rodolph L. Desdunes, *Our People and Our History*, ed. and trans. by Dorothea O. McCants (Baton Rouge, 1973), 144.

[2]Alan Barth, *Prophets with Honor: Great Dissents and Great Dissenters in the Supreme Court* (New York, 1974), 23.

[3]Don E. Fehrenbacher, *The Dred Scott Case: Its Significance in American Law and Politics* (New York, 1978), 384.

[4]Barth, *Prophets with Honor*, 52; Bernard Schwartz, *A Commentary on the Constitution of the United States* (New York, 1968), II, 567.

[5]C. Vann Woodward, *The Strange Career of Jim Crow* (3rd rev. ed.; N.Y., 1974), ch. 2; Henry C. Dethloff and Robert R. Jones, "Race Relations in Louisiana, 1877-1898," *Louisiana History*, IX (1968), 301-323.

[6]Milton R. Konvitz, *A Century of Civil Rights* (New York, 1961), 63.

[7]*E.g.*, Otto H. Olsen (ed.), *Reconstruction and Redemption in the South* (Baton Rouge, 1980), 7-8; J. Morgan Kousser, *The Shaping of Southern Politics: Suffrage Restriction and the Establishment of the One-Party South, 1880-1910* (New Haven, 1974), 250-265.

[8]Lawrence Grossman, *The Democratic Party and the Negro: Northern and National Politics, 1868-92* (Urbana, 1976), ch. 2.

[9]Otto H. Olsen, *Carpertbagger's Crusade: The Life of Albion Winegar Tourgée* (Baltimore, 1965), 306-309.

[10]These developments may be conveniently followed in Loren Miller, *The Petitioners: The Story of the Supreme Court of the United States and the Negro* (Cleveland, 1966), 102-164. See also Robert J. Harris, *The Quest for Equality: The Constitution, Congress, and the Supreme Court* (Baton Rouge, 1960); Robert Green McCloskey, *American Conservatism in the Age of Enterprise* (Cambridge, Mass., 1951); Konvitz, *A Century of Civil Rights.*

[11]*Strauder* v. *West Virginia*, 100 U. S. 303, 307-308. This passage was cited by Plessy's attorney and in Justice John Marshall's dissent in the Plessy case.

[12]Dethloff and Jones, "Race Relations in Louisiana," *Louisiana History*, IX (1968), 305.

[13]See especially Edmund S. Morgan, *American Slavery American Freedom: The Ordeal of Colonial Virginia* (New York, 1975), ch. 17; George Frederickson, *The Black Image in the White Mind: The Debate on Afro-American Character and Destiny, 1817-1914* (New York, 1971), ch. 1-2.

[14]My analysis of blacks in Louisiana politics and labor relies on William Ivy Hair, *Bourbonism and Agrarian Protest: Louisiana Politics, 1877-1900* (Baton Rouge, 1969); Joy J. Jackson, *New Orleans in the Guilded Age: Politics and Urban Progress, 1880-1896* (Baton

Rouge, 1969); John R. Kemp (ed.), *Martin Behrman of New Orleans: Memoirs of a City Boss* (Baton Rouge, 1977); Matthew J. Schott, "Progressives Against Democracy: Electoral Reform in Louisiana, 1894-1921," *Louisiana History*, XX (1979), 247-260; Edward F. Haas, "John Fitzpatrick and Political Continuity in New Orleans, 1896-1899," ibid., XXII (1981), 7-29.

[15]The quotations are from George E. McNeill, *The Labor Movement the Problem of Today* (Boston, 1886), quoted in Jackson, *New Orleans in the Guilded Age*, 226; and Philip S. Foner, *History of the Labor Movement in the United States. Volume II: From the Founding of the American Federation of Labor to the Emergence of American Imperialism* (New York, 1955), 203.

[16]Kousser, *The Shaping of Southern Politics*, 261-265. For judgments on Progressivism see also Raymond H. Pulley, *Old Virginia Restored: An Interpretation of the Progressive Impulse, 1870-1930* (Charlottesville, 1968); and F. Sheldon Hackney, *Populism to Progressivism in Alabama* (Princeton, 1969).

[17]*Louisville, New Orleans, and Texas Railroad* v. *Mississippi*, 133 U. S. 587 (1889); *Hall* v. *DeCuir*, 95 U. S. 485 (1878).

[18]*Official Journal of the House of Representatives of the State of Louisiana, 1890* (Baton Rouge, 1890), 127-128. Signers of the memorial were: P. B. S. Pinchback, A. E. P. Albert, A. S. Jackson, S. T. Clanton, T. A. Wilson, E. Lyon, J. T. Newman, I. E. Mullon, T. B. Stamps, Paul Trevigne, James Lewis, Laurent Auguste, R. L. Desdunes, L. A. Martinet, J. F. Marshall, W. S. Wilson, and J. L. Minor. The origins of the Plessy case may be followed in more detail in Otto H. Olsen (ed.), *The Thin Disguise: Turning Point in Negro History, Plessy* v. *Ferguson, A Documentary Presentation* (New York, 1967), and C. Vann Woodward, *American Counterpoint: Slavery and Racism in the North South Dialogue* (Boston, 1971), ch. 8. See also Desdunes, *Our People and Our History*, 141-148. Olsen, *The Thin Disguise*, 47-67, contains the full text of the memorial together with other responses to the law.

[19]Desdunes, *Our People and Our History*, xiv-xix, 67n, 131, 141-142, 146-148; L. A. Martinet correspondence in Albion W. Tourgee Papers, Chautaqua County Historical Museum, Westfield, New York; *Soard's New Orleans City Directory* (1874-1915). An L. A. Martinet is listed as a member of the state House of Representatives, 1876-1878, in A. E. Perkins, *Who's Who in Colored Louisiana, 1930* (New Orleans, 1930), 51.

[20]Ibid., ix-xxiii.

[21]Olsen, *The Thin Disguise*, 31-36.

[22]New Orleans *Daily Picayune*, July 10, 1890; New Orleans *Times-Democrat*, July 9, 1890.

[23]New Orleans *Crusader*, July 19, 1890.

[24]Stationary of the Citizens' Committee bears the organization date of September 1, 1891. See L. A. Martinet to A. W. Tourgee, October 5, 1891, Albion W. Tourgee Papers, Chautauque County Historical Museum, Westfield, New York. Committee members were Arthur Esteves (President), Firmin Christophe (Secretary), G. G. Johnson (Ass't Secretary), Paul Bonseigneur (Treasurer), Laruent Auguste, Pierre Chevalier, M. J. Piron, C. C. Antoine, N. E. Mansion, R. B. Baquie, L. A. Martinett, R. L. Desdunes, A. B. Kennedy, A. J. Giuranovich, L. J. Joubert, Alcee Labat, Eugene Luscy, E. A. Williams.

[25]Olsen, *Carpetbagger's Crusade, passim.*

[26]New Orleans, *Times-Democrat*, July 9, 1898; New Orleans *Daily Picayune*, July 9, 1898.

[27]For a contrasting concern see Woodward, *American Counterpoint*, 224.

[28]New Orleans *Crusader* quoted in Kansas City *American Citizen*, July 29, 1892; L. A. Martinet to A. W. Tourgee, July 4, 1892, Tourgee Papers.

[29]New Orleans *Times-Democrat*, November 19, 1892. Anti-miscegenation laws had fail-

ed passage in 1880 and 1888, but in 1894 laws were passed barring intermarriage and requiring separate accommodations in railroad depots. Dethloff and Jones, "Race Relations in Louisiana," 316.

[30]*State of Louisiana* v. *Homer A. Plessy*, Louisiana Supreme Court Records, 77-79, citing *Roberts* v. *City of Boston*, 59 Mass. (5 Cush.) 198 (1849), and *West Chester and Philadelphia Railroad Co.* v. *Miles*, 55 Pa. 209 (1867).

[31]Miller, *The Petitioners*, 136-147; *Civil Rights Cases*, 109 U. S. 3. For a more jaundiced view of the Civil Rights act itself see William Gillette, *Retreat from Resonstruction 1869-1879* (Baton Rouge, 1979), ch. 11.

[32]Olsen, *Carpetbagger's Crusade*, 312-320; G. Fabe Martin to Albion W. Tourgee, August 26, 1892, Tourgee Papers; Franklin Johnson, *The Development of State Legislation Concerning the Free Negro* (New York, 1918), *passim*.

[33]A. W. Tourgee to L. A. Martinet, Oct. 31, 1893, and J. C. Walker to A. W. Tourgee, April 9, 1896, Tourgee Papers.

[34]George Shiras, 3rd, and Winfield Shiras, *Justice George Shiras, Jr. of Pittsburgh, Associate Justice of the United State Supreme Court, 1892-1903* (Pittsburgh, 1953), 115.

[35]*Plessy* v. *Ferguson*, 163 U. S. 537. Justice Harlan was caustic in response to the social equality bugaboo: "That argument, if it can be properly regarded as one, is scarcely worthy of consideration; for social equality no more exists between two races when travelling in a passenger coach or a public highway than when members of the same races sit by each other in a street car or in a jury box, or stand or sit with each other in a political assembly, or when they are in the same room for the purpose of having their names placed on the registry of voters, or when they approach the ballot-box in order to exercise the high privilege of voting." The brief by Phillips and McKenney specifically distinguished between public transportation, public schools, and intermarriage, endorsing segregation in the latter two instances. S. F. Phillips and F. D. McKenney, Brief for Plaintiff in Error, 10-11, *File Copies of Briefs 1895*, VIII (October term, 1895), United States Supreme Court Records.

[36]David W. Bishop, "Plessy v. Ferguson: A Reinterpretation," *Journal of Negro History*, LXII (1977), 125-133; Richard A. Maidment, "Plessy v. Ferguson Re-examined," *Journal of American Studies*, VII (1973), 125-132. For a contrasting and still persuasive analysis see Barton J. Bernstein, "Case Law in Plessy v. Ferguson," *Journal of Negro History*, XLVII (1962), 192-198, and "Plessy v. Ferguson: Conservative Sociological Jurisprudence," ibid., XLVIII (1963), 196-205.

[37]J. Morgan Kousser, "Dead End: The Development of Nineteenth Century Litigation on Racial Discrimination in Schools," *Social Science Working Paper 349*, California Institute of Technology (Pasadena, 1980), is a thorough study of school case law precedent. My interpretation is heavily indebted to this study.

[38]A. W. Tourgee Brief of Plaintiff in Error, 19, 26, *File Copies of Briefs* 1895, VIII (October term, 1895), United States Supreme Court Records. Tourgee may have been unwise in the extent to which he attacked earlier court interpretations of the Reconstruction amendments. He was particularly hostile to *United States* v. *Cruikshank*, 92 U. S. 542, which he questionably described as "squarely against us." Ibid., 26.

[39]Richmond *Dispatch*, May 21, 1896; Baltimore *Sun*, May 19, 1896; Olsen, *The Thin Disguise*, 25-28, 123-130.

[40]Quotations from Arnold M. Paul, *Conservative Crisis and the Rule of Law: Attitudes of Bar and Bench, 1887-1895* (Torchbook ed.; New York, 1969), 229-230; Carl B. Swisher,

Stephen J. Field: Craftsman of the Law (Washington, 1930), 427. According to Swisher, Field "conceived it to be his function as a member of the Court, to declare the law, for the purpose of preserving order." Ibid., 427-430.

[41]C. Vann Woodward, "The Birth of Jim Crow," *American Heritage*, XV (1964), 100.

[42]Charles A. Kent (ed.), *Memoir of Henry Billings Brown Late Justice of the Supreme Court of the United States* (New York, 1915), 91-93, 133; Shiras, *Justice George Shiras*, 213; Louis D. Rubin (ed.), *Teach the Freedmen; The Correspondence of Rutherford B. Hayes and the Slater Fund for Education, 1881-1887* (Baton Rouge, 1959), I, xix.

[43]Donald Bruce Johnson (comp.), *National Party Platforms* (Urbana, 1978), II, 106. The People's Party did not advocate federal action in this crucial area, although it did ironically demand that "the Government should own and operate the railroads in the interest of the people and on a non-partisan basis, to the end that all may be accorded the same treatment in transportation. . . ." Their concern was economic, not racial. Ibid., 105.

[44]Paul, *Conservative Crisis*, 42, 198-204; Willard L. King, *Melville Weston Fuller* (New York, 1950), 85; Swisher, *Stephen J. Field*, 426-430; Alan Westin, "John Marshall Harlan and the Constitutional Rights of Negroes: the Transformation of a Southerner," *Yale Law Journal*, LXVI (1957), 637-710; Leon Freedman and Fred L. Israel (eds.), *The Justices of the Supreme Court of the United States Supreme Court, 1789-1969: Their Lives and Major Opinions* (New York, 1969), II, 1077, 1080, 1085, 1489, 1561-1562, 1584.

[45]New Orleans *Daily Picayune*, July 9, 1898; New Orleans *Times-Democrat*, July 9, 1898; Olsen, *Carpetbagger's Crusade*, 350-354; Succession Record, No. 120.958, Civil District Court, Parish of New Orleans.

François Xavier Martin (1762-1846), a member of the Louisiana Supreme Court and the reporter of the high court's decisions. Lithograph, *ca.* 1900. Unidentified artist. Louisiana State Museum.

LOUISIANA LEGAL HISTORY AND ITS SOURCES: NEEDS, OPPORTUNITIES AND APPROACHES

By
Warren M. Billings

When I was asked to prepare this essay, I hesitated to accept the assignment because my own scholarly interests and work lie mainly in a time and place far removed from Louisiana. Furthermore, my only claim to authority in the subject of Louisiana's legal heritage arises from a familiarity with the state's judicial archives—an acquaintance that developed while I helped rescue the records of our Supreme Court. Not being expert in the study of the state's law, I was somewhat reluctant to attempt to instruct scholars whose knowledge exceeds mine. To do so invited the hazard of unmasking my ignorance; nevertheless, at length it became a risk I was willing to assume. My reason for taking such a chance was this realization: Precisely because I am no specialist, I can play the part of the boy in the tale of the emperor's new clothes and thereby draw attention to some things that need doing in the uncharted regions of Louisiana's legal history. A step towards mapping those regions entails some reconsideration of the sourses in relation to a variety of needs, opportunities, and approaches to further research.

One of the more obvious needs is for legal scholars to maintain an abiding concern for the preservation of the sources because until fairly recently, the commitment of Louisianians to saving the records of their legal heritage can only be described as whimsical. The consequences of past failures are now all too readily apparent. For instance, the absence of a state department of archives until 1956—which even now lacks adequate facilities—compelled the state courts to retain their old records in places that were insufficient to insure their security. Under the circumstances, the result of poor care was predictable. Large portions of the earliest records were lost to disasters, carelessness, willful destruction, and pilferage. The colonial documents in the *Cabildo* came near to ruination because of improper storage and the tender ministration of those well-intended amateurs who attempted repairs with scotch tape. Legislative journals have disappeared, along with many of those of city councils across the state. Unhappily, while a limited number of papers belonging to members of the bench and bar have managed to stray into the holdings of our universities, no one ever undertook a systematic accumulation of such collections.[1] It is now therefore quite difficult to document the activities of the judges and lawyers who figured so prominently after 1803 in molding the civilian legal customs with those of the Anglo-American tradition. Equally unfortunate was the neglect of published sources. Often printed on paper highly infected with acid-producing compounds many reports, compilations, digests, treatises, or how-to-do it manuals have deteriorated to the point of no repair. Such a litany of losses or near losses could go on, but, in the words of a seventeenth-century friend of mine, that recital would "bee too tedious to mention."

More to the point however is a change in attitudes that has come gradually over the past two decades. There now exists among scholars, judges, lawyers, and laymen a keener sensitivity to how fragile are the sources and how great is the need to preserve what remains. The reason for this change is several-fold. During the period of the last twenty years, historians have abandoned the study of great men and great events and turned, in Jesse Lemisch's phrase, to writing "history from the ground up."[2] Accordingly, they now draw attention to the importance of blacks, women, native Americans, Hispanics, and so they have come to prize court records as the window through which to observe this mass of the American people.[3] In the 1960s and 1970s concern for historic preservation played a part, as did the bicentennial celebration, the "roots" phenomenon started by Alex Haley's book, as well as nostalgia for times seemingly less troubled than our own.[4] More specifically, certain individuals and institutions have led the effort to save things that might now be lost. Louisiana's genealogists, through their Friends of the Archives of Louisiana organization, have worked tirelessly to make public officials mindful of the need to secure surviving early records from further loss. The Louisiana Division of the New Orleans Public Library has gathered an impressive array of municipal archives having peculiar significance for studying our legal heritage. Not least among these are the historic records of the Civil District Court for Orleans Parish. The Amistad Research Center now houses an invaluable collection of papers of southern civil rights attorneys while the Louisiana State Museum has undertaken an ambitious project to repair, arrange, and film the colonial documents. Even the United States Court of Appeals for the Fifth Circuit has an archives-history committee presently at work on ways to preserve federal judicial records. And, my own university, the Supreme Court, and the State Archives are embarked upon a cooperative venture to save the high court records.

Myra Clark Gaines (1805-1885). Daguerrotype, *ca.* 1850. Louisiana State Museum.

These activities are encouraging and they must continue. They should not lull any one into believing that all is well, however, because there remain categories of sources that are not regularly collected, just as there are those that still face extinction through inadvertance or deliberate choice. For instance, no one routinely gathers the papers of modern law firms, and there is no systematic program of oral history to record the recollections of practitioners on the bench or at the bar. As yet, librarians have not taken many steps towards conserving their old law books, and until book conservation receives great attention, there is a continuing danger of losing the information which this rich source contains. The singular need in respect to preservation, though, may be deciding how to cope with the mountainous volumes of modern court records.

Since the mid-1950's our federal and state courts have been literally buried under a deluge of paper as the citizenry has come to regard the judiciary as the forum to remedy all manner of social ills. The example of the Supreme Court makes the point. In the past 25 years that court has produced more records than it did in its first 150 years of existence. Faced with such an onslaught, the inevitable question arose: "To make more space, what can we throw away?" The tempting answer was, those records nobody used anymore, meaning those that were of no value to pending litigation. Yet, giving into temptation was fraught with some peril, for it invited the opprobrium of those who cherished the records for the history they contained as it risked violating both state law and custom. Here, then, was a tension, the existence of which made the concept of selective destruction seem quite seductive. In archival parlance, this conception holds that while some documents have historic merit, others do not, and those that do not may be destroyed. Thus, by having someone earmark certain records insignificant and other significant, it becomes possible to satisfy the urge to retain sources of the past and still solve the problems of space and storage. The weakness in this calculus, though, has been the inability of those to whom the business of choosing has fallen to make their choices. My own experience with selective destruction makes me doubt the concept's value in records preservation, at least as the idea is currently understood. Perhaps it is time to consider an alternative.

In the place of selective destruction I would interpose a variant of what some historic building preservationists call "adaptive use." Restorers who save a building in this way return the structure's exterior form to its original condition while they transform its interior substance to a use other than its original purpose. As it applies to modern court records, adaptive use would reverse this formulation. The substance of the documents, that is their content, would remain unaltered, but their form would be reduced in size through a system of microprocessing.

What makes this variety of adaptive use possible is a fundamental difference between ancient and modern records. Ancient records have both a physical and a functional merit, while those of modern times are merely functional. This distinction arises from how the two types of records were generated. The media of early record keeping exemplify antique techniques of papermaking, printing, and bookbinding, as well as old court hands. Furthermore, a brief in the hand of Edward Livingston is prized not only for what it reveals of nineteenth-century practice, it is also cherished because that Moses of Louisiana law wrote it. In short, ancient records are prized as much for their physical characteristics as for their content. But, technological advances from the late nineteenth century to our day changed the nature of record keeping. The invention of the typewriter eliminated the handwritten record. Newer ways of making paper and books lessened their quality and durability. Dictaphones, tape recorders, word processors, computers, and even television opened new possibilities for information storage. The perfection of copyng devices from the typewriter to that ultimate copier, the xerox machine, made infinite reproduction a reality. Because one piece of xerox paper is like any other—cheap and short-lived—modern court records are valuable only for what they contain.[5] In their case, then, the medium is not the message; the message lies only in their content. That being so, their content is quite adaptable to some sort of microprocessing.

Microprocessing can be accomplished in one of two ways, employing conventional microfilm or storing the records' texts on computer tapes or discs. The latter technique is still at an experimental stage of development and its possibilities have yet to attract widespread notice or acceptance.[6] Whatever technique of miniaturization is used, though, the result remains the same. The need for paper records diminishes as cases close and they can then be destroyed after being microprocessed. Microprocessing would do more than merely reduce the amount of space required to house retired records. It would also eliminate the need for someone to distinguish records according to their presumed historical significance because they could all be kept in miniature.

Lest it appear that I have concocted a sovereign remedy, let me hasten to caution adaptive use is still in its infancy. Just as some building preservationists argue the folly of applying the concept to the salvation of old houses, there are archivists and other scholars who balk at the suggestion of destroying paper documents. Others decry microfilm as inconvenient or harmful to the eye, while some undoubtedly object to learning how a computer terminal works. Besides these objections, there are as yet unresolved concerns about the longevity of microfilm or computer tapes, as well as questions about efficient means of retrieval or the costs and staff requirements of a microprocessing system. Admittedly, each of these cares is genuine, but their expression should not be the occasion to ignore this salient fact: If we wish to reduce the tension between the demands of records management and the needs of history, then we cannot continue to blink our eyes to advances in the technology of information storage.

Of course, the object of exploring any means of records preservation is to assure the survival of the greatest array of legal sources. Obviously, the wider scope of the surviving evidence, the broader is the opportunity to understand the impression Louisiana law has made upon the shaping of our state's unique culture and how in turn that culture has helped to fashion our law. It is this bond between law and culture which suggests the need of new formulas to interpret Louisiana legal history.

To date, the scholars of the history of our law are not all that dissimiliar from their colleagues who write in the general field of American legal history. That is to say, they fall into two distinct groups, each of which sees the study of things legal as serving particular ends. One of these groups is a band of students who trained primarily as lawyers and only incidentally as historians. Here, as elsewhere, this company consists not only of academicians, but practicing attorneys and judges as well. Their central interests lie in describing the evolution of judicial doctrines developed by the statutes or the courts, studyng the growth of legal institutions, or doing legal biography.[7] But their emphasis upon these seemingly autonomous features of the legal order enhances the idea that only those who speak the special language of Louisiana law are capable of interpreting its history to others. This species, which may be styled "internal legal history," therefore frequently separates the law from its cultural links to the past, as it often renders its study mechanical and a trifle tedious. The consequences of these tendencies has been largely to keep professionally-trained historians from entering a field of study that appears beyond their ken.[8] Those who do make the venture comprise the second group, and to judge from their work, two reasons draw them to it. Some see in the legal sources numerous rich episodes that give flesh and color to the Louisiana story, and so they seek to devise diverting narratives about gamblers, highwaymen, or trollops. Others work the sources for evidence of how previous generations used the legal order to settle social imperatives that may now have modern relevance. They are curious, for example, to learn how our ancestors handled women rights or other personal relationship.[9]

Even though such scholars bring different backgrounds and perspectives to their studies, they are drawn together by common threads. The most obvious of these is a shared assumption about the nature of the legal variety of history. Both groups freight it with didactic or utilitarian ends. They take for granted that the purpose of examining the past is to find the keys to reconciling modern legal problems or maintaining fictions that serve professional purposes.[10] Another of these drawstrings is the fact that existing scholarship was bounded long ago within some fairly narrow limits, and since their drawing they have seldom been crossed.

An outsider like myself therefore discovers that the refrain of the questions asked by Louisiana legal historians is remarkably the same. Among them are these. Is Louisiana a civilian or common law jurisdiction, or is it a mixture of both?[11] If wholly civilian, which tradition, the Spanish or the French, predominated?[12] Parenthetically, those who debate that proposition, really never indicate the importance of that distinction to the growth of law or culture. What were the sources of Louisiana law? When was the law first codified? Was James Brown's and Louis Moreau Lislet's handiwork of 1808 a code or a digest?[13] After 1803, how were the conflicts between Louisiana and American legal customs resolved?[14] What is the role of our judges?[15] Do they follow something called civilian methodology or do they act like their brethern elsewhere in the union?[16] Apart from these queries, there is a fascination for demonstrating the uniqueness of Louisiana law that borders on the obsessive, just as there is a frequent preoccupation with comparative analyses.[17]

To be sure, these are vital questions; had they not been asked, there would be no Louisiana legal history, and we would not now be pondering that heritage. Still, constantly asking them yields basically the same results, even as they lead scholars to the same types of sources.

Only a tiny portion of the manuscript sources are now in print, a fact which could open many possibilities for documentary publishing.[18] Unhappily, though, any large-scale documentary project is unlikely to materialize because of the costs in bringing it to publication. At a time when the goal of cutting public spending is being pursued with the dogged conviction of the New England Puritans, it is probably sanguine to expect the state or federal governments to subvene such undertakings. Indeed, if the national administration succeeds in killing the National Historic Records and Publication Commission, documentary publication may cease altogether. In short, unless private philanthropists create endowments similar to the Holmes Devise or the American Historical Association's Littleton Griswold-Fund we are unlikely to see many legal manuscripts rendered into print.

Opportunities for doing legal bibliography also abound. So long as there are no comprehensive guides to the manuscripts, they will be underutilized. Even as simple a compilation as an annual listing of theses, dissertations, articles, and books on Louisiana legal topics, published in a law review or a scholarly journal, would be valuable, as would a union list of Louisiana legal imprints.[19] Apart from the late Kate Wallach, however, Louisiana never produced rivals to the great Virginia bibliographer Earl Gregg Swem or his successor W. Hamilton Bryson. Bryson's bibliographies of the Old Dominion's law and legal history could serve as models here.[20] Despite advances in librarianship that make composing such reference aids easier to accomplish, bibliography remains unfashionable because the investment is great and the return small.

More pointed than these examples are the chances to examine the sources anew for a fresh, broader appreciation of how Louisiana came to possess its distinct legal heritage. The opportunities for imaginative research are manifold, especially in the manuscript court records. These documents are the last great untapped body of evidence about Louisiana's past, and they await exploration and exploitation.

Among the possibilities for further investigation are detailed studies of the courts from colonial to modern times. Nothing that is written on colonial Louisiana compares to the vast literature on the Virginia country court or the Massachusetts township.[21] Apart from Henry P. Dart's essay in the *Louisiana Reports*,[22] there is not a single general history of the Supreme Court, let alone any on the lower courts. Neither the federal district courts nor the Fifth Circuit Court have been subjected to vigorous study, despite their prominent role in refashioning the character of Louisiana's social institutions over the last quarter-century.[23]

It is also possible to achieve a greater appreciation of how legal practices evolved through time. From 1812 onwards, the Supreme Court, by its rule-making power and its control over admissions to the bar always exerted a profound influence on the way in which the legal order routinely worked. Consider the impact of two of the court's earliest rules not only upon practices but upon the social habits of early Louisianians. In 1819 the court declared that "candidates for admission to the bar who shall give satisfactory assurances to the Court that they have received a good classical education, altho' they may not have degrees in any college, may be examined on shewing that they have studied two years under an attorney duly admitted to practice in this state."[24] And in 1821, the court promulgated this rule:

> The Judges find it necessary to make known that they expect that no application for a licence to plead will be made by any Gentleman not acquainted with the legal language of the State [*i.e.*, English]. It is true we have translations of our laws, and those may suffice to direct the citizen in the ordinary transactions of life. But he who aspires to the high honor of being consulted on, and to explain these laws to his fellow Citizens, and the Court, must be able to read the text. Very few of the acts of Congress, which form a considerable proportion of our written laws, paramount to the acts of our state legislature are translated. The records of suits must be preserved in the samed language as the laws, and the judges cannot designate as learned in the laws, and qualified to give legal advice and to carry on a lawsuit, [anyone] who is ignorant of the legal language of the state as not to be able to read the text of the laws or to undergo an examination in it.[25]

Quite apart from such matters, the records could also be thrown into the debate that swirls around the question of the origins of Louisiana's law. They incorporate hundreds of inventories of personal estates. A systematic analysis of these inventories can furnish clues as to what compilations, digests, treatises, or how-to-do it manuals circulated in Louisiana during the law's formative period.[26] Such hints can therefore inform us how men of law came by their erudition, just as they can lead to a deeper apprehension of legal education and the rise of the professional bar.

Someone interested in explaining the evolution of procedural rights would do well to look to these records too. The examples of a criminal defendant's rights to counsel and appeal suffice as illustrations. At the time of Louisiana's admission to the union, American law did not guarantee a criminal defendant the right of counsel, and his opportunities for appealing a conviction were few or non-existent. By the second third of the nineteenth century, however, attitudes changed and these changes were reflected in the state's courts. At first, appeals went not to the Supreme Court, but to a special tribunal known as the Court of Errors and Appeals. That arrangement proved unworkable, and so the authors of the Constitution of 1845 assigned the jurisdiction to the Supreme Court. From that point forward, the high court began to assume responsibility for developing procedural rights that it has continued to exercise down to the present day.[27]

Then too, the records could be combed for life data on the judiciary. In some instances they are the only evidence of how individual judges discharged their office. The facts accumulated through such a search could be compiled into a biographical dictionary that expands upon the work of Judge Cleveland Frugé, who has done a directory of the state's modern judges.[28]

Moreover, it is worth pondering anew how conceptions of law transferred to Louisiana and were translated into indigenous legal traditions. In this regard, there are discernible parallels between early Louisiana and Virginia. Both were settled by people who sprang from rule-bound cultures that stressed the importance of law for regulating social conduct. Settlers in both places showed penchants for creating their own laws and legal institutions, for each group believed there could be neither order nor stability without such trappings of civility. For their models, both could draw from richly complex legal inheritances that were somewhat too complicated for the primitive social organisms that first took life on the shores of the James and the Mississippi. Inevitably, there was a good deal of casting about to discover what suited the needs of a frontier existence, and because of the character of the population in both settlements these experiments were initially carried off by laymen. Their concern was always for what met the demands of the moment rather than for professional niceties or what ought to be. By determining what out of the Old World legal baggage could actually be made to work in new settings, these laymen laid the ground-work for indigenous bodies of law that remained receptive to later additions by other hands. Those other hands belonged, of course, to members of the professional bars that arose in the century after 1740. Obviously, the parallels are not exact. They are near enough however to convey the value of comparing Louisiana's legal tradition not only with those of continental Europe but with those of other states in the union as well.

A final possibility is to take a closer look at the bond between law and culture. Today, Louisiana law represents an accretion of cultural values that accumulated haphazardly over nearly three centuries. It has come to say how this state's institutions and people ought to be arranged and governed, just as it stands as the measure against which to gauge all manner of conduct. In this way, then, throughout the state's history, the law has always shaped the social order. But that law has also been influenced by the social, political, and economic imperatives that have fashioned Louisiana since its beginnings. Just as its civil law ancestors ultimately defined French and Spanish culture, Louisiana's legal heritage came gradually to describe an identity that set Louisianians off from their antecedents and the rest of the nation as well.

Since the Purchase, some Louisianians have understood this nexus. The rivalry between Louisiana law and American law after 1803 was no mere intellectual exercise for the edification and material benefit of lawyers; it was a conflict of culture in which Franco-Spanish Louisianians sought to preserve their identity. The courts quickly became the forum in which the competing legal systems were harmonized, but the story of that accommodation requires telling.

These examples represent only a tiny sampling of the many opportunities for further study that await the curious researcher. Even so, they testify to the richness of the sources. And, if that evidence is linked to and made part of the larger history of Louisiana, then the importance of the state's singular legal heritage will take on a newer, deeper meaning.

[1]Connie G. Griffith, "Collections in the Manuscripts Section of Howard-Tilton Memorial Library," *Louisiana History*, I (1960), 320-27; V. L. Bedsole, "Collections in the Department of Archives and Manuscripts, Louisiana State University," ibid., 328-34; Kate Wallach and Elsa B. Meier, "Dear Father-Dear Son, About Southern Law Students, 1800-1860," *Louisiana Law Review*, XXIII (1962-63), 680-708.

[2]Jesse Lemisch, "The American Revolution Seen from the Bottom Up," in Barton J. Bernstein, ed., *Towards a New Past: Dissenting Essays in American History* (New York, 1969), 3-46.

[3]For example, see John Demos, *A Little Commonwealth: Family Life in Plymouth* (New York, 1970); and Thad W. Tate and David Ammerman, eds., *The Seventeenth-Century Chesapeake: Essays in Anglo-American History* (Chapel Hill, N. C., 1979).

[4]One of the projects that the Louisiana American Revolution Bicentennial Commission was subvening is the Louisiana Bicentennial Reprint Series. The series is a reissue of early books on the state's history. It is under the general editorship of Joseph G. Tregle, Jr. of the University of New Orleans, and it is published under an LSU Press imprint.

[5]On the evolution of the idea, see Warren M. Billings *et al.*, "Towards a Comprehensive Judicial Records Management Program in Louisiana," a report submitted to Chief Justice Joe W. Sanders by the Committee on Records Maintenance and Storage, March 15, 1978, and Billings to Judge Albert Tate, Jr., Nov. 19, 1980.

[6]The idea for the use of computers for full text storage of court records derives from the example of the Henry Laurens Papers Project. There, the editor, David K. Chestnutt employs the computer to hold transcribed texts of Laurens items. How the Laurens system works is described in David K. Chestnutt, "Comprehensive Text Processing and the Papers of Henry Laurens," Association for Documentary Editing *Newletter*, II, #2 (1980), 12-14; II, #3 (1980), 3-5.

[7]Erwin C. Surrency, "Legal History and Rare Books," *Law Library Journal*, LIX (1966), 71; Alice M. Magee, "History of the Courts of Louisiana," ibid., XXXIII (1940), 253-59; Elizabeth Gaspar Brown, "Legal Systems in Conflict: Orleans Territory, 1804-1812," *American Journal of Legal History*, I (1957), 35-76; Henry P. Dart, "Courts and Law in Colonial Louisiana," *Louisiana Historical Quarterly*, IV (1921), 255-89; Howard Newcomb Morse, "Federal Equity Jurisdiction in Louisiana," *Loyola Law Review*, VII (1953), 1-22; Henry G. McMahon, "The Case Against Fact Pleading in Louisiana," *Louisiana Law Review*, XIII (1952-53), 369-94; John T. Hood, Jr., "The Louisiana Judiciary," ibid., XIV (1953-54), 811-24; and "The Louisiana Lawyer," ibid., XVIII (1957-58), 661-70; J. Denson Smith, "Law Revision in Louisiana in Retrospect, ibid., XIX (1958-59), 34-42; Hood, "History of Courts of Appeal in Louisiana," ibid., XXI (1960-61), 531-53; Ginger Roberts, "Edward Livingston and American Penology," ibid., XXXVII (1976-77); Mitchell Franklin, "The Foundations and Meaning of the Slaughterhouse Cases," *Tulane Law Review*, XVII (1943-44), 1-88, 218-62; Walter E. Joyce, "Edward Douglas White: The Louisiana Years, Early Life and on the Bench," ibid., XLI (1966-67), 752-68; Philip English Mackey, "Edward Livingston on the Punishment of Death," ibid., LXVIII (1973-74), 25-42; Max Nathan, Jr., "In Search of a Missing Link: Edward Livingston and the Proposed Code of Commerce," ibid., 43-54; Anne L. Simon, "Inequality under the Law: The Louisiana Story, *Southern Studies*, XVI (1977), 293-308.

[8]The most recent single-volume history of the state all but ignores legal developments, Joe Gray Taylor, *Louisiana, A History* (New York, 1975).

[9]Jack D. L. Holmes, ed., "O'Reilly's Regulations on Booze, Boardinghouses, and Billiards," *Louisiana History*, VI (1965), 293-300; Germaine E. Reid, "Race Legislation on Louisiana, 1864-1920," ibid., 379-93; Robert B. Murray, "Mrs. Alexander's Cotton," ibid., 393-400; David E. Everett, "Free Persons of Color in Louisiana," ibid., VII (1966), 21-50; James D. Hardy, Jr., "Probate Racketeering in Colonial Louisiana," ibid., IX (1968), 109-21; E. Russ Williams, ed., "Slave Patrol Ordinances of St. Tammany Parish, Louisiana, 1835-1838," ibid., XIII (1972), 399-412.

[10]Perhaps the most obvious of these fictions is the one which holds that *the law* has an ex-

istence independent of those who make or enforce it. It is therefore a neutral, external gauge against which all human conduct may be impartially measured. The necessity for such a fiction is beyond doubt, for it invests the law and its minions with an awesome majesty that compels social obedience. Sometimes the fiction is disbelieved, however. In that case the law is powerless, as in the celebrated confrontation between John Marshall and Andrew Jackson over Marshall's ruling in *Cherokee Nation* v. *Georgia*. Marshall's opinion upholding the validity of treaties guaranteeing the Cherokee the integrity of their lands ran counter to the President's avowed aim to remove all eastern Indians across the Mississippi. Upon learning of the decision, Jackson is reputed to have remarked, "John Marhsall has made his decision, now let him enforce it." Apocryphal or not, the fact remains that Marshall had no power to make Jackson obey, and so the Cherokee were removed.

[11]John H. Wigmore, "Louisiana: The Story of its Legal System," *Tulane Law Review*, I (1916), 1-45; Henry P. Dart, "The Legal Institutions of Louisiana," ibid., III (1918), 254-80; Gordon Ireland, "Louisiana's Legal System Reappraised," ibid., XI (1936-37), 585-98; Leonard Greenburg, "Must Louisiana Resign to the Common Law?" ibid., 598-601; Hood, "A Crossroad in Louisiana History, *Louisiana Law Review*, XXII (1961-62), 709-26; Sidney Pugh Ingram, "Administration of Successions: Anglo-American Influence upon Louisiana Law," ibid., XXIV (1963-64), 54-105.

[12]Dart, "The Influence of the Ancient Laws of Spain on the Jurisprudence of Louisiana," *Tulane Law Review*, VI (1931-32), 83-93; Mitchell, "The Place of Thomas Jefferson in the Expulsion of Spanish Medieval Law from Louisiana," ibid., XVI (1941-42), 319-38; and "The Eighteenth Brumarie in Louisiana: Talleyrand and the Spanish Medieval Legal System of 1806," ibid., 514-61; C. Russell Reynolds, "Alfonso el Sabio's Laws Survive in the Civil Code of Louisiana," *Louisiana History*, XII (1971), 137-47.

[13]John H. Tucker, Jr., "Source Books of Louisiana Law," ibid., VIII (1933-34), 396-405; Ferdinand Stone, "The Civil Code of 1808 for the Territory of Orleans," ibid., XXXIII (1958-59), 3-6; Hood, "The History and Development of the Louisiana Civil Code," ibid., 7-20; Louis Baudouin, "The Influence of the Code Napoleon," ibid., 21-28; Radolfo Batiza, "The Influence of Spanish Law in Louisiana," ibid., 24-39; Franklin, "An Important Document in the History of American Roman and Civil Law: The De la Verque Manuscript," ibid., 35-42; Thomas W. Tucker, "Sources of Louisiana's Law of Persons: Blackstone, Domat, and the French Codes," ibid., XLV (1970-71), 264-95; Batiza, "The Louisiana Civil Code of 1808: Its Actual Sources and Present Relevance," ibid., XLVI (1971-72), 4-165; Joseph Modeste Sweeney, "Tournament of Scholars over the Sources of the Civil Code of 1808," ibid., 585-603; Robert A. Pascal, "Sources of the Digest of 1808, A Reply to Professor Batiza," ibid., 603-28; Batiza, "Sources of the Digest of 1808, Facts and Speculation: A Rejoinder," ibid., 628-53; and "The Actual Sources of the Louisiana *Project* of 1823: A General Analytical Survey," ibid., XLVII (1972-73), 1-115; Joseph Dainow, "Moreau Lislet's Notes on Sources of Louisiana's Civil Code of 1808," *Louisiana Law Review* XIX (1958-59),43-51; Pascal, "A Treatise on the Reprint of Moreau Lislet's Copy of a Digest of the Civil Laws," *Publications of the Louisiana Historical Society*, 2nd Ser., I (1974), 43-48.

[14]George Dargo, *Jefferson's Louisiana: Politics and the Clash of Legal Traditions* (Cambridge, Mass., 1975).

[15]Albert Tate, Jr., "The Role of the Judge in Mixed Jurisdictions," *Loyola Law Review*, XX (1973-74), 231-44; and "The Role of the Judge in the American Republic," *Louisiana Law Review*, XVI (1955), 386-90.

[16]Mack E. Barham, "A Renaissance of the Civilian Tradition in Louisiana," ibid., XXXIII (1972-73), 357-89.

[17]E. Fabre-Surveyes, "The Civil Law in Quebec and Louisiana," ibid., I (1938), 649-64; Dainow, "The Early Sources of Forced Heirship: Its History in Texas and Louisiana," ibid., IV (1942-43), 42-69; Leonard Oppenheim, "The Law of Slaves: A Comparative Study of the Roman and Louisiana Systems," *Tulane Law Review*, XIV (1939-40), 384-406; Daniel J. Flanigan, "Criminal Procedure in Slave Trials in the Antebellum South, *Journal of Southern History*, XL (1974), 537-64.

[18]What is in print appears variously in the old *Louisiana Historical Quarterly*, *Southern Studies*, and *Louisiana History*, as well as in such collections as the Claiborne papers and the *American State Papers*.

[19]Back in the 1960's both *Louisiana History* and *Southern Studies* published annual listings of theses and dissertations on Louisiana topics, but the practice was soon discontinued. There does exist a bibliography of doctoral dissertations, Edward F. Haas, *Louisiana: A Dissertation Bibliography* (Ann Arbor, Mich., n.d.).

[20]Swem, of course, was the compiler of the monumental *Virginia Historical Index* (Roanoke, Va., 1934), that is keyed a variety of published sources, many of which relate to the commonwealth's legal history. Bryson has compiled three bibliographies, *Census of Law Books in Colonial Virginia* (Charlottesville, Va., 1977), *The Virginia Law Reporters Before 1900* (Charlottesville, Va., 1978), and *A Bibliography of Virginia Legal History Before 1900* (Charlottesville, Va., 1979). While useful, Bryson's work is not flawless; see my review of *A Bibliography of Virginia Legal History*, in the *American Journal of Legal History*, XXV (1981), 80-81.

[21]Jerry A. Micelle, "From Law Court to Local Government: Metamorphasis of the Superior Council of French Louisiana," *Louisiana History*, IX (1968), 85-107; Ronald R. Morazan, "The Cabildo of Spanish New Orleans, 1769-1803," *Louisiana Studies*, XII (1973), 591-607; Donald Lemieux, "Some Legal and Practical Aspects of the Office of *Commissaire Ordonnateur* of French Louisiana," ibid., XIV (1975), 378-93.

[22]Vol. 133 (1913), xxx-lxxiv.

[23]The appeals court has however designated Professor Harvey Couch of the Tulane law school as its official historian.

[24]Ms. Minute Book, 1818-23, 38. This and all other minute books kept between 1812 and 1921 are part of the Court's records that are deposited in the Department of Archives and Manuscripts at the University of New Orleans.

[25]Minute Book, 1818-23, 239.

[26]For an example of such a study, see Billings, "English Legal Literature as a Source of Law and Legal Practice for Seventeenth-Century Virginia," *Virginia Magazine of History and Biography*, LXXXVII (1979), 403-17.

[27]Upon the demise of the Court of Errors and Appeals, its records were turned over to the Supreme Court. The remnants of that deposit are now housed at UNO.

[28]J. Cleveland Frugé, ed., *Biographies of Louisiana Judges* (Lake Charles and New Orleans, 1971, 1977).

INDEX